Carl and Susie,

Honored and blessed

these years and to sh

Christ together. May He continue to g

bigger in our hearts and lives in the years ahead.

Much love,

Doug

Jesus Changes *Everything*

Advance Praise for

Jesus Changes *Everything*

"*Jesus Changes Everything* is an intriguing and inspiring book that offers invaluable lessons about living an abundant life, drawn from the fascinating experiences of the author and the captivating stories about people from all walks of life who were blessed by spiritual enlightenment."

—**Edwin Meese III,** *former U.S. Attorney General, Ronald Reagan Distinguished Fellow Emeritus at Heritage Foundation*

"There comes a time for each of us when, mindful of the manifold blessings we have been given, we desire to discern what God expects of us. Why are we here? In his compelling memoir, *Jesus Changes Everything,* Doug Burleigh recounts how, through his years of work with Young Life, he has held the hands of countless young adults, and in more than a hundred countries has prayed for and challenged Prime Ministers and Parliamentarians to become one with Jesus Christ, to put on the 'armor of God,' and to build relationships of trust, mutual respect, and commitment toward fulfilling their calling from God. Throughout his remarkable life, he has been devoted to biblical scholarship and ministry, to mentoring two generations of aspirants toward becoming disciples, to vindicating the sacred trust of life, and to improving the human condition. This is both a timely wake-up call and an inspiring way forward for every American."

— **Robert McFarlane**, *Career Marine Officer, President Reagan's National Security Advisor, Chairman of an International Energy Company*

"This is a great book for anyone who is interested in deepening their faith journey. Doug has written beautifully of his extraordinary life, following the person and principles of Jesus. It's a road map to a journey to Love, Peace and Hope."

— **Jack McMillan**, *President of Nordstrom (Retired)*

"My very first encounter as a teenager with Young Life over forty years ago included listening to Doug Burleigh share the story of God's love for us through his Son, Jesus Christ. I still remember his words all these years later. Whether you have been following Jesus for decades, have recently made that commitment, or are just beginning to consider who he is, *Jesus Changes Everything* lives up to its title. Jesus jumps off the pages of the Bible and into remarkable stories from Doug's own life, even as he faithfully points us to the most amazing person to ever walk the face of the earth."

— **Newt Crenshaw**, *President of Young Life*

"Doug Burleigh's book, aptly named, is an everything changer. It lays the foundation of a lifelong faith for the new believer and, for those who've had a lifelong faith, it renews and inspires. As he clearly explains the fundamentals of discipleship, with God's Word as the source of all knowledge, Doug weaves many personal stories to show how Jesus is the redeemer of all. Finding it hard to love a difficult neighbor? Doug's story brought tears of joy as I read it.

I began reading *Jesus Changes Everything* expecting to finish it quickly, but within a few pages, was compelled to slow down and treat it as a devotional text. A daily measure of Doug's profound teaching, personal stories and Scripture challenged me to seek a deeper relationship with Jesus, because He indeed changes everything.

Doug Burleigh's lifetime of ministry to teens and adults forms the narrative of this amazing book that teaches the fundamentals of our faith, challenges us to read and memorize God's Word, and inspires us to seek a real relationship with Jesus. Doug does not burden us with efforts to achieve God's grace and mercy; he shows through personal stories that God's grace and mercy is there for the asking. What a joy to know that *Jesus Changes Everything*!"

— **Susan Hutchison**, *Former CBS Anchor in Seattle and Chair of Washington Republican Party and Board of Young Life*

"This book is vintage Doug Burleigh–winsome, superbly told, and centered on Jesus. Capturing the essence of Doug's heart and lifelong mission, readers are encouraged to surrender to grace, live out Jesus' values in every aspect of life, pursue reconciliation, and share the good news. *Jesus Changes Everything* is a wonderful primer on faithful discipleship."

— **Alec Hill**, *author of* Living in Bonus Time: Surviving Cancer and Finding New Purpose, *and President Emeritus of InterVarsity Christian Fellowship*

"Doug Burleigh is extremely knowledgeable about the Bible, and in *Jesus Changes Everything*, he well articulates his experience and understanding of

Jesus. Regardless of one's own beliefs, everyone can find something to celebrate in his book."

— **John Dalton,** *Former Secretary of the Navy*

"Indeed, Jesus changes everything. But it takes someone like Doug Burleigh who has committed a lifetime to introducing people to Jesus to help us realize how powerful and transformative that change can be. Imparting vivid insights from his fifty-plus years of experience discipling young adults, Doug unwraps the mysteries of Scripture, and carefully, generously, and humbly reveals how God has used him to make the Gospel accessible and alive to countless men and women across the globe. In *Jesus Changes Everything*, Doug shares personal and poignant stories of challenge and doubt, success and consequence, with those of us who have been on the Jesus journey all along but who may have forgotten, lost, or never understood how Jesus can use even a 'motley crew' like us. But Jesus changes everything—including us. Jesus calls us to acknowledge and live into the transformative, loving, and merciful relationship Jesus reveals in these pages and in our own lives."

— **Margaret Grun Kibben, DMin**, *Chaplain, US House of Representatives; Rear Admiral, Chaplain Corps, United States Navy (Retired)*

"The passion, love, and faith of Doug Burleigh are on full display in this book. Grounded in Scripture yet seeking application in everyday circumstances, Doug presents a chapter-by-chapter picture of what it means to be actively seeking truth through faith in today's day and age. Further, he continues to draw attention to how our relationships define our faith: relationships with family and friends, relationships with the world around us, and our relationships with and through God. Doug's extensive experiences through his years of travel and his own relationships bring this book to life and will provide relatable anecdotes for countless numbers of people."

— **Tony Hall**, *Twelve-Term Member of Congress, Former US Ambassador for World Hunger*

"When a prominent US Senator and statesman died, his colleagues held a remembrance in his state legislature. They began chanting, 'Jesus. Jesus. Jesus.' Because Jesus had changed everything in his life, that was his memory, not his political accomplishments. Doug Burleigh beautifully shares how Jesus is not just the way to personal salvation but the way to all of life. That is because Jesus changes everything—not just some things, but everything. Doug then lays down the foundation of walking as a disciple of Jesus for a lifetime. He does not paint a simplistic formula for success, but a life totally and completely fulfilled by following Jesus."

— **Jerry White, PhD**, *Major General, USAF (Retired), The Navigators International President Emeritus*

"A once-a-century pandemic has dramatically altered careers and transactions across the globe. Quarantines and isolation have forced upon the world's citizens new patterns of living and much-needed introspection. In the summer of 2020, during one of the pandemic's infection peaks, Doug Burleigh penned this provoking narrative, gently asking his readers to consider an alternative path in their pursuit of happiness—a highway that can transform careers into ministries and transactions into lasting and mutually-enhancing relationships. Despite its title, *Jesus Changes Everything* isn't a traditional 'Christian' book any more than the Book of Psalms is a Jewish book. Rather, it is a spiritual autobiography rooted and inspired by the Bible and the life, ideas, and achievements of Jesus, the Nazarene prophet. As a diligent student of the Bible, the author has constructed a coherent, accessible, and above all practical list of principles and practices which have transformed his life and, through his ministry, the lives of countless young people throughout the world, including the fifteen former Soviet republics. And, he has ordered and expounded on them in nineteen compelling chapters. At a moment in time when forces beyond our human control have pushed pause on careers and transactions, *Jesus Changes Everything* is a special and welcome gift from a friendly fellow traveler."

— **Stephen I. Danzansky, Esq.,** *Former Deputy Assistant to the President for Cabinet and Economic Affairs, Chief of Staff, US Department of Education*

"This a great book for someone who is wanting to know Jesus and a great book for some who knows Jesus as their Lord and Savior but want a deeper and closer relationship. A great resource to assist in sharing the God News with others. Very Jesus-centric, written on a biblical foundation. I plan to keep a copy of this book close at hand."

— **Claude M. (Mick) Kicklighter**, *Lieutenant General, US Army (Retired)*

"Doug Burleigh has spent more than fifty years sharing the Gospel of Jesus with young and old all over our country and around the world. He has now written an amazing book that captures the essential teachings of Jesus and how to apply them as a modern-day disciple. This book could be titled, 'Jesus Distilled.' If anyone is interested in learning more about the Jewish carpenter from Nazareth and how He changed everything, I highly recommend Doug Burleigh's new book."

— **Jim Slattery,** *Lawyer, Businessman, and Former Democrat Congressman, Kansas 2nd District*

"Luke recorded the things Jesus began to do and to teach. It is this order that changes everything. Too often religious leaders teach with the hopes that listeners will do what they hear and usually they don't. I have known Doug Burleigh for fifty years and this book records, with wonderful insights, his life of doing and teaching in ways that have helped scores of people connect to Jesus in life-transforming ways."

— **Kent Hotaling**, *Senior Associate, International Foundation*

"For the thirty years I have known Doug Burleigh, he has lived out and shared the principles found in his long-awaited book. They have impacted my own ministry and my personal walk with Christ. I commend enthusiastically this work to you."

— **Mark Toone**, *Senior Pastor at Chapel Hill Presbyterian Church*

Jesus Changes *Everything*

DISCOVERING A TRULY CHRIST-CENTERED LIFE

Doug Burleigh

NASHVILLE

NEW YORK • LONDON • MELBOURNE • VANCOUVER

Jesus Changes *Everything*
DISCOVERING A TRULY CHRIST-CENTERED LIFE

Published in New York, New York, by Morgan James Publishing. Morgan James is a trademark of Morgan James, LLC. www.MorganJamesPublishing.com

For more information or contact details, please email at jesuschangeseverything2021@gmail.com.

ISBN 978-1-63195-411-5 paperback
ISBN 978-1-63195-412-2 eBook
Library of Congress Control Number: 2020922532

Cover Design by:
Chris Treccani
www.3dogdesign.net

To my wife, Debbie, and our four awesome offspring:
John, James, Katie, and Peter.
You five have been the inspiration and examples
for so much of my experiencing the truth that
"Jesus Changes Everything."

Table of Contents

Acknowledgments

I never planned to write a book. However, after over fifty years of meeting with people to share the principles of Jesus and the attributes he challenged his disciples to embrace, it seemed right to set these thoughts, coupled with many stories, down in print.

I first want to acknowledge that I would have nothing so important to share were it not for the presence of Jesus in my life and his loving revelations that he imparted to me over the years, and my realization that Jesus never called us to a religion, to a set of doctrines, or a code of rules: he called us to himself! That stunning realization provided all the valuable content of these thoughts and experiences I have shared here.

I want to thank my great wife, Debbie, and her mom, Jan Coe, who lives with us, for their incredible patience with me. During the time I was writing this book, they were packing boxes in a house we were selling after fourteen wonderful years living there. I was very little help in that process, and they cheerfully supported my efforts. As I would spend long hours in the study, they would take on the endless number of duties to empty a three-story house.

I dedicated this book to my wife and our four offspring—John, James, Katie, and Peter. These wonderful family members and their spouses and sixteen grandchildren have provided so much inspiration and content for the thoughts I have shared. We have developed an annual tradition of meeting together at some resort location and enjoying one another's company. I have learned so much about family, friendship, loyalty, and love from being together with them. I am convinced family is the very best place to learn about unconditional love and loyalty.

There are a handful of small groups that have been very meaningful in my life's journey. Forty-seven years ago, I believe God called six of us on Young Life staff in the Pacific Northwest to walk together through life. We didn't realize it at the time, but Bob Krulish, Jim Eney, Jim Brown, Tom Jonez, and Gordy Anderson have been anchors in life for me. Their counsel, encouragement, and unconditional love have provided me a window to see more clearly the love of Jesus Christ and how to live it out in the everyday.

Several other groups have also been very meaningful. Over forty years ago, Terry Olsen, Dr. Jack Miller, and Connie Jacobsen and I began to meet together to share life. While Connie graduated to Heaven, I treasure these brothers and their commitment to grow together as brothers and value one another's families.

Finally, a core of brothers that began meeting together to dream about the ministry of Jesus in Washington State has endured for decades and seen God do amazing things, both in our lives and in many around the state. Wes Anderson, Jack McMillan, Scott Hardman, Jeff Vancil, George Petrie, Skip Li, and Russ Johnson have been faithful friends and partners in ministry, along with their spouses.

A number of men and women that comprise the Youth Cores in six cities in Russia, and one each in Ukraine, Armenia, and Kazakhstan, have walked together over the past twenty-five years. Some of them I initially met while serving with Billy Graham at the 1992 Moscow Crusade. We have done numerous Jesus Conferences across the former Soviet Union and gathered regularly together over the years at "Acts 2:42 Conferences" (breaking bread, prayer, fellowship, and study of Scripture, as well as time to play together). These young friends have provided so much of the inspiration and stories, as well as helping me see Jesus more clearly by their example. They are too many to mention by name, but I would be remiss to not acknowledge my gratitude to my administrative partner in all of this, Yessa Serkina. She has faithfully been the glue that helped keep all the teams meeting and growing together over the years.

I want to acknowledge the wonderful team at The Cedars in Arlington, VA. For the past sixteen years, I have had the privilege to serve alongside a tremendous group of young men living at Ivanwald House, young women at Potomac Point, and a number of gifted, enjoyable, and committed men and women who volunteer their time and talents at this beautiful seven-acre property, just minutes from the Capitol. Doug Coe would call the thousands of friends from all over the world who would come to The Cedars "the walk-in business." This home, dedicated to the poor, is a place where Jesus is our unseen host. I have been awed by the amazing individuals who have come to meet together in the Spirit of Jesus. People of all religious, political, and ethnic backgrounds come together, and so much of my learning about what our Lord is doing around the world has come from the friends who come to this special place. Much of what I write has been learned from meeting with friends at The Cedars.

I want to thank my editor, Arlyn Lawrence, a longtime friend, who many years ago challenged me to write this book. It took a pandemic to provide the window to get started with it, but her encouragement and experience have been invaluable in this process. And, she steered me to Morgan James Publishing, who have been helpful and understanding of my desire to provide a book that provides practical wisdom in navigating a relationship with Jesus Christ in an increasingly secular world.

Finally, I want to acknowledge the mentors that I have oft quoted in this book. First and foremost is my late father-in-law, Doug Coe. Words cannot express what his life and example have meant to me. Someone asked me shortly after his passing in 2017 what it was like to work with him for over forty years. What immediately came out of my mouth was, "My Jesus got bigger and bigger." As I pondered that hasty response, I thought that perfectly expressed my deepest sentiments. Hanging around him caused the Jesus I was getting to know and follow to continue to grow bigger. I couldn't have written these thoughts without his example.

Other mentors I have mentioned also contributed to the content I have shared in these pages. Bruce Larson, Juan Carlos Ortiz, Connie Jacobsen, Earl

Palmer, Vernon Grounds, Ed Meese, C. Davis Weyerhaeuser, and Bob Reeverts have been a handful of the people God has used in my life to point me closer to Jesus and help me navigate the dangerous shoals that take place in our lives. As I have sought to mentor young men, each of these men has provided a wonderful example of how to live out their faith in the respective arenas in which God has placed them. I am forever grateful to them for making time to help me in my journey through life.

Foreword

Doug Burleigh writes a book about what never gets old: the transforming of human lives by Jesus Christ. To quote, he states that his work represents " … the culmination of many years of walking with Jesus, of seeing God work in my life and other people's lives in astounding and transformational ways." Having served for twenty-five years on the staff of Young Life and then twenty-five years with The Fellowship in Washington DC, Doug has earned the right to give voice to a much needed conversation. I like his book. I believe that how he shares practical learning and gives teaching examples of God's grace at work is a fresh breeze of air for every one of us today.

Doug divides his work into three parts. The first points to the character and teaching of Jesus. He begins with Jesus and the greatest commandment,

> *"… and one of them, a lawyer asked Jesus a question to test him. 'Teacher, which commandment in the law is the greatest?' He said to him, 'You shall love the Lord your God with all your heart, and with all your soul, and with all your mind. This is the greatest and first commandment. And a second is like it: You shall love your neighbor as yourself.' On these two commandments hang all the law and the prophets.'" (Matthew 22: 35-40)*

This text is paramount and sets the foundation for Doug's ministry that puts the relationship with Christ at the center.

Christian relationships and the resulting discipleship flow from the love of God; we can order our priorities and ministry objectives based on this text. Jesus says all the law and the prophets depend on these two mandates. For us, as Christians, every behavior is tested by these two commands. Doug's goal in teaching about the Kingdom of God seeks to preserve the mystery. In his words, he describes the kingdom as a living relationship rather than as a place: "I tell them, it is the reign and rule of the King, and it starts right here pointing to each of our hearts."

In the next part, Doug describes the challenges of decision-making that face young Christians. He presents a strong, practical edge. He tells about his own personal experiences of ministry through relationships where he was mentored and where he was a mentor, not only in America, but also in Eastern Europe, especially Russia. Here, too, Doug offers guidance for those who want to grow in biblical faith.

He espouses the importance of mentors and gives credit to key people in his own life, during the formative years of his service in Young Life. His words on discipleship are offered in natural, non-self-serving ways and based on his own growing edge experiences with mentors such as Connie Jacobsen, John R.W. Stott, Juan Carlos Ortiz, Bruce Larsen, and Vernon Grounds. As Doug expresses what he learned from these men of faith, the moderating and wisdom markers show up in the guidance principles he offers.

In the last part of his book, Doug gives personal witness to the truth that the faithfulness of God lasts and endures even through our own personal mistakes and the confusion caused by temptation. Citing C.S. Lewis, who faces up to temptations of the devil and warns against an "unhealthy interest in the devil," Doug steers his readers away from destructive fascination with spiritual evil and how we, as followers of Jesus, should view this warfare. Lewis writes, "There are two equal and opposite errors into which our race can fall about devils. One is to disbelieve their existence. The other is to believe and feel an excessive and unhealthy interest in them. They themselves are equally pleased by both errors and hail a materialist or a magician with the same delight." (Preface to *Screwtape*

Letters) Lewis warns that there are believers in Christ who are tempted to come under the influence of religious and cultic conspiratorial movements. Doug's approach stays faithful to the biblical teaching and points to St. Paul's whole-armor-of-God strategy (Ephesians 6:10-17).

As he writes, Doug adds two more mentors who have been key encouragers. He shares the poem of Dr. Sam Shoemaker, "I Stand by the Door." In so doing, Doug brings out the warm-hearted invitation to readers and reminds us that wherever we are on our journey to discover for ourselves the door where Jesus knocks, *"If any one hears my voice and opens the door I will come in"* (Revelation 3:20).

True to Doug's character, he honors his father-in-law, Doug Coe, who offered what is an unforgettable sentence in this book because of its humility and the openness to grace. It was Doug Coe who set the stage for us all when he repeatedly said, "Don't convert others, convert yourself." The influence of this man was deep and wide. It built on the basic nature of the young man who then continued on to mentor thousands of others over these many years. I say these words with honesty, as I have known Doug Burleigh since he was a teenager. I have watched him grow. I am witness to how the Lord has used his life to bring good into the world by offering the grace that comes from God.

The final biblical theme in the book is Doug's attention to the ministry of reconciliation that naturally flows from humility and the surprise of grace. Doug writes, "There appears to be a very close connection between my truly experiencing God's love personally and passing it on to all of those I meet. Yes, we love because he first loved us."[1]

Permit me to turn to the very first story in the book because it is an example of what discipleship mentoring is about and what makes possible healing and reconciliation ministry between people of different national backgrounds, and those who each have unique racial, cultural, religious, and self-understandings. Doug begins with a simple story, telling of a time with a young attorney who had been encouraged by friends that he met at The Cedars in Arlington, Virginia. Doug asked this new friend, who was at a crossroad in his own life, if he would like to get together to read and talk about the texts from the teaching of Jesus,

---

1 See 1 John 4:19

and even memorize memorable parts. What gradually happened is that the New Testament's teaching of Jesus came into focus and all pointed to the living center, Jesus, who is the teacher. And that Jesus won the respect of Doug's friend. Some years later, his friend narrated from memory to Doug the entire gospel text of the Lord's Supper event of Holy Week (John 13-17).

What has always been and still is at the center of Doug's life is recognizing that God's love can change everything, even those feelings and experiences that have historically separated people from each other. Faith happens when the promises of the teacher become ours to trust. As Doug has represented throughout his life, it is the relationship with this Jesus that changes everything. I commend the ministry of Doug that bears testimony to this truth.

—**Reverend Earl F. Palmer**, *Pastor Emeritus:*
The First Presbyterian church of Berkeley,
Union Church of Manila and
University Presbyterian Church in Seattle.

(Upon retirement, Earl served for two years as Preaching Pastor in Residence at The National Presbyterian Church of Washington, DC. He is now Pastor-at-Large with Earl Palmer Ministries, Seattle, Washington.)

Introduction

Winkey Pratney, a longtime friend, author, and disciple maker from New Zealand, once noted, "The unmistakable evidence of being in Christ is a changed life." Jesus changes lives! That truth never gets old.

As I reflect on my life's journey, the most thrilling memories are the testimonies of countless lives that have been radically transformed by the power of Jesus working in their lives. Hundreds of stories flood through my mind. Perhaps for me the accounts of friends who emerge from total unbelief to a life-changing encounter with Jesus are the most exciting.

One recent such encounter was with Matt. I first met him about nine years ago when a friend from the West Coast called and asked if I would meet his friend at The Cedars in Arlington, Virginia, where I have lived and worked for the past fifteen years. Matt was Jewish, a Stanford Law graduate from Miami. His father, a lawyer, was disbarred in the 70s, and turned to developing strip clubs and moving in the underworld. As a multimillionaire in his mid-seventies, he married a young woman forty years younger. Matt, realizing the motives were unmistakably about money, pondered how to get rid of her.

One morning on an early run, anguishing about this woman's motives, he struggled over his response. He came to a church and decided to go inside and think. It was locked. He couldn't even enter a place called the "House of God" to consider such an enormous decision? As he left, another door opened and a middle-aged man came out from a men's Bible study group. They briefly talked, and Matt was invited to come the next week. For reasons unknown even to him, he found himself there the following week. And the following week, he came back.

Shortly afterward, he moved to Washington, D.C. to take a job as an attorney for the U.S. Department of Justice. At this point, we met at The Cedars. I always ask new friends to tell me their story. You learn so much by listening to a person's story, especially in the manner that they tell it. One of my favorite scenes in Scripture is when Jesus was on his way to the home of synagogue president, Jairus, where his daughter was sick and dying. On the way, the woman with longtime internal bleeding touched the hem of his garment. Mark 5:33 notes that he listened as "she told her whole story."

As I listened to Matt's story, I realized his life was truly at a crossroads. I offered to meet together, only asking that he would be willing to memorize Scripture each time we met to go over the teachings of Jesus. Nine years later, I am witnessing a miracle—Matt is a new creation, one that is talked about in 2 Corinthians 5:17 … "If anyone is in Christ, they are a new creation. Old things are passed away; all things have been made new." A thrilling addendum to that recently unfolded as Matt sat with me and recited nearly word perfect the Upper Room account from John 13-17.

I am convinced that knowing and practicing God's Word is essential to allowing His Holy Spirit to do His quiet work in our hearts. It never gets old to watch what the Spirit of God quietly does in his transformative work. In Matt's case, this even involved the heartbreaking loss of a loving wife to cancer, leaving him to raise two young daughters.

One of the greatest joys of my life is the privilege of meeting with folks like Matt, always asking them to do something concrete to commit themselves to growth, because growth and change always involve our steps of faith combined with his life-changing transformation. Paul summarizes it well, "Continue to work out your salvation with fear and trembling, for it is God who works in you to will and to act according to his good purpose."[2]

This book is the culmination of many years of walking with Jesus, of seeing God work in my life and other people's lives in astounding and transformational ways. Through the years, certain principles and practices have emerged, tested and true, that have contributed to this discipleship process. Now, for the first time, after much urging from friends, family, and ministry colleagues, I have written these principles and practices down in hopes that others will be able to apply them to their own lives and discipling relationships.

I have organized them into three parts: "Principles of Jesus," "Attributes of a Disciple," and "Thoughts and Afterthoughts" (those topics that didn't seem to fit neatly into the other two categories). I wanted to write them all down for you, in the hopes that you, too, will experience the same dynamic relationship with Jesus that I and so many millions of others have experienced—and the privilege of helping others know him as well.

When this happens, you and I—and anyone we reach for Jesus—will never be the same. He changes everything!

—**Doug Burleigh**, The Cedars

---

2 Philippians 2:12-13, NI

PART 1
Principles of Jesus

Chapter One

The Purpose

"One of them, an expert in the law, tested him with this question, 'Teacher, which is the greatest commandment in the Law?' Jesus replied: 'Love the Lord your God with all your heart and with all your soul and with all your mind.' This is the first and greatest commandment. And the second is like it: 'Love your neighbor as yourself.' All the Law and the Prophets hang on these two commandments." (Matthew 22:35-40, NIV)

The trap was set. *All he has to do is step into it,* thought the Pharisees, who were desperate to discredit Jesus in the eyes of an increasingly adoring and growing throng of followers. First came a howitzer of a question.

"Teacher," they queried, "we know you are a man of integrity and that you teach the way of God in accordance with the truth. You aren't swayed by men because you pay no attention to who they are. Tell us then, what is your opinion? Is it right to pay taxes to Caesar or not?"[3] In short, they were challenging him to

3 See Matthew 22:15-22

choose: was he a supporter of the hated Roman oppressors, or a rebel whose fate would be swift and certain?

Jesus, knowing their hypocritical motive, asked to be shown a Roman coin. "Whose image is this?" he asked them.

"Caesar's," they responded warily.

"Then give to Caesar what is Caesar's, and to God what is God's," Jesus replied.

The Pharisees were momentarily deflated, but undeterred. Later, the interrogation continued until an expert in the Law asked a significant question: Out of the 613 commandments contained in the Torah (the first five books of the Old Testament), which one was most important? Certainly, this was a carefully thought-out question, designed to either create unending theological arguments or—at the very least—sheer bewilderment.

Jesus' reply reveals to us the loving and relational heart of God, and the purpose for which we exist. Jesus said, "'Love the Lord your God with all your heart and with all your soul and with all your mind.' This is the first and greatest commandment. And the second is like it: 'Love your neighbor as yourself.'"

In a nutshell, Jesus was telling them: it's not about the religion. It's about the *relationship*!

The Purpose Is All about Love

Jesus' answer to the lawyer's question invites each one of us—you and me—to respond to God's great love for us by eagerly turning in love toward him, and then toward others as we love ourselves. Jesus then makes the incredible statement that all of the Old Testament Scriptures—the Law and the Prophets—*depend* on these two commands.

Jesus responded to the question about which was the greatest of the 613 commandments with two. First, he referred to the *shema* in Deuteronomy 6:4-5, well known to every Orthodox Jew as the words they would speak daily and before each entry to the local synagogue. Jesus then joined the *shema* with the latter part of Leviticus 19:18, "Do not seek revenge or bear a grudge against one of your people, but love your neighbor as yourself. I am the Lord."

To the religious mindset of the Pharisees (and even to many religious people today), this was a stunning revelation. Jesus pointed to a God who calls us to intimate relationship with himself, with our neighbors, and even with ourselves. This was in sharp contrast to the legalistic rule-bound religious tapestry of first-century Judaism.

RELIGION	JESUS
Rules and Performance	Love Relationship

The Purpose for Which You Were Made

One of the most important questions any of us will ever be asked is, "What is your purpose in life?" Another, more practical way to ask the question is, "Why do you do what you do?"

How would *you* answer? Why did *you* get up this morning? Why did you go to school or work today? According to Jesus, the answer to each of these questions is penetrating and practical: **our purpose is to love God, and to love our brothers and sisters as we love ourselves**. In other words, life is all about *relationships.*

Conversely, isn't it interesting how much our world seems to be all about the acquisition of *things*? About focusing on the false gods of the world, like money, sex and power? All of these things are temporal, and none of them will truly make us happy.

Over forty-six years ago, my father-in-law and longtime mentor, Doug Coe, said to me around the time I was marrying his daughter, Debbie: "Doug, invest your life in things that are eternal. I can think of two: a relationship with Jesus Christ, and relationships *in* Christ with family and friends." Then he smiled at me and concluded, "Ten thousand years from now, these things will still matter." Several years after his passing, I note that hardly a day goes by without friends around the world mentioning his influence in their lives, always pointing them to Jesus. Relationships in Jesus Christ are precious and eternal gifts.

The only truly lasting legacy for any of us is our deep and loving investment in relationships—with God and with people. This principle that Jesus was articulating in the Matthew 22 passage is true and timeless, and he wonderfully modeled it in his life during those thirty-three years over two thousand years ago.

The Apostle John captured the essence of Jesus' example to us in his letter written decades after Jesus' resurrection: "God is Love. Whoever lives in love lives in God, and God in him. In this way, love is made complete among us so that we will have confidence on the day of judgment, *because* in this world we are like him."[4] (Or, as the King James version notes, "As he is, so are we in this world.") The Scriptures seem to tell us that love is a Person! Knowing him opens us up to a new world of love and relationship, a relationship to which Jesus calls us to commit as our purpose and primary goal in life. The happiest people in the world are those fortunate ones who heed this clarion call of Jesus.

Living Our Purpose in Real Life

Someone might easily ask the question, "How do I live out my purpose? It sounds great, but what does it look like in everyday life?"

To answer this question, it's helpful to look at the whole of Scripture, not just the New Testament. The New Testament Scriptures were written in Greek, and first-century Greeks tended to be very cerebral, philosophical thinkers. Knowing this makes it easy to understand how Jesus' instructions that we should "love God with all of our heart" (heart is synonymous in Scripture with spirit), "all of our soul" (the soul was thought to be the intellect, the emotions, and the will—the thinking and reasoning part of us), "and all of our mind" (seemingly at least partially repetitive of the soul), would be related in this more conceptual way.

The Old Testament, on the other hand, was written in Hebrew—a much more earthy, practical, and illustrative language. Note the difference in the parallel passage that communicates the same principle: "Hear, O Israel: The Lord our God, the Lord is one. Love the Lord your God with all your heart, and with all your soul, and with all your strength."[5] The Hebraic translation is seemingly more eclectic and practical—we love Him with spirit, soul, and body. In other words, all of our being is involved in this holistic response of love to God.

---

4 1 John 4:6-17, NIV

5 Deuteronomy 6:4-5, NIV

Continuing in the passage in Deuteronomy 6, it appears that this intensely practical Hebrew mind is exhorting us to live this out in ten concrete ways in our daily lives. The writer (likely Moses) offers to us a list of opportune suggestions as to how this purpose can be fleshed out in the day-to-day grind of life:

1. **"Upon your hearts."** When something is a "heart thing," it is the first thought you have each day and the last thought at night. It is precious and ever present. It seldom leaves your mind. It brings you endless happiness, hope, and joy. It is number one, always front and center in your daily existence. It brings sheer delight.
2. **"Impress them on your children."** As our four children were growing up, I regularly tried to engage them in conversation about matters of life, the most important being what was their purpose or goal. My wife remembers the same practices in her childhood home. As Debbie vividly recalls from her years of growing up with five siblings, they would be asked a host of questions by their father, always concluding with this same quintessential question. She noted, "I could say it all in three seconds!"
3. **"Talk about them when you sit at home."** As I write this chapter, we are in the middle of the epic Corona virus quarantine. While we are all self-isolating at home for weeks on end, we might be asking ourselves, "What are the most important things to be talking about?" What a tremendous opportunity! I believe there is no more relevant and revolutionary topic to reflect upon and discuss amongst our closest relationships than our heart motivation for what our lives are truly about. *What does it look like for each of us to love God with all of our being? How can we encourage one another to embrace these three loves as a practical hallmark of who we are and what we do?* Whether during a quarantine or at any other time, these are crucial conversations.
4. **"When you walk along the road."** There is no part of our lives that is meant to exclude this all-encompassing mandate. There is no "time off" or "time on" for those who embrace this relational challenge. I often am reminded of this when I borrow my wife's car and hear the worship

songs that play loudly as she travels hither and yon. Our daily lives can be moment-by-moment opportunities to commune with Jesus in thought and in action. As we go from here to there, it is yet another chance to spend time with the Lord. In the words of the old hymn, "And He walks with me, and He talks with me, and He tells me I am His own. And the joy we share as we tarry there, none other has ever known."[6] As my good friend, Dr. Tony Campolo, used to say, "Don't sing it if you aren't doing it."

5. **"When you lie down."** After a long day, our last thought at night is hopefully one that is in communion with the One whom we seek to live for and live with each hour of the day. We can so easily be beaten down by the bumps and bruises our daily lives often bring. What a great way to conclude the day, to review it through the lens of our loving friend and leader, Jesus Christ. It is also a great time to reflect on any relational work that needs to be done with our brothers and sisters in forgiveness and reconciliation. I have a strong hunch that we sleep better and more peacefully when as the hymn intones, "It is well with my soul."
6. **"When you get up."** Hopefully, our first thought of the day is to be in tune with God. My longtime friend, Wes, shares, "When I am awake, I like to ask, 'Lord, what is it you have in mind for today? And can I join you?'" What a great way to start every day! Wes and I often talk about the fact that we both used to think we were supposed to work *for* God. Then, we realized he wanted us to work *with* him. That makes all the difference. No more burnout. Jesus' tender calling to us is clear: "Come to me, all you who are weary and burdened, and I will give you rest. Take my yoke upon you and learn from me, for I am gentle and humble in heart, and you will find rest for your souls. For my yoke is easy and my burden is light."[7]
7. **"Tie them as symbols on your hands."** We do so much with our hands. Each of us can likely recall a time in life when we either sprained a digit or cut it severely. Simple, routine tasks like buttoning a shirt or tying a

---

6 *In the Garden,* by C. Austin Miles
7 Matthew 11:28-29, NIV

shoe became monumental challenges. That's when we realize how much we rely on our hands to do so much each day! A generation ago, tying a string around your finger was a common way to remember something important. I have worn a ring on my finger the past forty-five years to REMIND me of a covenant that was made with my wife and the Lord. Our hands symbolize activity and getting things done. The reminder of tying this all-important purpose on our hands helps us to remember the words of our Lord in the Upper Room to his disciples, "I am the vine; you are the branches. If a man remains in me and I in him, he will bear much fruit; apart from me you can do nothing."[8]

8. **"Bind them on your foreheads."** The most visible part of us is our forehead. (Some of us regrettably with receding hairlines more than exemplify this truth.) Certainly, it is of primary importance for what is most important in our lives to be prominently displayed. In addition, behind our forehead is our mind. So, in addition to having this purpose firmly placed upon our hearts, it also is to be very much on our minds. Romans 12:2 tells us to "not conform to the pattern of this world, but be transformed by the renewing of your mind." To embrace in our minds the enormity of this purpose requires it to be prominent in our thought process.
9. **"Write them on the doorframes of your houses."** My late friend, Connie, exemplified living a life that clearly modeled this magnificent purpose. I would often visit him at his home. One time, as we were entering the dining room, I remember seeing the *shema* written upon the arch above us. I am most assured he and his family kept it visible as a constant daily reminder of what was most important. In the busyness of life, it is so easy to substitute what seems immediately urgent versus what is a long-term commitment in life.
10. **"And on your gates."** In the first century, gates often served as protection from intruders, but also provided an opportunity to display a message to neighbors and passersby. The warmth and welcome of those who have chosen to live with this lofty purpose as their life's goal would most

8 John 15:5, NIV

surely beckon the casual onlooker to gaze a second time at this unusual place.

These suggestions point us to a lifestyle of practically living out "loving God, others, and ourselves" day after day, year after year. They remind me of the concluding words of the Apostle Paul's message to the Greeks at the Areopagas in Athens: "For in him we live and move and have our being.'"[9] I am firmly convinced that the closer we are able to embrace this lofty purpose as the most important goal of our lives, the more we will gradually become the special and unique individuals created in His image that reflect His likeness: "As he is, so are we in this world."[10]

Good-Bye Religion, Hello Relationship

I would venture to speculate that a large number of conventional church-goers primarily live in the first box in the illustration above. I am not questioning their salvation (Isn't it good to know that is beyond "our pay grade"?), but rather simply observing that the doing of good deeds—tithing, regular church attendance, practicing the Golden Rule, being a good person, etc.—are many people's ultimate reality. The development of a love relationship with Jesus, on the other hand, through feasting on His Word, communing with him, sharing His life with other followers, and reaching out in love to care for others are where the joy and life of Jesus are truly found and demonstrated.

A wonderful Bible story that supremely illustrates the contrast between religion (a commitment to rules and performance) and a love relationship with Jesus (a commitment to grace and intimacy) is the miraculous, autobiographical account of Saul of Tarsus. Saul's conversion, as related in Acts chapter 9, is the beginning of this incredible story: "Saul, still breathing out murderous threats against the Lord's disciples, went to the High Priest and asked him for letters to the synagogues in Damascus, so that if he found any there who belonged to the Way, whether men or women, he might take them as prisoners to Jerusalem."[11]

---

9 Acts 17:28, NIV
10 1 John 4:17, KJV
11 Acts 9:1-2, NIV

The story goes on, "As Saul headed toward Damascus, seeking to arrest followers of Jesus, believing them to be heretics who followed a false messiah, he was suddenly blinded by a light flashing from Heaven. A voice spoke from the light, 'Saul, Saul, why do you persecute me?'

'Who are you, Lord?' Saul asked.

'I am Jesus, whom you are persecuting,' (the voice) replied. 'Now get up and go into the city, and you will be told what you must do.'"[12]

Paul tells his story in his own words in Philippians 3:3-14, providing us with an autobiographical account of one person's miraculous journey from the legalistic confines of the religious box to the liberating position of finding his place in Christ Jesus. In summary, Paul describes what happened in the process:

1. He threw off his old basis for identity (religion and performance).

"For it is we who are the circumcision, we who worship by the Spirit of God, who glory in Christ Jesus, and who put no confidence in the flesh—though I myself have reasons for such confidence. If anyone thinks he has reasons to put confidence in the flesh, I have more:

"Circumcised on the eighth day, of the people of Israel, of the tribe of Benjamin, a Hebrew of Hebrews; in regard to the law a Pharisee; as for zeal, persecuting the church; as for legalistic righteousness, faultless."[13]

Paul reflects upon his former life, and seems to boast when he says, "If anyone thinks he has reason to put confidence in the flesh (the performance standard), I have more." (In other words, if you put your ladder up on the wall of religious performance, his went much higher!)

Then he goes through his credentials. To a first-century follower of Judaism, they are the top of the heap. He begins by noting his new reason for rejoicing—worshiping by the Spirit of God rather than by seeking to climb the religious ladder of works. He recites his impressive list of credentials for the latter.

Paul was well known in Jerusalem as a leading Pharisee, a respected and articulate teacher. His zealous commitment to his faith tradition was emphasized by his ferocious desire to seek out and arrest the followers of Jesus. The beginning

---

12 Acts 9:4-6, NIV

13 Philippians 3:3-6, NIV

of Acts 8, relating the stoning of Stephen, notes, "And Saul was there, giving approval to his death."

The final capstone to this impressive list of accomplishments is his boast to having faultlessly obeyed all six hundred and thirteen commandments in the Torah. This is a staggering accomplishment to any of us who have sought to wade through all the ceremonial washings of the Sabbath and the unending list of religious duties contained in the first five books of the Old Testament. Saul of Tarsus was truly a devoted religious man, seeking to climb the ladder of performance he thought was the way to God.

2. He underwent a metamorphosis.

"But whatever was to my profit I now consider loss for the sake of Christ. What is more, I consider everything a loss compared to the surpassing greatness of knowing Christ Jesus my Lord, for whose sake I have lost all things. I consider them rubbish, that I may gain Christ and be found in him, not having a righteousness of my own that comes from the law, but that which is through faith in Christ—the righteousness that comes from God and is by faith."[14]

The word "rubbish" in the passage above is actually a very kind translation. The actual Greek word, *skýbalon,* is best translated "dung." We all know that, these days, one is not even supposed to walk a dog without a "pooper scooper." We've been taught that dung is something to be removed and eliminated as quickly as possible. What an analogy to use—all the things Paul had previously valued were as dung to him that he "might gain Christ and be found in him"!

As we consider the transformation in Paul's life after his encounter on the road to Damascus, perhaps the appropriate term to use is "metamorphosis," meaning a radical change. Most of us identify it with the transformation from caterpillar to butterfly or from tadpole to frog. As we think about the stages of metamorphosis, we can envision the hand of God throughout that miraculous process. This can help us understand the radical nature of the Spirit of God in transforming an extremely religious zealot into a passionate lover of Jesus.

The response of the religious leaders to Paul's "metamorphosis" cost him everything he had earned over the years in advancing in the religious hierarchy.

---

14 Philippians 3:7-9, NIV

He lost his status and the admiration and respect of all of his peers. For the rest of his life until his martyrdom, he experienced repeated persecution, imprisonment, and harassment. Perhaps the time is coming when the followers of Jesus in the Western world will experience persecution. Certainly, religious persecution is rampant around the rest of the world.

Having traveled frequently to the Soviet Union—and now the nations of the former USSR—for the past fifty-five years, I have rubbed shoulders with many who have lost everything for their stand for Jesus. I particularly remember a visit to Moscow in 1990, just a year before the Soviet Union fell. It was a gathering of 1500 Soviet pastors and church leaders sponsored by the Lausanne Committee, a network founded in 1974 by Billy Graham in Lausanne, Switzerland, and dedicated to world evangelization.

I was serving as President of Young Life at the time, and was part of a group of six para church presidents, including Youth for Christ, Navigators, Campus Crusade, Inter Varsity, and Fellowship of Christian Athletes, most of whom were at the event. After several days of meetings, toward the conclusion of the conference, we were all asked to stand for a moment of silence to remember all those who had given their lives or were imprisoned and tortured for their faith in the previous fifty years in the Soviet Union.

As we quietly stood in prayer, the realization struck me that I was one of the only ones in that vast assembly who had not lost a spouse, child, mother, father, or friend in those years when standing for your personal faith often meant death, imprisonment, exile, torture, and, for any young person, exclusion from any opportunity of higher education or position of prestige. I began to quietly weep as I realized that what I had so often taken for granted—the freedom to express and practice my faith—was a privilege to be cherished, not a universal right to be taken for granted.

So many of my heroes are the friends I have met over these fifty-five years, whose sacrifice was extraordinary. They understand losing everything, but every one of them emerged with an ebullient joy that radiates from their countenance. My longtime friend and brother, Pastor Joseph Bondarenko, endured repeated imprisonments and beatings which he chronicles in his wonderful book, *The KGB's Most Wanted.* This was routine for so many of these dear souls who counted everything they possessed before as "dung" compared to being counted as a follower of Jesus.

3. He established a new basis for his identity.

> *"I want to know Christ and the power of his resurrection and the fellowship of sharing in his sufferings, becoming like him in his death, and so, somehow, to attain to the resurrection from the dead. Not that I have already obtained all this, or have already been made perfect, but I press on to take hold of that for which Christ Jesus took hold of me. Brothers, I do not consider myself yet to have taken hold of it. But one thing I do: Forgetting what is behind and straining toward what is ahead, I press on toward the goal to win the prize for which God has called me heavenward in Christ Jesus."*[15]

Paul's frequent use of the term "in him" or "in Christ" is informative. One of my prized possessions is a book, *In Christ,* given to me many years ago. It was authored by the late E. Stanley Jones, a British missionary to India is the early twentieth century. Jones notes in the preface that he had looked for many years for one term that would summarize the essence of the mystery of following Jesus Christ. He concludes that he found it in the Greek phrase, *en Christo*—"in Christ." It is a term used one hundred and seventy-two times in the New Testament and, according to Jones, is the quintessential summary of what it means to follow Jesus.

He notes, "You are either in Christ or out of Christ." He likens it to marriage. One would never answer to the question, "Are you married?" by saying, "Sometimes." You either are or you aren't! Similarly, Paul employs the term "in Christ" to indicate that in his metamorphosis he has found a new identity—in a loving and close relationship with Jesus.

Paul concludes his autobiographical testimony by affirming a brand-new vision for his life—to know Christ and to experience the power of the Risen One, even to the point of suffering and perhaps martyrdom, which in the end he experiences. What strikes me in this new affirmation is the humility of

---

15 Philippians 3:10-14, NIV

this new man in Christ. He seems very clear about the ultimate destination in this journey of faith—to know Jesus by "taking hold of that which Christ Jesus took hold of me." And, as he reaffirms that he is not yet there, he refers to "winning the prize." The winner of the Greek races usually received a prize, which might be a beautiful wreath or even a cash remuneration. The follower of Jesus possesses the incredible hope of being with Jesus in glory. It is this association that now forms the basis of his or her identity. This is our purpose—this is our prize!

Risking It All for Jesus

On my visits to the former Soviet Union when it was in bondage under Communism, I noted that one of the most frequent subjects of the Sunday sermons I heard was this hope of eternal life. In the midst of withering persecution and suffering, the followers of Jesus would cling to the hope of being with Jesus. That living hope would give them purpose and buoy them in times of distress and seeming hopelessness. As I write this, we are all aware of many places in the world where this kind of suffering is a daily menu for followers of Jesus.

Over the past twenty-five years, I have had the privilege to do about sixty-five conferences about the principles of Jesus in all fifteen former Soviet republics and in every region of Russia. A number of these were secretly held in "closed countries." I recall in one occasion in Uzbekistan, as we drove to a remote setting in the countryside outside of Tashkent, I was told that if discovered, the likely sentence for the leaders would be five years in prison. (As an American, I would most likely be quickly escorted out of the country.)

As I asked them whether it was worth it to them to risk a four-day gathering in secret for a hundred and seventy-five young people, I recall the beaming faces that turned my way to give unbridled assent to my query. As we arrived for the conference, I remember walking into the meeting place several hours before we began, and seeing over a hundred young people singing and worshipping the Lord. I sat in the back, my eyes filled with tears, and thanked the Lord for the inexpressible privilege of being with these kids and lifting up Jesus. Those memories in Tadjikhistan, Kazakhstan, Turkmenistan, Azerbaijan, Kyrgystan, Eastern Siberia, and Chechnya remain embedded in my mind and heart and continually remind me what a gift we all too often take for granted in the Western world.

It is humorous to note Paul's concluding word in Philippians 3:15, after he shares his journey: "All of us who are mature should take such a view of things. And if on some point you think differently, that too God will make clear to you." In other words, he is telling all of us, "Trust me, friends, if it doesn't make sense right now, it absolutely will down the road." It might be his way of reminding us of that reality described in 2 Corinthians 5:7, "We live by faith, not by sight." It certainly indicates his abiding confidence in the veracity of the journey he has been privileged to walk before us.

Perhaps the journey of Saul of Tarsus, religious zealot and persecutor of the followers of Jesus, to the Apostle Paul, one who longed to know and follow the Lord Jesus at all cost, is one of the very best examples to consider and to emulate.

Loving Others … As We Love Ourselves

We have already thought much about love for God and others, but I would be remiss to not consider the subject of love for self. It can make us uneasy to address the topic of self-love. It is many times confused with selfish love, in which I make my own wants, needs, and pleasures the center of my life. Narcissism is unfortunately common in our day, and it evokes revulsion in us when our lives intersect such a one.

However, I believe the most accurate definition of self-love is agreeing with God about who I am. He made each of us unique, never another one like us in the history of the world. The Psalmist graphically illustrates this beautiful reality:

> *"For you created my inmost being; you knit me together in my mother's womb. I praise you because I am fearfully and wonderfully made; your works are wonderful, I know that full well. My frame was not hidden from you when I was made in the secret place. When I was woven together in the depths of the earth, your eyes saw my unformed body. All the days ordained for me were written in your book before one of them came to be. How precious to me are your thoughts, O God. How vast is the sum of them! Were I to count*

> *them, they would outnumber the grains of sand. When I awake, I am still with you."*[16]

What a beautiful, relational description of God's purpose and desire to continue the intimacy He began when He created each of us! How could each of us not realize how loved we are by the intricacy of His design as described in this Psalm?

For many years I have quoted Herb Barks, who famously said, "God don't make no junk." A few years ago, as I walked into The Cedars, I introduced myself to a stranger in the doorway. "Dan Barks is my name, from Tennessee," he responded. I asked him if his father was Herb, and he jumped back in surprise and said he was. Then I told him I had been quoting his father for years without absolute assurance I was on target.

As I repeated the above quotation, Dan beamed in assent. And, friends, God beams in assent to us that, indeed, "He don't make no junk." I am convinced that our deep and unconditional love for others is always crafted by a sincere regard and affection for the design of our God when He created us. We often quote the verse, "We love because He first loved us."[17] In the same way, we can love others only out of an appreciative reverence for the skillful handiwork of God as was demonstrated when He designed each of us. Once again, Scripture beautifully undergirds this thought:

> *"But now, this is what the Lord says—he who created you, O Jacob, he who formed you, O Israel: Fear not for I have redeemed you; I have summoned you by name; you are mine. When you pass through the waters, I will be with you; and when you pass through the rivers, they will not sweep over you. When you walk through the fire, you will not be burned; the flames will not set you ablaze. For I am the Lord, your God, the Holy One of Israel, your Savior; I give Egypt for your ransom, Cush and Seba in your stead. Since you are precious and honored in my sight, and because I love you, I will give men in exchange for your life. Do not be afraid for I am with you."*[18]

---

16 Psalm 139:13-18, NIV

17 1 John 4:19

18 Isaiah 43:1-5, NIV

I believe the reason our Lord included self in the three loves in the Great Commandment is that self-love is intricately woven into the fabric of God's amazing design for love that He beckons us toward in this life. He calls us and woos us to Himself in Jesus Christ. This lofty purpose is the most worthy goal for any of us as we consider what is of supreme importance in our lives.

Jesus, the One who is Lord of all, calls us to himself in love. He beckons us to give what we have to him—to love him with all of our heart, all of our soul, and all of our mind. In return, he has already offered himself to us—his love, his guidance, his leadership in our lives. It is the best offer we will ever have. We have the privilege and opportunity to bring everything we have and everything we are to Jesus. He not only awaits us but, like the father in the Prodigal Son story,[19] he sees us a long way off, and runs to us in a loving embrace.

---

19 See Luke 15

Chapter Two

The Work of God

"Then they asked him, 'What must we do to do the works God requires?' Jesus answered, 'The work of God is this: to believe in the one he has sent.'" (John 6:28-29, NIV)

The excitement around Jesus had reached a fevered pitch. The previous afternoon, he had fed five thousand men, plus women and children, with five barley loaves and two fish, the single lunch of a young boy. Later that night, he walked across stormy waves to reach the boat carrying his disciples, and at once they reached their destination.

The growing crowds were realizing this was no ordinary man, and as they encountered him on the other side of the lake, they asked an important question. They wanted to know how one might do the *works* (plural) they thought God required. Jesus responded with one singular but profound answer: the true work of God is to believe in the One sent by God.

Are you surprised that this was Jesus' simple answer? If someone had come up to *you* and asked this question, what answer would you have given? Sit back and ponder this for a moment, because this is intensely practical—and supremely important. Perhaps, like the crowd to whom Jesus spoke, you gasp. What? That's all there is to it? All I have to do to fulfill the work God requires is … *believe*? In *Jesus*?

Before we seek to address this very practical and powerful principle, it would be important to recognize that believing is central to making an initial commitment to Jesus. In my Young Life years, I often had the privilege to speak to kids at camp for a week. On the sixth night, I would address commitment. Ironically, this was generally after the whole camp had been on the ropes course.

The last stage of the ropes course would have each young person standing next to me, forty feet in the air, on a platform. They have to leap through the air to grab the trapeze, which then will lower them to the group. While each person is belayed, it is still frightening for many, including myself who has never loved heights. It is a wonderful example to use, because a commitment to Jesus Christ, like that leap into the air, involves "a leap of faith."

I would tell the kids it is as simple as A-B-C:

1. ***Admit*** **my need for Jesus.** *(1 John 1:9 "If we confess our sins, he is faithful and just and will forgive us our sins and purify us from all unrighteousness." NIV)*
2. ***Believe*** **that he is the son of God** and the one that is best qualified to lead my life. *(Romans 10:9-10 "If you declare with your mouth, 'Jesus is Lord,' and believe in your heart that God raised him from the dead, you will be saved. For it is with your heart that you believe and are justified, and it is with your mouth that you profess your faith and are saved." NIV)*
3. ***Commit*** **as much of myself as I know to as much of him as I know**, realizing both will surely grow in the years ahead. *(Psalm 37:5 "Commit your way to the Lord. Trust in him, and he will act." ESV)* Without this step, the rest of our discussion is irrelevant.

Listen to Your Spiritual Smoke Alarm

Let's stop for a moment and look at the flip side of belief—unbelief. Every time you worry, or get angry or fearful, it is a symptom of *unbelief* (the opposite of the work of God).

When we worry, we are really saying that there is no one to trust or rely upon to help us in our quandary. When we become angry, it is often because a right we feel entitled to is being trampled upon. Our Lord would have us surrender those rights to him, and he will give them back to us as privileges. This results in an attitude of gratitude.

I often tell the young men I meet with at The Cedars that we can ask the Lord to install a "spiritual smoke alarm" in our head and heart, so that every time we worry, get angry, or become fearful it goes off and reminds us—*do the work of God*. And, I'm not just talking to them when I encourage them; I find that my own "spiritual smoke alarm" is also frequently triggered! I need to remind myself constantly of this principle.

Some years ago, I traveled to Moscow for several days to meet with members of the Russian Duma. Then I flew to Armenia to spend several days with young men and women in a Youth Core community that had started in the nineties. I was joined a day later by a physician friend who was committed to supporting these young friends.

As he arrived, he looked concerned. He told me the Russian visas I had earlier secured for us were only single entry. I disagreed, telling him I had specifically requested double entries. As I checked my passport, to my astonishment he was correct. I had already used my entry. It was Friday afternoon in Yerevan, the capital, and the Russian Embassy had already closed for the weekend. I had a flight back to Moscow on Monday afternoon, and one hundred young people from ten cities in five different nations were coming for a four-day leadership retreat. I was also in possession of financial support for many of them.

As I lay in bed at night over the weekend, I found myself fighting worry, some anger at the person who ignored my important request, and fear about the seemingly inevitable consequences. (That's right, *unbelief*.) I felt that I was in a serious battle regarding my trust in Jesus' provision. But, as Monday morning came, I found an amazing peace sweeping over me. The Lord gave me the strong impression that I should go to the Russian Embassy with my Armenian translator and seek to connect with the administrator in the visa office—a dubious hope.

As I arrived, there was a long line at the door. I sensed I should ask the guard if I could go inside and ask a question. He motioned me ahead. Inside was a young man who spoke perfect English. I suddenly had the thought that I should tell him I was from Washington D.C. and needed to get to Moscow later that day, avoiding placing blame on the consular agent who had failed to heed my request for a double entry. I had received an impression that reaching out as a friend was better than any other path.

The man smiled and told me about his years in Washington when his father worked in the Russian Embassy. He invited me to sit down, and soon I was able to share my dilemma with him. Then he asked a surprising question—did I have any Russian friends in influential positions? I handed him the business card of a longtime friend. Fifteen minutes later, he returned from calling him, noting how badly this friend wanted me to return to Moscow. Since I lacked the required formal letter of invitation, and despite the usual seven-day waiting period, he asked me if I had a hundred and fifty dollars in Armenian money. I called my Armenian translator for help, and she soon returned with the money. Leaving with the new visa in hand, my new friend embraced me and expressed his hope that we would meet again in Washington someday.

I was overcome by the goodness of the Lord and his guidance in a seemingly hopeless situation. I was also aware that, after the events of the weekend, my spiritual smoke alarm probably was in need of new batteries!

What It Means to "Have Faith"

The subject of faith (to "believe") is very prominently mentioned in the four Gospels; in fact, its frequency is only exceeded by mention of the Kingdom of God. So, in studying it, I find it helpful to explore several accounts of Jesus' interaction with people on the issue of faith.

One arresting story is found in Mark 9, where a man comes to Jesus with an enormous and heartbreaking dilemma: his son is plagued with an evil spirit.

> *"A man in the crowd answered, 'Teacher, I brought you my son, who is possessed by a spirit that has robbed him of speech. Whenever it seizes him, it throws him to the ground. He foams at the mouth, gnashes his teeth, and becomes rigid. I asked your disciples to drive out the spirit, but they could not.'*

'O unbelieving generation,' Jesus replied, 'how long shall I stay with you? How long shall I put up with you? Bring the boy to me.'"

Trying to understand this account through the eyes of Jesus, we might observe that everywhere he went, he encountered unbelief. He had come from the Father. He knew what was possible, and the absolute supremacy of believing, even in the face of impossible circumstances. Therefore, it is understandable that his brief, exasperating utterance in the face of continuous unbelief is more of a heavenly sigh than an expression of contempt. Jesus knew that his Father was totally up to the task. So, following this brief pause, he asked for the boy.

"So they brought him. When the spirit saw Jesus, it immediately threw the boy into a convulsion. He fell to the ground and rolled around, foaming at the mouth. Jesus asked the boy's father, 'How long has he been like this?' 'From childhood,' he answered. 'It has often thrown him into fire or water to kill him. But if you can do anything, take pity on us and help us.' 'If you can,' said Jesus. 'EVERYTHING IS POSSIBLE FOR HIM WHO BELIEVES.' Immediately the boy's father exclaimed, 'I do believe; help me overcome my unbelief.'"

Who in the Gospel accounts always instantly recognized Jesus and spoke out? It was the demons. The book of James tells us that these demons believe and they tremble (but don't obey!)[20] Here we clearly see that all kinds of "belief" do not necessarily qualify as the "work that God desires." Not all belief is the same as faith. I love the faith of the father in this story. Perhaps we are a lot like him—we *believe*, but even in that belief, we need help with our *unbelief.*

Imagine entering a room that is illuminated by the light—all except one corner that is completely black. We wonder why the light doesn't penetrate this part of the room. It may be similar to our own lives, in which we want to trust God but have several reservations. We want to determine our future—maybe we grew up in poverty and swore years ago it would be different for our life. Or we hesitate to trust God with our choice of a life partner—we think we

20 James 2:19

know what we are looking for. Maybe we secretly have a list of requirements. So the light, strangely, doesn't get to those remote places of my heart and thinking… where I have quietly determined that I know best what I want for the future.

That is why this principle is so basic. It meets me right where I live—in every corner of my heart, imploring me to trust him with all of it—my future, my life partner, my work, my pocketbook, my dreams—all of it. God wants not only my head knowledge "belief," but more importantly my heart posture belief, which is faith.

Jesus went on to heal the boy, but I love this story because we can so easily identify with the father. Life delivers some crushing blows, and it is often very hard work to believe in the face of pain and adversity. Clearly, the man also made an impression on Jesus. In fact, in the four Gospels, there are only two places where the phrase "Jesus was amazed" is used. Both have to do with the subject of faith. I would invite us to learn from Jesus in each of these encounters.

Belief and Unbelief

> *"When Jesus had finished saying all of this in the hearing of the people, he entered Capernaum. There a centurion's servant, whom his master valued highly, was sick and about to die. The centurion heard of Jesus and sent elders of the Jews to him, asking him to come and heal his servant. When they came to Jesus they pleaded earnestly, 'This man deserves to have you do this, because he loves our nation and has built our synagogue.'*
>
> *So Jesus went with them. He was not far from the house when the centurion sent friends to say to him: 'Lord, don't trouble yourself, for I do not deserve to have you come under my roof. That is why I did not consider myself worthy to come to you. But say the word, and my servant will be healed. For I myself am a man under authority, with soldiers under me. I tell this one, 'Go', and he goes, and that one, 'Come', and he comes. I say to my servant, 'Do this,' and he does it.'*
>
> *When Jesus heard this, he was amazed at him, and turning to the crowd following him, he said, 'I tell you I have not found such great faith even in*

Israel.' Then the men who had been sent returned to the house and found the servant well.'"[21]

Obviously, this Gentile Roman officer was unusual. Unlike most Roman soldiers, he cared for the local people. He built their synagogue, showed love for their nation, and likely had a Jewish servant whom he highly valued. He had never met Jesus, but had heard much about him since Jesus had frequently come to Capernaum and done many miracles.

As Jesus approached his house, his incredible faith showed itself as he sent a delegation to tell Jesus that he recognized the Master need not come personally—he knew simply a word from him would be sufficient to heal his servant. This centurion understood authority, and he felt unworthy that Jesus would enter his house.

I have often thought that one of the greatest things that any of us could ever do would be to amaze Jesus. How would we do it two thousand years after this Roman centurion? **We would do it by believing that Jesus is completely adequate for the problem that appears impossible for me today.** Wouldn't it be a thrill to amaze Jesus by believing him to do that impossible thing! I believe each of us will have that opportunity in the years ahead. And isn't it thrilling that a Gentile Roman officer who had never met Jesus was one who did.

The second time in the Gospels that the phrase "Jesus was amazed" is used is in sharp contrast to the inspiring story of the Roman centurion. On this occasion, Jesus had returned to his hometown, Nazareth. This small, dusty town in Galilee was like any small town—everyone knew one another! It is generally understood that Joseph and Mary settled there when they returned from Egypt, where they had taken the infant/toddler Jesus to protect him from King Herod's efforts to kill all male babies under two.

Jesus began his public ministry at about age thirty, so Nazareth was his home for most likely twenty-seven or twenty-eight years. There he was well-known as a carpenter, like his earthly father. After several years of itinerant ministry, Jesus returned to Nazareth:

---

21 Luke 7:1-10, NIV

> *"Jesus left there and went to his hometown, accompanied by his disciples. When the Sabbath came, he began to teach in the synagogue, and many who heard him were amazed. 'Where did this man get these things,' they asked. 'What's this wisdom that has been given him, that he even does miracles! Isn't this the carpenter? Isn't this Mary's son and the brother of James, Joseph, Judas, and Simon? Aren't his sisters here with us?' And they took offense at him. Jesus said to them, 'Only in his hometown, among his relatives and in his own house is a prophet without honor.' He could not do any miracles there, except lay his hands on a few sick people and heal them. And he was amazed at their lack of faith."*[22]

Upon Jesus' return to Nazareth, he entered the synagogue, where his teaching and perhaps a few miracles amazed the onlookers. What happened after this speaks directly to the dilemma all of us can face: our supposed familiarity often breeds skepticism and even contempt. Rather than ponder the amazing teaching, the people of Nazareth chose to disparage this familiar carpenter, Mary and Joseph's son, whose brothers and sisters continued to live in their midst. As they reasoned in their natural minds, the supernatural event was quickly dismissed. The next day's headlines in *The Jerusalem Times* may well have read: "Jesus Does Nothing at Nazareth"!

We might well ask if this could happen in our own day and age. Is there any situation, even now, where Jesus would choose to do less than his followers would expect? This encounter at Nazareth seems to suggest that, in a climate of unbelief, it might be so.

Jesus Uses Our Faith

To frame it in the positive sense, Jesus responds to the faith of ordinary people in extraordinary ways. Many times in, the Gospel accounts, we see he responded to people, "Be it unto you according to your faith." That is why this principle of the work of God is so fundamental to each of us in our respective journeys of faith.

---

22 Mark 6:1-6, NIV

The writer of Hebrews summarizes the importance of this: "And without faith, it is impossible to please God, because anyone who comes to him must believe that he exists and that he rewards those who earnestly seek him.[23] "This verse highlights two very important points:

1. believing that God exists, and
2. that he rewards those who earnestly seek him

When I first memorized this passage, years ago, I learned it in the Revised Standard Version, which reads," He that comes to God must believe that he is, and he is a rewarder of those who diligently seek him." It sounded repetitive to my mind, until someone pointed out to me that God told Moses in Exodus 3:14 what his name was: "God said to Moses, 'I Am who I Am. This is what you are to say to the Israelites: I Am has sent me to you.'" That helped me understand a little better the emphasis of repetition. Similarly, in the Hebrews passage, we see that in coming to God by faith, we are to believe that—in every situation good or bad—HE IS, and he rewards those who seek him with all of their heart.

What a practical and helpful summary of the essence and importance of faith in our lives. What is it right now where God is challenging *you* to believe that "He Is"? I find that when I am worrying, getting angry, or fearful, I am in actuality saying, "He isn't!" What a deflating lack of faith that is!

Hebrews chapter eleven is often called "the faith chapter," because in its forty verses it chronicles many Old Testament characters who are often viewed as members of the "Hall of Fame" of faith. Upon a closer view, each of them had noticeable flaws of character, but found their place in these hallowed accounts because of their profound faith at very important junctures in history.

I have loved the stories of these heroes of faith for many years. In the early seventies, one of these accounts became very practical in my own life. I had been serving as the area director of Young Life for a suburban part of Seattle for five years, and, as a bachelor, I devoted nearly all my time and energy to seeing the work grow to every high school. As I was preparing for my sixth year, I was at Malibu, the Young Life resort in British Columbia, Canada, for a weekend

23 Hebrews 11:6, NIV

retreat. I was invited to an afternoon meeting, which I entered to find four senior staff members and my soon-to-be replacement. To my surprise, I was told that I would be moving in a week to an area that was in disarray, with a large financial deficit.

That very evening, as the retreat's program director, I was tasked to lead entertainment that evening—hardly what I was excited to do. My world was collapsing around me, and late that night as I sat alone on the boardwalk, I seriously considered resigning, feeling a bit like an unimportant pawn in the organization rather than a valued team member. (I know this was not the intent of my supervisors, but it surely felt that way at the time.) That was precisely when a young woman from the camp office walked up to me and handed me seven letters that had arrived there since my departure from my August assignment. Each was an amazing encouragement from kids who had met the Lord that month, volunteer leaders from home, and adult guests from previous weeks!

As I sat alone late at night, my disappointment in one fist and the encouragement from these letters in the other, I heard God's still small voice speaking to my thoughts, "Trust me. Believe me. The best is yet to come." I'm happy to say, the next few years of ministry were some of the best of my life. The new trainee I picked up the following week became the best man in my wedding several years later, and so many lifelong friends were made in those wonderful years.

A Tale of Two Cities

The Lord also impressed upon my heart a gold nugget from Hebrews 11 that served as a roadmap for the years ahead. To this day, fifty years later, this picture the Lord painted for me speaks volumes.

As I prayed about what God wanted to do in my new assignment, he gave me a vivid illustration from Scripture that I call "The Tale of Two Cities." Borrowing the title from Charles Dickens' classic novel, this picture contrasts the building of two cities: one from Genesis 11, and the other from Hebrews 11.

The first city, famously known as Babel, began with its residents formulating their own plan: "Then they said, 'Come, let us build for ourselves a city, with a tower that reaches to the heavens, so that we may make a name for ourselves and not be scattered over the face of the whole earth.' But the Lord came down to see the city and the tower that the men were building."[24]

No one asked God for his leadership or his plans; he had simply heard the commotion and came to take a look. The result is well known to us: "So the Lord scattered them from there all over the earth, and they stopped building the city."[25] Isn't this so common, even among followers of Jesus? We make our plans, and then we ask the Lord to bless them. What is amazing is that often he does! Yet, there is such a better way, as illustrated in the building of the second city.

Early in Genesis, it is recorded that God spoke to Abraham and asked him to leave his comfortable life in the Ur of Chaldees. However, God's call didn't inform him of the ultimate destination: "By faith Abraham, when called to go to a place he would later receive as his inheritance, obeyed and went, even though he did not know where he was going. By faith he made his home in the promised land like a stranger in a foreign country … For he was looking forward to the city with foundations, whose architect and builder is God."[26]

Here are two different cities, but two radically different strategies. One is constructed the world's way—building something to honor men (or self), totally leaving out the counsel and guidance of the Creator. The second is God's way—stepping out in faith and seeking to bring honor to Him. For Abraham, it meant starting out with the ultimate destination unknown, but with an eye toward "the city that has foundations, whose builder and maker is God." This contrast truly served as a roadmap for me in watching God do amazing things in those following years. It continues to be a reminder that God is always the best architect in building a city or anything else that he calls us to join in with him.

God Delights in Our Faith

Once again, it is an encouragement to each of us that God delights in those who want to work with him rather than just for him. Hebrews 11 concludes by giving a long list of the suffering and martyrdom of many members of this Faith Hall of Fame, and concludes by noting, "These were all commended for their faith, yet none of them received what had been promised. God had planned

24 Genesis 11:4-5, NIV
25 Genesis 11:8, NIV
26 Hebrews 11:8-10, NIV

something better for us so that only together with us would they be made perfect."[27]

What a wonderful conclusion to this blessed chapter of Scripture, chronicling the heroes of faith! All of us find the fulfillment of God's promises throughout history to be found in Jesus Christ. He is the one, and the only one, who perfects our faith. He is the one for whom all of history was waiting. This is why the work of God for each of us is "to believe in the one whom he sent." Jesus answers the yearnings of all of history as he tells us, "I am the resurrection and the life. He who BELIEVES in me will live, even though he dies; and whoever lives and BELIEVES in me will never die. Do you BELIEVE this?"[28]

As I consider the importance of this principle of Jesus, it occurs to me that it is so practical that every minute of the day I am practicing this—believing him. Foundationally, I believe in his redeeming work that makes me a child of God through faith. And then every minute of every day after that, with every fiber of my being, I believe him for every step I make in life, and every situation I encounter. This "work of God" for me is significant because, rather than being merely a static guideline, it is inherently dynamic—growing, relevant, revealing, and a constant reminder that "without faith, it is impossible to please God."

---

27 Hebrews 11:39-40, NIV
28 John 11:25, NIV, emphasis added

Chapter Three

The Message

"You diligently study the Scriptures because you think that by them you possess eternal life. These are the Scriptures that testify about me, yet you refuse to come to me to have life." (John 5:39-40, NIV)

In one of the most startling of Jesus' miracles recorded in the Gospels, He heals a man who has been immobilized for thirty-eight years. That's right—paralyzed and completely unable to move for thirty-eight long, lonely, desperate years.

Like many other disabled individuals in Jerusalem in Jesus' time, this man spent his days lying by a pool that supposedly had healing powers when an "angel" would agitate the water. (If you visit the ruins of this pool today, guides will tell you that the waters of the ancient pools would be intermittently stirred by shifts in water pressure in the pipes that carried water in from nearby springs. This effect created ripples that people superstitiously believed were caused by angels.) Popular legend at the time held that if a person could just get himself to the water when it was being stirred, and be the first one in, he could be miraculously healed. Sadly, this poor man was so profoundly disabled he couldn't even get himself into the water, much less anywhere else! John's account tells us:

> *Afterward Jesus returned to Jerusalem for one of the Jewish holy days. Inside the city, near the Sheep Gate, was the pool of Bethesda, with five covered porches. Crowds of sick people—blind, lame, or paralyzed—lay on the porches. One of the men lying there had been sick for thirty-eight years. When Jesus saw him and knew he had been ill for a long time, he asked him, "Would you like to get well?"*
>
> *"I can't, sir," the sick man said, "for I have no one to put me into the pool when the water bubbles up. Someone else always gets there ahead of me."*
>
> *Jesus told him, "Stand up, pick up your mat, and walk!" Instantly, the man was healed! He rolled up his sleeping mat and began walking!*
>
> *But this miracle happened on the Sabbath, so the Jewish leaders objected. They said to the man who was cured, "You can't work on the Sabbath! The law doesn't allow you to carry that sleeping mat!"*
>
> *But he replied, "The man who healed me told me, 'Pick up your mat and walk.'"*
>
> *"Who said such a thing as that?" they demanded.*
>
> *The man didn't know, for Jesus had disappeared into the crowd. But afterward, Jesus found him in the Temple and told him, "Now you are well; so stop sinning, or something even worse may happen to you." Then the man went and told the Jewish leaders that it was Jesus who had healed him. (John 5:1-15, NLT)*

Jesus had just healed a man who had been an invalid for thirty-eight years, which you would think would be an occasion for celebration. But there was a problem—a big problem. He had done it on the Sabbath.

The Jewish leaders quickly jumped on Jesus for this egregious religious violation, and a long and testy exchange ensued between Jesus and the zealots, whose traditions were being challenged by this One who had the audacity to claim God was his father.[29] As the argument wound toward a conclusion, Jesus recognized that the Pharisees, who knew the Old Testament exceedingly well, had missed the fact that over two hundred and sixty times the Scriptures prophetically referred to the coming Messiah. Entrenched in their rigid mindset, they missed the very One who had been promised to come in those Scriptures—even though, right in front of them, he had healed a man they had all seen lying in utter filth and despair for THIRTY-EIGHT YEARS! Talk about blindness!

But here's a sobering question: Is it possible that many of us who are followers of Jesus can just as easily, 2,000 years later, also miss the essence of the message communicated in the Gospel accounts? It's a question worth looking into …

The Essence of the Gospel

After many years of ministry to young people, my own life was revolutionized some years ago by the realization that the gospel is not information with six points or eight points, but *the gospel is a PERSON.* I can't emphasize enough the significance of this realization.

Think back to the last days of Jesus' life. In the Upper Room, he was spending the evening before his crucifixion with his disciples. John saw him wash his friends' feet, predict his betrayal, and serve them the first communion, after which Judas slipped out into the night (recorded for us in John 13). Then, he dropped a bombshell: he was leaving them (chapter 14). He did tell them he would come again, but most likely that went unheard. These ones who had left everything three years before to follow Jesus became unhinged: "Thomas said to him, 'Lord, we don't know where you are going, so how can we know the way?'

"Jesus answered, 'I am the way and the truth and the life. No one comes to the Father except through me.'"[30]

Consider what Jesus is telling them here. First of all, by using the phrase "I am," as he does numerous other times in John's Gospel, he is identifying himself with God the Father. As we ponder this incredible statement, Jesus is telling us the way to God is a *person*, not a set of directions. He is telling us *truth* is a

29 "For this reason the Jews tried all the harder to kill him; not only was he breaking the Sabbath, but he was even calling God his own Father, making himself equal with God." (John 5:18, NIV)

30 John 14:5-6

person, not a collection of important information. He is also saying, finally, that life's meaning is ultimately found in *relationship* with this person.[31]

Let's stop here. This is important. It was a real revelation to me and maybe it will be for you too. If I truly believe the *way* is a person, that ultimate *truth* is a person, and my *life* can only be found in Jesus, then my journey of faith will be all about … knowing Jesus better and better! He truly is the all in all!

" … in order that they may know the mystery of God, namely Christ, in whom are hidden all the treasures of wisdom and knowledge." (Colossians 2:2-3)

"And this is the testimony: God has given us eternal life, and this life is in his Son. He who has the Son has life; he who does not have the Son of God does not have life." (1 John 5:11-12)

"Moreover your own completeness is realized in him, who is ruler over all authorities, and the supreme head over all powers." (Colossians 2:10, Phillips)

The way becomes a *person*; truth is found in a *person*; life is fulfilled in relationship with this *person*.

Jesus Yes, Religion No

In contrast, if I look up "Christianity," it tells me it is "the religion founded by the early disciples of Jesus." I have been searching for that elusive passage anywhere in Scripture. (If you find it, you will be the first.) If we consider Scripture to be authoritative, it never mentions any religion Jesus came to establish. He never told anyone to convert to a religion, sect, or denomination. He simply said to all manner of people, "Follow me."

In the past twenty-five years of working with the National Prayer Breakfast in Washington, DC, I have regularly encountered people who come from all over the world—from all religious backgrounds. I have listened to testimonies of friends worldwide from every religious background who have met Jesus in the most incredible ways—through dreams, visions, horrific suffering, and miracles. For example, my friend Ahmet, born and raised in Kosovo in a moderate Islamic culture, said, "I learned something I had not known before … that the Gospel is a Person, not information or a set of rules. This was one of the most powerful

31 There are several other times that the person of Jesus is equated with life are equated. John 11:24, "I am the resurrection and the life," and John 1:4, "In him was life and that life was the light of men.")

and transformational things in my life. It was a revolution in my mind, heart, and way of living.

"Jesus' teachings made me different. They made me stronger and even taught me to forgive my enemy of genocidal killings of many close to me. Since then I have felt free—totally released and cleansed from hate. I have felt full of love and warmth in my heart, mind, and soul. I have felt that Jesus entered me, and I have been transformed into a new person. Living with Jesus' principles of unconditional love, forgiveness, and hope is a joy. It is a miracle in my life."

On the other hand, it is so common to read a mission statement or fundraising brochure by a Christian organization or denomination and see it filled with references to Christianity and Christians.[32] Sadly, such documents quite often never mention the name of Jesus, the person from whom all the power and authority is derived!

Maybe this will help illustrate my point. Think about the encounter of Peter and John at the gate Beautiful in Acts 3:6, "Silver and gold I do not have, but what I have I give you. In the name of Jesus Christ of Nazareth, walk!" Did Peter tell the lame man to walk in the name of Christianity? No, he did not. If it had been in the name of Christianity, the man would still be paralyzed!

It's All about Jesus

I often have the privilege to speak at a downtown men's gathering called "His Deal" in Seattle. After one session a few years ago, a businessman came up to me and remarked, "Every time you come here, all you talk about is Jesus." I think he might have meant it as a curiosity. I received it as a badge of honor: our message is him!

Like the Apostle Paul said, " … the mystery that has been kept hidden for ages and generations, but is now disclosed to the saints. To them God has chosen to make known among the Gentiles the glorious riches of this mystery, which is Christ in you, the hope of glory. WE PROCLAIM HIM, admonishing and teaching everyone with all wisdom, so that we may present everyone perfect in

32 While the word "Christian is a scriptural term—used three times in the New Testament, twice in the Book of Acts and once in 1 Peter—across the world in religious hot zones like India or the Middle East it can often feel tainted because of the perceived actions of those claiming its name.

Christ. To this end I labor, struggling with all his energy, which so powerfully works in me."[33] Paul's beautiful message to the Colossians, and to all of us, captures the essence of this powerful message—it is Jesus living in us.

The term "perfect" in the Greek is *teleios*, which means "fully mature." Jesus used it in his Sermon on the Mount when he said, "Be perfect, therefore, as your heavenly father is perfect."[34] In practical terms, it means to be the person God had in mind when he created each one of us. I often tell the young men I meet with that if there would ever be reason for sadness in Heaven, it might be when we catch a glimpse of what our Designer had in mind when he uniquely created each of us—unlike anyone else in the history of the world—with our unique DNA—in body, soul and spirit. We are created in his image, and the closer we come to Jesus, the more we discover who we are.[35] David Benner, in his book, *The Gift of Being Yourself*, summarizes, "It is like putting on a perfectly custom-tailored dress or suit after wearing clothes made for other people. Our self-in-Christ is a self that fits perfectly because it is completely us. Sadly, our world is ravaged by depression, mental illness, addictions, and so many other things that are often symptoms of a frantic and fruitless search for identity and meaning. We only discover that meaning and value in the one "who holds all things together."[36]

Many years ago, I helped lead a Young Life basketball trip to Australia. We had assembled a dozen young men from around the country and embarked on a month-long tour to play various teams from Down Under. It was a great time. One of the highlights of the time was meeting and hearing from Major Ian Thomas, the renowned author of *The Saving Life of Christ.* His singular message to us was drawn from Galatians 2:20: "I have been crucified with Christ and I no longer live, but Christ lives in me. The life I live in the body, I live by faith in the Son of God, who loved me and gave himself for me." I remember that this message deeply resonated in me. He called it, "the exchanged life." I put to death the old man, and Jesus brings to life the one he created unique in his

33 Colossians 1:26-29, NIV
34 Matthew 5:48
35 Colossians 1:16-17
36 Benner, David G. *The Gift of Being Yourself: The Sacred Call to Self-Discovery*. Downers Grove, IL: IVP Books, 2015, p. 95.

image. My new life is defined by the power and presence of Jesus living in and through me.

The late Dr. Richard Halverson, former Chaplain of the U.S. Senate and the man who married my wife and me, had a little formula in which he sought to capture this reality:

"Jesus + nothing = everything."

When I first heard this, it was confusing. As I reflected upon it, and life's experiences seemed to validate it, I realized it is so easy to unconsciously add something to Jesus. I think we seldom do this intentionally, but the enemy sure loves it when it happens.

For example, we hear a lot about the prosperity gospel—supposedly, if we follow Jesus, he will "prosper" us. Most certainly there is a grain of truth in this, but to make it a key part of our message is to misappropriate that truth. That single misappropriation can take people down the wrong path very quickly and very destructively. And it doesn't have to be prosperity that is our "plus" when it comes to adding to Jesus; it can be anything. In my years of ministry through Young Life, I think I unconsciously thought a week at Malibu was all but indispensable for a young person to meet Jesus. Jesus + Malibu!

Perhaps the most humorous example I have heard of adding to the gospel was from an eighteen-year-old girl from a village six hours out of Ashkhabad, Turkmenistan. While I was at a Jesus conference in that country, she shared what *she* had added to Jesus: "No lipstick, no makeup, no rouge." Her Baptist pastor had legalized some New Testament teachings about women's behavior and presentation. She received it as part of the message. The Holy Spirit revealed to her that, as she encountered women wearing makeup, she was having a judgmental heart toward them. This was not from Jesus, but a divisive thing that got in the way of her walk with Jesus—and her relationship with some of his followers.

Surrendering the Need for Control

So often, the adding of something to Jesus is all about control. When Jesus overturned the tables in the synagogue, he was reacting to the control of religion by the scribes and Pharisees. Jesus famously told his disciples, "So, if the Son sets you free, you are free indeed."[37] Obviously, this freedom in Christ has boundaries, but when we are operating in it, we are no longer subject to a long list of dos and don'ts.

I mentioned earlier that this realization that the gospel is a person has revolutionized my life. There are several notable ways in which it has. I find that I have quietly discarded terms like "Christianity," "Christian," "saved," and other such popular terms, not because they are wrong, but because they can so easily be misconstrued by their connotations.

For instance, if I am sitting on an airplane reading my Bible, and the person next to me asks, "Oh, are you a Christian?" I might respond, "I used to be, and then I met Jesus." I am not wanting to be evasive or "cutesy," but what are we going to be talking about next? Most likely it will be the difference between religion and a love relationship with Jesus. I would be most willing to wager that this person is highly likely to have experienced judgmentalism, legalism, or hypocrisy in his or her encounters with religion or with people of faith. I would love to talk about a love relationship with Jesus, and also to listen to his or her story of their respective journey and its joys and/or heartaches.

Another way this has changed my life is I no longer find myself getting into religious arguments. My longtime friend, Jim, formerly the athletic chaplain at Stanford University for over forty years, in his book, *One on One* notes, "In over forty years of ministry, I never brought a person to Christ by winning (or losing) an argument." When I read this, I totally agreed. In almost fifty-five years of working with young people, I have also never convinced anyone to follow Jesus through argument. As Paul exhorts us, "Warn them before God about quarreling about words; it is of no value, and only ruins those who listen."[38] With this in mind, when I am meeting with someone and the discussion moves toward argument, I quietly step back and listen rather than take the person on. I find that if I do further engage, it rapidly becomes my ego versus theirs, and tempers flare and no one wins.

A third area that has become very clear is the realization that I don't convert or change anyone—the Spirit of God does! Therefore, I find that as I am preparing

---

37 John 8:36, NIV
38 2 Timothy 2:14

a message, I am increasingly asking the Lord what he wants to say to this group, realizing the truth of Paul's words, "No eye has seen, no ear has heard, no mind has conceived what God has prepared for those who love him—but God has revealed it to us by his Spirit."[39] In other words, the Lord knows the hearts of this crowd—their hopes and fears, their joys and sorrows—and what is needed to be said today. Wouldn't it be great if, indeed, Jesus showed up to speak to these folks! I think he wants to. The only person standing in the way is myself—and my flesh that decides what needs to be said.

I experienced this recently when I was at a church in Seattle where I have often preached over the years. My message was prepared, but I strangely lacked a peaceful feeling about it. As I sat in the back of the Sunday School class before the worship service, I felt the Lord speaking to me: "Share your pain and be very specific." I had no idea what this might look like. Then I had a picture in my mind's eye of playing ping pong with Jesus—I would share from a painful area of current difficulty in my life, and his response would be from God's word: "And as for those who try to make your life a misery, bless them. Don't curse, bless."[40] As the ball came back to me, I would further respond about a perceived injustice from others. Jesus would hit back, "'It is mine to avenge; I will repay,' says the Lord, and 'If your enemy is hungry, feed him; if he is thirsty, give him something to drink.'"[41] So, as I shared some pain in my life, Jesus helped me to respond in the opposite manner of how I would naturally have chosen.

As I continued with another area of current challenge and pain, I hit it back to Jesus. He responded, "When all kinds of trials and temptations crowd into your lives, my brothers, don't resent them as intruders, but welcome them as friends! Realize that they come to test your faith and to produce in you the quality of endurance. But let the process go on until that endurance is fully developed, and you will find that you have become people of mature character…"[42]

Obviously, it helped that I had earlier committed these passages to memory, but the ping pong match continued for ten to twelve returns—me sharing my pain and struggle, and our Lord giving me comfort and solace in his amazing

39 1 Corinthians 2:9-10
40 Romans 12:14, PHILLIPS
41 Romans 12:19-20, NIV
42 James 1:2-4, PHILLIPS

perspective. When I finished, I felt pretty naked—having shared some painful struggles with the audience, but also offering God's healing words to these painful situations. As the service concluded, I had one of the surprises of my life—a line of people, many weeping, thanking me for this sharing (which I admit was done with some initially begrudging thoughts). It was a powerful lesson to me that the Lord, and he alone, knows the hearts and minds of those we encounter in ministry.

Several days later, I spoke with my younger sister, Jan, who attends this church with her husband. She asked me, "Do you have any idea what happened Sunday?"

I answered, "Not really, but I think I am beginning to understand."

She said, "I have listened to you preach for fifty years. I have never heard anything from you that powerful."

Today, it is slowly becoming more natural for me to surrender control and ask God for *his* words and his thoughts. Even the gifted Apostle Paul confessed, "In myself, I was feeling far from strong; I was nervous and rather shaky. What I said and preached had none of the attractiveness of the clever mind, but it was a demonstration of the power of the Spirit. Plainly, God's purpose was that your faith should rest not upon man's cleverness, but upon the power of God."[43] This is a significant part of what it means to surrender control. As I grow in my understanding that the gospel is a person—not a religion, system, or body of rules—I find myself relying more and more upon him to speak and act through me. It is a blessed journey.

Over the years of sharing this principle of the gospel message, I have witnessed the work of the Holy Spirit in communicating and authenticating the veracity of the gospel being a person. One of the most memorable occurred about twenty years ago while I was driving a fifteen-passenger van filled with college students from the University of Washington. We were taking several days to drive to Spokane, five hours away, to meet with fellow students at Whitworth and Gonzaga Universities and to attend the Mayor's Prayer Breakfast.

As we drove over the mountain pass on Interstate 90, I was talking with the dozen or more students about the principles of Jesus. As we discussed the gospel

43 1 Corinthians 2:3-5, PHILLIPS

as a person, suddenly Ramesh, a gifted and engaging senior at the UW whose Islamic family had emigrated from Iran (and who was a recent follower of Jesus), suddenly declared, "Oh, my goodness. Oh, oh my word, the gospel is Jesus … The way is a person; truth is a person … Jesus is life. Oh my … "And on and on she intoned as all of us sat in the van, riveted by the power and reality of the words she spoke as this realization dawned on her. In a very clear and observable way, the Holy Spirit fell upon Ramesh, and the truth of this powerful message resonated in her heart. I have witnessed this numerous times all around the world and strongly identify myself with the fact that this beautiful spiritual reality is often better caught than taught. Jesus authenticates this truth, and blesses us and draws us nearer to him as we realize it in our daily lives.

That the Whole World May Know

One final realization about this principle of "the Message"—that the message is a *person*—comes as we consider the intended audience of the four gospels. Unlike the rest of the New Testament, which seems to be written primarily to the followers of Jesus, the gospels were written for the whole world. For anyone doubting this fact, it is interesting to note that the term, "Lord Jesus" is used only a handful of times in the gospels. The term "Jesus Christ" is similarly only mentioned a half dozen times, mostly in the introductory words. However, the word "Jesus," and the personal pronoun "he" or "his" referring to Jesus, are used over twelve hundred times in the four gospels. In other words, these accounts of Jesus' life—written by Matthew, a Jewish tax collector, by Mark, in the wider circle of disciples, by Luke, an esteemed physician, and by John, a close disciple of Jesus—are addressed to the whole world.

Some see Jesus as a great teacher—and that he most certainly is, though that is not all he is. Our Muslim friends see him as a great prophet, and absolutely he is that, though that is not all he is. And some of us, because the Holy Spirit has revealed it to us,[44] see him as more than both of those things: the very Son of God. These gospels are addressed to all of us, that we might know him fully, and in coming to know him, to give him our whole lives.

---

44 Matthew 16:15-17

Chapter Four

The Ministry

"So from now on we regard no one from a worldly point of view. Though we once regarded Christ in this way, we do so no longer. Therefore, if anyone is in Christ, he is a new creation; the old is gone, the new has come! All this is from God, who reconciled us to himself through Christ and gave us the ministry of reconciliation: that God was reconciling the world to himself in Christ, not counting men's sins against them. And he has committed to us the message of reconciliation." (2 Corinthians 5:16-19, NIV)

What is the greatest problem in the world? As I write this, the Covid-19 pandemic is still impeding most people's daily lives, the news is filled with stories of riots, anger, division, and brutality, and political tensions rage like most of us have never seen before. What IS the greatest problem? There are so many problems to choose from.

It is an intriguing and painful question that, as we survey not only today's headlines but thousands of years of history, is important to ask. We might immediately think of murder, genocide, hatred, selfishness, greed, and a plethora of other ills that have plagued our planet throughout its history. God's Word would suggest that these are but the *symptoms*. They merely point to the real core problem that threatens humanity: ALIENATION. Where does this alienation begin? Most certainly, the Scriptures contend, it begins with alienation from God.

You might have thought of the word "sin" to answer the question about the world's greatest problem. In fact, an accurate depiction of sin would be alienation from God. Sin is, at its root, a relationship problem. It started in the beginning with Adam and Eve and has continued throughout the history of humankind.

More often than not, when we think of "sin," we are tempted to point to the symptoms of sin—like hatred, killing, rape, theft, envy, and the list goes on and on.

But it all starts with a broken relationship with God, then moves on a breathless pace from there. We see it between husband and wife, father and son, mother and daughter, explaining the heartbreaking disintegration of the nuclear family. Alienation relentlessly continues ... neighbor against neighbor, race against race, religion against religion, nation against nation, until the whole world is affected and infected with the pandemic of being alienated from our Creator and, as a result, from one another.

What is God's solution to this perilous problem? RECONCILIATION. God's massive rescue attempt is beautifully summarized in the verse many of us learned as children: "For God so loved the world that he gave his one and only Son, that whoever believes in him shall not perish but have eternal life. For God did not send his Son into the world to condemn the world, but to save the world through him."[45] This was the most massive rescue effort in the history of the world.

Sometimes a human illustration helps us put this in perspective. In 1987, Jessica McClure Morales, also known as "Baby Jessica," fell down a twenty-two-foot well in her aunt's backyard in Midland, Texas. Within hours, the world was focused upon events in this backyard. For fifty-eight hours workers frantically sought to rescue her. Subsequently, efforts to drill a hole next to her caused the dirt to begin to collapse. The decision was made to drill a hole adjacent to the

---

45 John 3:16-17, NIV

well and tunnel over to Jessica. All the while, the cries of the toddler could faintly be heard from the depths of the dark hole that entrapped her. Finally, two and half days later, after tunneling horizontally through dense rock to connect the two holes, two paramedics reached Baby Jessica and carefully brought her back to the waiting arms of her father. What a picture! It gives us a tiny emotional snapshot of this herculean rescue effort by our Lord.

The Ministry of Reconciliation

As we seek to understand the "ministry of reconciliation," it is helpful to see its four components. Let's consider them in the order of their importance:

1. Reconciliation with God

Scripture tells us that when we are initially reconciled to God through salvation, our sins are forgiven. The Psalmist notes, "As far as the east is from the west, so far has he removed our transgressions from us."[46]

When I asked Jesus to be my Lord and Savior as a high schooler, he forgave my sin. However, like the rest of us, I continued (and continue to this day) to sin. Sin separates us from our God. But he doesn't give up on us. He keeps providing ongoing forgiveness as we follow him and allow him to lead us, humbly confessing our sin when we fall into it: "If we confess our sins, he is faithful and just and will forgive us our sins and purify us from all unrighteousness."[47]

Once again, love is the guiding force in this journey—we follow him because we love him—a much stronger motivation than rules or legalism. Perhaps the magnitude of God's reconciling love for us is best illustrated in the "prodigal son" account in Luke 15, where Jesus tells the story of the son who demands his inheritance, in essence communicating his father is dead to him, and squandering his wealth in lavish parties until he is penniless.

As he is feeding the pigs and longing to eat their swill himself, he decides to go back to his father and ask to be a servant. Jesus notes that the father, looking down the road every day for his lost son, sees him a long way off and runs to him, embracing him. He puts a ring on his finger and shoes on his feet, ignoring his

---

46 Psalms 103:12, NIV
47 1 John 1:9, NIV

pleas to be a hired servant, and prepares a feast in his honor. What an expression of unconditional love! And yet, the older son, caught up in his faithful service to the father, not only cannot rejoice at his brother's return, but refuses to go in to the celebration.

Some years ago, I recall hearing Tim Keller, noted author and pastor of Redeemer Church in New York City, reflect, "I wonder how long the father stayed outside trying to get his older son to come in and celebrate?" This is a beautiful picture of God's loving and reconciling heart as compared to an understandable human legalistic response. Thank God for his incredible, loving and forgiving heart toward us!

2. Reconciliation with Self

I firmly believe that being reconciled to oneself is the wonderful result of first being reconciled to Jesus Christ. David Benner, in his book, *The Gift of Being Yourself,* says it well, "In order for our knowing of God's love to be truly transformational, it must become the basis of our identity. Our identity is who we experience ourselves to be—the "I" each of us carries within. An identity grounded in God would mean that when each of us thinks of who we are, the first thing that would come to mind is our status as one that is deeply loved

How deeply God loves each of us is wonderfully articulated throughout the Scriptures, such as when David wrote, "O Lord, you have searched me and you know me. You know when I sit and when I rise; you perceive my thoughts from afar ... You hem me in—behind and before; you have laid your hand upon me. Such knowledge is too wonderful for me, too lofty for me to attain."[48]

We need to understand that being reconciled to God also includes be reconciled to ourselves—learning to love our *self* as much as God does. David Benner observes this truth in his book *The Gift of Being Yourself.*

> *"Knowing the depths of God's personal love for each of us as individuals is the foundation of all genuine self-knowledge. But, there is yet more to be learned from reflecting on how God knows us. The self that God persistently loves is not my prettied-up pretend self; it is my actual self—the real me!*

48 Psalm 139:1-2, 5-6, NIV

But master of delusion that I am, I have trouble penetrating my web of self-deceptions and knowing the real me. I continually confuse it with some ideal self that I wish I were."[49]

The closer I get to experiencing the vast, unconditional love that Jesus has lavished upon me, the more I am able to get in touch with the shimmering diamond that he created in his image.

In our day, there is an all-out assault on self-worth. We cannot gain it from success in the world's eyes, or from comparison with others. We can most certainly not get it from narcissism, but only from seeing our own reflections as mirrored in the loving eyes of Jesus. We are truly being reconciled to ourselves as we experience the overwhelming reconciling love of God.

3. Reconciliation with Others

"If your brother or sister sins, go and point out their fault, just between the two of you. If they listen to you, you have won them over. But if they will not listen, take one or two others along, so that 'every matter may be established by the testimony of two or three witnesses.' If they still refuse to listen, tell it to the church; and if they refuse to listen even to the church, treat them as you would a pagan or a tax collector." (Matthew 18:15-17, NIV)

Obviously, it would not become a priority to mend the fractured relationships with others if we have not experienced the healing, forgiveness, and reconciliation that Jesus offers us. Jesus spoke very specifically about our responsibility to reconcile with those we have offended or who have offended us, not by way of request, but as a commandment! He said, "Therefore, if you are offering your gift at the altar and there remember that your brother has something against you, leave your gift in front of the altar. First go and be reconciled to your brother; then come and offer your gift."[50] This has to do with my becoming aware that someone has something against me.

---

49 Benner, David G. *The Gift of Being Yourself: the Sacred Call to Self-Discovery*. Downers Grove, IL: IVP Books, 2015, p. 57.

50 Matthew 5:23-24

Often when this happens to us, our first reaction is to take issue with their offense. We also can minimize it, accusing them of the wrongdoing. My responsibility is clear—ask forgiveness for *my* wrong.

I equate this with going to the teller at the bank and making a transaction. I confess my wrong to my brother or sister, then ask if there is anything else. That's me initiating my transaction. They respond with specific wrongs (offenses), which I take responsibility for by asking if they will forgive me. As they respond, "I forgive you," a transaction in the heavenlies is recorded, just like when the bank teller punches the computer keys and we hear the machine whirr, knowing it is now recorded. (We even get a receipt!) I believe the Lord smiles as two of his beloved are reconciled! I know that well as a parent; each time my kids reconciled with each other, it gave me great joy.

It is also startling to realize that Jesus is telling us that making things right with our brother or sister supersedes "bringing our gift before the altar," which could mean worship, prayer, or the giving of ourselves in ministry. Being aggressive to make relationships right appears to trump much of the religious activity that we universally celebrate in our lives.

It is noteworthy that this passage actually gives us four concrete steps in responding to a brother's offense. Initially, we are commanded to go to him alone. I believe over 90 percent of offenses can be healed by this simple step of obedience. Instead, we often get others involved who are not a part of the problem or the answer. Then, Jesus says in the same passage, if our brother listens, the relationship can be restored.[51]

If this does not succeed, we are told to gather one or two others who are neutral and will be responsible and unbiased listeners. So often, because these witnesses have objectivity, they can help to resolve the broken relationship.

I recall, years ago, when I was asked to sit with two couples who were estranged through a previous business breakup. As each former business partner shared his grievances, understanding, forgiveness, and reconciliation miraculously took place. It was a celebration!

If, after this step, resolution has not taken place, the offense is brought before the whole fellowship. This fourth step is often misunderstood. Matthew, the

51 Matthew 18:15-17

former tax collector, writes to "treat him as you would a pagan or a tax collector." In other words, you still love him, but you don't work with him anymore. I believe our Lord was so specific in these steps because he loves his sons and daughters and places a high priority on our reconciling with and loving one another. If we do not, we open a door to Satan in our lives: "In your anger do not sin: Do not let the sun go down while you are still angry, and do not give the devil a foothold."[52]

In this final exhortation, we are urged to reconcile quickly, lest the enemy gain a foothold. The Greek word used here is *topos.* It is referring to gaining terrain in our lives. The term" topology" is derived from this word, indicating "the study of geometric properties." In the same way, the enemy loves to elevate his entry into our lives by taking this foothold and making it a stronghold, a place of operation from which he can gain greater access and exert greater influence.

4. Reconciliation with the World

> *"We are therefore Christ's ambassadors, as though God were making his appeal through us. We implore you on Christ's behalf: Be reconciled to God." (2 Corinthians 5:20, NIV)*

As we are reconciled to God and then to one another, one of the highest honors in life can become ours—to join Jesus in his work of reconciliation around the world. Let's consider the role of an ambassador, who lives temporarily in a foreign land as a representative of his homeland and its government. We, similarly, are temporary residents in this life, but have our permanent home in Heaven,[53] and we represent its government here on Earth. An ambassador carries the full authority of the leadership of the nation he represents. Similarly, as Christ's ambassadors, God actually makes his appeal to mankind through us!

There are several ways in which we can serve in this esteemed role. We can join Jesus in his ministry of reaching out to the lost (evangelism). We

---

52 Ephesians 4:26-27
53 2 Corinthians 5:1

can also represent him in seeking to encourage his followers to reconcile with one another (exhortation). Finally, we can join him in addressing the many calamities of the world: world hunger, sex trafficking, promoting religious freedom, healing infectious diseases, seeking to address the ravages of poverty in the world, and more (mercy and justice). There are many ways God uses our unique gifts, talents, passions, and callings. Isn't it incredible that, if we are reconciled to Jesus and to one another, Jesus invites us to partner with him in his reconciling and healing ministry in the world? Once again, the greatest joy is to work *with* him rather than just for him! It really is all about relationship.

My late friend, Joe Aldrich, the former President of Multnomah School of the Bible in Portland, Oregon, wrote about an imaginary encounter between Jesus and the angel, Gabriel, after his return to Heaven from spending thirty-three years on this earth. Gabriel congratulates him on the amazing commitment of leaving the splendor of Heaven to love so many he encountered in his years of life and ministry. Finally, he lauds Jesus for his willingness to suffer, for dying as a sacrifice for the sins of mankind on the cross, and for completing his work by rising again from the dead, thus conquering the power of sin and death.

Then Gabriel asks Jesus what his plan for the future is. Jesus responds that he has entrusted responsibility to Peter, James, John, Andrew, Phillip, and the other disciples, who will tell others about him and God's love for each of them. Those people, in turn, will tell others about him, and they will also become salt and light—reflecting his love—wherever they go.

Gabriel frowns. He knows well of humanity's shortcomings and often lack of faithfullness. He shares his doubts with Jesus, who responds, "I have no other plan. I am counting on them."

Though this is a fictional encounter, the truth remains that Jesus' plan for redeeming the world has each of us, his followers, playing a key role.[54] The magnitude of Jesus' love for us is beautifully illustrated in his desire for us to join him in his redemptive work around the world. It is, indeed, the highest honor, privilege, and responsibility of our lives to be God's ambassador!

---

54 Aldrich, Joseph C. *Lifestyle Evangelism: Crossing Traditional Boundaries to Reach the Unbelieving World.* Portland, OR: Multnomah, 1981.

Learning to Seek and Extend Forgiveness

Because the highest priority of an ambassador is relationship, someone in this position is always keenly sensitive to protecting relationships from what may seek to destroy them. Probably the greatest threat to relationships is offense. In fact, the title of John Bevere's practical book on this subject calls it what it is: *Bait of Satan.* That's right, a favorite tactic of the enemy is to offend and divide, many times over the smallest of infractions.

Our immediate inclination when someone offends us is to tell others—gathering allies. Satan delights in this, because he knows the greatest magnetic attraction the Church has is its love for one another. If we truly love Jesus, we manifest it by our love and obedience. He tells his disciples this over and over in the Upper Room discourse in John 13-17. Forgiveness toward one another is one way we demonstrate that love and obedience.

Bitterness, the advanced fruit of unforgiveness, has opened many doors in the lives of people who are unwilling to forgive. A graphic example of this is forever etched in my psyche. Nearly twenty years ago in Seattle, the Green River Killer, Gary Ridgway (believed to be the largest mass murderer in American history), was apprehended after a two-decade search. He had raped and killed at least forty-eight young women over a period of years and buried their remains in the Green River area, south and east of Seattle. He accepted a plea bargain to life in prison without parole on the condition that he would help authorities find the bodies.

As a part of the process, one member from each of the families of the 48 victims had the opportunity to speak briefly to the murderer of their loved one. It was an unforgettable picture— one person from each aggrieved families addressing Gary Ridgway. Most were sadly similar rants of rage and epithets against this heinous killer. Ridgway appeared unfazed as their angry torrents continued.

After about a dozen similar angry messages, an elderly woman rose to speak. She said, "Gary Ridgway, you raped and killed my only daughter. I have been angry for years … no more! In the name of Jesus of Nazareth, I forgive you." What happened after that caused my jaw to drop: the camera panned to Gary

Ridgway, and a tear rolled all the way down his face as he listened to this woman's amazing words of forgiveness. The hardest hearts in the world can be melted by these healing words, "I forgive you."

I have often thought about those unfortunate ones who could not forgive. They are locked into an unending, daily cycle of bitterness that eats away at the soul. The offense that is not forgiven seems to remain in a present tense reality, even though it may have taken place decades ago. Satan thrives on unforgiveness—it is one of his best open doors into our lives.

I had an unforgettable, if very painful, experience with forgiveness and reconciliation many years ago. Serving in a leadership role, I had several folks under me come together to confront me with a list of shortcomings in my leadership and relationships with them. It was hurtful, but as time went by and I prayed about these things, realizing my strained relationships with these people, the Lord quietly spoke to me. I sensed he was saying, "Ask each of them for forgiveness for your wrongs." I was stunned by the specificity and clarity of this message.

As I continued to ponder and pray about these things, I began to write down the areas in which I had fallen short in these relationships. I will remember each of those encounters for the rest of my life as I met with each person and asked forgiveness for the wrongs and offenses revealed.

The result was the restoration of those relationships, and, in several cases, actually growing to deeper friendships. It was a gracious and humbling reminder that the Lord helps us in our weaknesses, as the Apostle Paul noted, "...being confident of this, that he who began a good work in you will carry it on to completion until the day of Christ Jesus."[55]

A Ministry Magna Carta

> *"So from now on we regard no one from a worldly point of view. Though we once regarded Christ in this way, we do so no longer." (2 Corinthians 5:16, NIV)*

---

55 Philippians 1:6

I have one final reflection as we consider the ministry of reconciliation, one I would consider the "Magna Carta" of ministry. Think about someone who is very hard for you to love. Gordon MacDonald, a longtime colleague of mine and former President of InterVarsity, used to call such people "VDP's"—Very Difficult People. We all encounter these folks in our lives. How do we love them?

My problem is that I tend to see them from a worldly point of view, or, as one translation of the Bible put it, "according to the flesh."[56] In the NIV version of the Bible, it says, "Though we once regarded Christ in this way, we do so no longer."[57] This great verse tells me, that because of the finished work of Jesus, I can see these "very difficult people" through the eyes of Jesus. The takeaway for me is that I really can't love people by myself—I need help.

Thankfully, in Jesus, help is on the way. His Spirit working in me gives me a new set of eyes to see beyond the difficult characteristics of a person to be able to love him or her unconditionally. Isn't this exactly what Jesus has done for us? He loved us even when we were "very unlovely." This is an incredible manifestation of the scriptural truism, "We love because he first loved us."[58] Because he first reached out to reconcile with us, we too, can extend that ministry of reconciliation to the world around us.

This is God's Plan A to save the world. There's no Plan B.

---

56 2 Corinthians 5:16, KJV
57 2 Corinthians 5:16, NIV
58 1 John 4:19

Chapter Five

The Church

"I tell you the truth, whatever you bind on earth will be bound in heaven, and whatever you loose on earth will be loosed in heaven. Again, I tell you that if two of you on earth agree about anything you ask for, it will be done for you by my Father in heaven. ***For where two or three come together in my name, there am I with them.****" (Matthew 18:18-20, NIV, emphasis added)*

On the heels of sharing with his disciples how to reconcile with one another after difficult conflicts, Jesus invites us to understand the incredible power of agreement and unity in the Holy Spirit. What a tremendous statement: "… if two of you on earth agree about anything you ask for, it will be done for you …"[59] It feels like a blank check to access the presence and power of God as we walk together in agreement in Jesus' name!

As we consider the Church of Jesus Christ in the world two thousand years after these words were spoken, it would be important to ponder the import of

59 Matthew 18:19, NIV

this wonderful promise of Jesus and to remind ourselves that the Church is most certainly, "people together in Jesus Christ," and he only has one Church in the world. Where we get bogged down, oftentimes, is the "agreement" part.

We Are One

The conversation was a bit stiff and formal at this initial meeting with a senior official from the Russian Orthodox Church. We were sitting at lunch at the Washington Hilton, several days before the National Prayer Breakfast. Our host, a Russian business leader who had been a friend to each of us for a number of years, was wanting to introduce us.

After a few minutes of informal introductions, my new Orthodox friend asked me, "What denomination are you affiliated with?" As I considered the dubious ramifications of a swift reply on my part, the encounter of Jesus with the religious leaders in Mark 12 came to mind. He was asked by what authority he was doing these things. He briefly deferred his answer until they would first reply to the question of the baptism of John—was it from heaven or purely human? This caused the chief priests, the scribes, and elders to realize however they answered the question would bring undesirable consequences. In that Scripture account, we read, "So they answered Jesus, 'We do not know.'

'Then I cannot tell you by what authority I do these things.' returned Jesus."[60]

With this story in mind, I politely asked if I could first offer a question to my new Russian friend. He appeared a bit taken aback, but nodded his assent. I asked him, "How many churches does Jesus have in the world today?"

My obviously learned new acquaintance quietly pondered this question for what seemed to me an unusually long moment. Then he answered, looking me squarely in the eyes, "He has one." I then named the denomination I grew up in and in which I was ordained for ministry years before. The whole tenor and spirit of the conversation changed—there was a warmth that entered our lunch together. Three days later, when twenty-five of us were gathered for the Russian dinner following the Prayer Breakfast, he shared that those days had been a wonderful blessing to him, and he wanted to bring some colleagues with him to a future Prayer Breakfast.

---

60 Mark 12:33, PHILLIPS

As we consider the state of the Church of Jesus Christ around the world today, we see thousands of various sects and denominations. I recall it being said that the late Billy Graham, when criticized for making a bold pronouncement about the Church of Jesus Christ that listeners feared would set it back for centuries, replied, "That's too bad. I would like to set it back two thousand years!"

It would be good to reflect on the strategy of Jesus two thousand years ago. Elton Trueblood, distinguished theologian and author of the renowned classic, *Incendiary Fellowship,* writes,

> *"There is no person in history who has impacted all of mankind more than Jesus of Nazareth. Jesus was deeply concerned for the continuation of his redemptive work after the close of his earthly existence, and his chosen method was the formation of a redemptive society. He did not form an army, establish a headquarters, or even write a book. All he did was to collect a few unpromising men and women, inspire them with the sense of his vocation and theirs, and build their lives into an intensive fellowship of affection, worship, and work.*
>
> *"One of the truly shocking passages of the gospel is that Jesus indicates that there is absolutely no substitute for the tiny redemptive society. If this fails, he suggests, all is failure; there is no other way. He told the little bedraggled fellowship that they were actually the salt of the earth, and that if this salt should fail there would be no adequate preservative at all. He was staking all on one throw. What we need today is not intellectual theorizing or even preaching, but a demonstration."*[61]

Today, Jesus' Church in this modern world finds itself divided on a number of topics and issues—even above and beyond denominational differences. In light of our culture's changing morality, it is considered by some to be narrow-minded and irrelevant, and—as we have seen in the wake of recent pandemic lockdowns—even "non-essential."

---

61 Trueblood, Elton. *The Incendiary Fellowship*. New York, NY: Harper & Row Publishers, 1967.

I would like to attempt, in this brief chapter, to reflect upon what God might have in mind as he views the Church of Jesus Christ. My reflections are informed by thoughts from the late British Bible teacher and scholar, Derek Prince, taken from a cassette tape I first listened to over fifty years ago. Prince took the first sixteen verses of Ephesians chapter four, calling them, "The Blueprint for Building the Body of Christ." Even though it has been over a half century since I initially heard his words, they have been of immense help to me in considering God's vision for his church.

God's Design for His Church

> *"As a prisoner for the Lord, then, I urge you to live a life worthy of the calling you have received. Be completely humble and gentle; be patient, bearing with one another in love. Make every effort to keep the unity of the Spirit through the bond of peace."*[62]

A blueprint is an essential document for any builder to have within easy access. It isn't to be filed away in the business office—it is necessary right on the site to refer to at every point in the building process. So, if the builder has the blueprint, the tools, and the workers as well, what is still absolutely necessary to build the house? Of course, it is the materials.

For the Church, the building materials are the people, and the character qualities they bring. In this passage above, the Apostle Paul lists six character qualities:

1. living a life worthy of one's calling
2. complete humility, gentleness, patience, forbearance (hanging in there with one another)
3. eagerness to keep the unity of the Spirit

These are the kind of qualities that should be foundational—like building materials— in the lives of those members of Jesus' family, his Church. When these are cultivated, we can grow together.

---

62 (Ephesians 4:1-3, NIV)

I remember a few years ago at Ivanwald, the young men's house at The Cedars, where I live and work, when we had eight young men join us one September—each from a different country. They began to live together, work together, eat together, and generally do life as one group. These young men rapidly realized there were a myriad of different expectations, values, and habits they had brought with them from five different continents in the world. These qualities were essential in helping them to coalesce into a family of brothers in Jesus Christ. These character qualities were absolute requisites in forging a spirit of love and unity in their house. The journey was often a bumpy one, but six months later, there was an unmistakable sense of love and bonding that could never have happened without the necessary materials. They found themselves living out the next part of Paul's encouragement to the Ephesians:"There is one body and one Spirit—just as you were called to one hope when you were called—one Lord, one faith, one baptism; one God and Father of all, who is over all and through all and in all."[63]

We would all likely agree to the truism that out of unity diversity must flow (as contrasted with the opposite, that unity can come from diversity). As God's blueprint for building the Church (Big "C") in our world continues, it is important to crystallize what it is that all the disparate parts of Christ's Body can agree upon—where we have unity. In addition, it is important that there be great simplicity and clarity in our points of unity and agreement.

Seven basic unities are listed in these three verses above. So, whether it be related to Orthodox, Catholics, Lutherans, Presbyterians, Pentecostals, Baptists, different ethnic and racial diversities, and many more parts of Christ's body, these are the essentials:

One body: The Church of Jesus Christ—there is just one with many members worldwide.

One Spirit: The Holy Spirit promised by Jesus in the Upper Room to his disciples and poured out to the Church at Pentecost.

One hope: Heaven. The promise of eternal life with Jesus Christ buoys all of us in our lives.

63 Ephesians 4:4-6, NIV

One Lord: Jesus Christ, the matchless one.

One faith: The Scriptures. Romans 10:17 tells us, "So then faith cometh by hearing, and hearing by the word of God" (KJV). The holy Scriptures represent the inspired word of God to all believers. They authoritatively articulate all matters of faith and practice for believers.

One baptism: Death, burial and resurrection—following Jesus in his journey. The outward sign of our inward journey. (Some immerse, some sprinkle, but one baptism.)

One God and Father of us all: He is over all, through all, and in all.

It was St. Augustine many centuries ago who said, "Unity on the essentials, liberty on the non-essentials, and love (charity) overall." This incredible list of seven unities comprises the absolute rock-bottom essentials that followers of Jesus must find agreement upon. Only out of this unity can the faithful exercise of the diverse gifts be manifested, as Paul goes on to say in his letter to the Ephesians: "It was he who gave some to be apostles, some to be prophets, some to be evangelists, and some to be pastors and teachers, to prepare God's people for works of service, so that the body of Christ may be built up."[64]

Gifted to Serve

Next, out of the unity of the Spirit, flow the diverse gifts of the Holy Spirit, which are meant to "build up" the Church. These are commonly called the five main ministries. In the New Testament, there are also lists of spiritual gifts such as tongues, interpretation, and prophecy, discussed in I Corinthians 12 and 14, and another list of the more practical gifts, including leadership, service, mercy, and helps in Romans 12. These five are all intended to be used in the functioning of Christ's Body.

The **apostle**, or "one sent forth," originally included the twelve disciples and Paul. Today, an apostolic calling is generally seen as one who pioneers a new movement in the Church. A **prophet** is one who speaks forth God's thoughts to the people, always in accordance with the Scriptures; the word literally means "a seer." An **evangelist**, of course, is one who is called to share the good news

64 Ephesians 4:11-12, NIV

of Christ with the lost. A **pastor**, from the Greek word *poimen,* literally means "one who shepherds God's flock." Unfortunately, all too often today, a pastor is so saddled with preaching and administrative duties that he often lacks the time, experience, or understanding to care for God's people.

The **teacher** is one skilled in articulating the truths of God's word to his people. The original intention of this gift was that the leadership of the local church or *ecclesia* would include the functioning of all five ministries. Bill Johnson, the renowned pastor of Bethel Church in Redding, California, strongly advocates that one of the great needs in the local church today is the effective interplay of these five main ministries. Verse twelve underscores this as it reminds us these ministries are "to prepare God's people for works of service, so that the body of Christ may be built up." What an important equipping ministry the church needs to embrace today so that every member may be seen as a minister of Jesus Christ.

Reaching Unity

"... Until we all reach unity in the faith and in the knowledge of the Son of God and become mature, attaining to the measure of the fullness of Christ." (Ephesians 4:13, NIV)

When I first heard Derek Prince speak about this verse over fifty years ago, chills went up my spine. He calls this passage "the ultimate goal of God's blueprint for building His body." The word "until" gives us the hint that the end result is unfolding. And that end result—of finally coming to the unity of faith and doctrine and growing in the knowledge of Jesus—is maturity: the body of Jesus two thousand years later reflecting the image of Jesus to the world. In other words, a people who walk like Jesus, talk like Jesus, live like Jesus and love like Jesus.

Occasionally I will preach on this subject, and as I reach this point of declaring the goal, I look out at the crowd and say, "I'm looking at Him now—eyes, ears, arms, legs, big toes, etc.—the body of Jesus, this year's rollout! (It reminds me of that blessed verse in I John 4:17, "As he is, so are we in this world.")

In Paul's letter to the Ephesians, he goes on to say, "Then we will no more be infants, tossed back and forth by the waves, and blown here and there by every wind of teaching and by the cunning and craftiness of men in their deceitful scheming. Instead, speaking the truth in love, we will in all things grow up into him who is the Head, that is Christ."[65] I recall that the Revised Standard Version, which I was using many years ago, began verses 14 and 15 with "either" and "or." This contrast might be called "the great either/or." Either God's people will be like little children, quarreling about various doctrines and beliefs—which has most certainly taken place so often in the church's history, or we will grow up in every aspect into Jesus Christ.

I have sixteen grandkids whom my wife and I adore. At this writing, they are between two and twelve years old. Each of their parents has worked very hard to love and discipline them. But, I would guess that if I put all of them in our basement, filled it with toys, and then left them alone for the next hour, upon our return there would likely be some tears, hurt feelings, and some degree of commotion. They are children—they are learning. Their parents are training them for adulthood—they are in process, like all of us in Christ's body.

In contrast, Paul cites two crucial elements that, when joined together, make for maturity—speaking the truth, and combining it with love. In many years of supervising people in ministry, I have learned the great value of joining these two. If I just tell someone the unvarnished truth, it will likely be hurtful, even if it is true. If I avoid such confrontations and just choose love, that ends up as "sloppy *agape*." But when the two are merged together, even in the hardest circumstances, genuine change and healing is the usual and happy result. This has proved to be an invaluable understanding for me over the years, confirming that, "From him the whole body, joined and held together by every supporting ligament, grows and builds itself up in love, as each part does its work."[66]

Building up the Body

One of my least favorite exercises in my senior English class in high school was to diagram sentences. Ironically, it has proved to be a most helpful exercise.

65 Ephesians 4:14-15, NIV
66 Ephesians 4:16, NIV

If you recall, the goal is to isolate the subject, a noun, and the predicate, which includes the verb and the object. What is eliminated are prepositional phrases, descriptive or adjectival phrases, and other descriptive adjectives or adverbs. (Probably more than you wanted to remember about English class!)

The end result of the process, if we diagram the passage above, tells us "the body builds itself up" or, more simply, "the body builds the body." That realization changed my life and ministry!

My old biology teacher would tell me that a healthy animal or plant would reproduce that health; similarly, an unhealthy organism would reproduce that lack of health. As I was working in Young Life at the time, I came to realize that a healthy team of leaders in a Young Life club would reproduce healthy spiritual disciples. The opposite, sadly, is true. This truth helped me to affirm the mantra of "people over program." Jesus lived and died for people. We use programs as tools. It is so easy to end up prioritizing programs over people. I don't think we set out to do this deliberately, but in our urge to get things done, we sometimes end up actually giving ourselves for programs and using people. Living this principle out sometimes meant I would actually ask a staff person or a volunteer to step away for a time if it seemed that the result of his or her ministry involvement was harmful to him or to others around him. The takeaway was that people should love Jesus more and become healthier in their journeys of faith rather than to be burned out or totally discouraged in the process of serving. One result that thrills me to this day is the number of folks with whom I did ministry years ago, who remain dear friends and colleagues. I believe it is what God intended for his family. Remember: the body builds the body!

Unity: Our Witness to the World

I hope I have communicated the significance of this wonderful blueprint for building the Body of Christ as set forth in the first sixteen verses of Ephesians four. I believe it is meant to be a practical encouragement and a roadmap of sorts as we grow in our individual and corporate journeys in the Church of Jesus Christ.

Each of us values our own nuclear family, and considers it a precious gift to us in life. Similarly, our family of brothers and sisters, both locally and worldwide in the Body of Christ, is an incredible gift from Jesus to each of us. To view it through the eyes of our Savior is not only thrilling, but will allow us to cooperate with him as we seek to live out our respective roles of service.

Three times in the Upper Room discourse in John 13-17, Jesus makes note of the powerful influence of the body of believers upon the outside world. The first occurs earlier in the evening when he tells them, "A new command I give you: love one another. As I have loved you, so you must love one another. *By this all men will know you are my disciples, if you love one another*."[67] Jesus waited three years before he shared this quintessential command to his followers. Why? Because he wanted first to show them! And today, the outside world needs to see it fleshed out in our lives.

Finally, in Jesus' high priestly prayer in John 17, he concludes by praying for us, the distant descendants of the original disciples. He repeats himself in noting their (and our) influence to the watching world: "Father, just as you are in me and I am in you, may they also be in us so that the world may believe that you have sent me."[68] And then, " … May they be brought to complete unity to let the world know that you sent me and have loved them even as you have loved me."[69] Our love communicates to the watching world!

Many years ago, I read an article titled, "The Greatest Method of Evangelism," challenging all the churches in Portland to consider taking an extended period of time to abstain from any of their efforts of evangelism and instead to embark on intentional acts of love and service across denominational lines to other churches in Portland—Baptists with Pentecostals, Presbyterians with Catholics, Lutherans with Assemblies of God, etc.[70] The hope was that if this were done, with vigorous, loving and wholehearted effort, the end result might be that they would not be able to contain the number of nonbelievers who would flock to their doors out of sheer wonderment and curiosity to find out what they had that was so special and unusual. I believe the point was to emphasize what Jesus was telling his disciples on his final evening with them before his crucifixion.

---

67 John 13:34-35, emphasis added

68 John 17:21, NIV

69 John 17:23, NIV

70 Article authored by Earl Rademacher, then the president of Western Baptist Seminary in Portland, Oregon.

To sum this up, I think of what the late Elton Trueblood wrote, reminding us of the strategic importance of the Church, from Jesus' small, first-century band of followers to today:

> *"There is only one way of turning people's loyalty to Christ, and that is by loving others with the great love of God. We cannot revive faith by argument, but we might catch the imagination of puzzled men and women by the exhibition of a fellowship so intensely alive that every thoughtful person would be forced to respect it. If there should emerge in our day such a fellowship, wholly without artificiality and free from the dead hand of the past, it would be an exciting event of momentous importance. A society of loving souls, set free from the self-seeking struggle for personal prestige and from all unreality, would be something unutterably precious. A wise person would travel any distance to join it."*

The Church—the way God planned it—is not irrelevant, impersonal, or non-essential. Rather, it was designed to be the living, vibrant, representation of Jesus on the earth, through his disciples then and now. If we could all break free of our misconceptions, differences, and personal disappointments in this regard, and truly become what Jesus intended us to be … imagine what the Church could be!

Chapter Six

The Method of Leadership

"Jesus called them together and said, 'You know that those who are regarded as rulers of the Gentiles lord it over them, and their high officials exercise authority over them. Not so with you. Instead, whoever wants to be great among you must be your servant, and whoever wants to be first must be slave of all. For even the Son of Man did not come to be served, but to serve, and to give his life as a ransom for many." (Mark 10:42-45, NIV)

It happened during one of those insufferably long walks from place to place on the hot and dusty roads of Galilee. The disciples were most likely strung out in little pockets of two or three as they trudged on under the hot sun. James and John, sometimes dubbed "the Sons of Thunder," were known for their occasional hotheadedness. (They actually asked Jesus at one time to call down fire upon an unresponsive Samaritan town!)[71] On this day, they had finally positioned themselves to be walking alone with Jesus, seemingly out of earshot from the other ten disciples who were lagging behind. They seized the moment.

71 See Luke 9:54

"Teacher,' they said, "we want you to do for us whatever we ask." (A humble request!)

"What do you want me to do for you?" Jesus asked.

They replied, "Let us sit at your right and the other at your left in your glory."

"You don't know what you are asking," Jesus said. "Can you drink the cup I drink or be baptized with the baptism I am baptized with?"

"We can," they answered.

Jesus said to them, "You will drink the cup I drink and be baptized with the baptism I am baptized with, but to sit at my right or left is not for me to grant. These places belong to those for whom they have been prepared."

The Push for Position

Unfortunately, at that moment the Sons of Thunder discovered they were being overheard by the others. One can only imagine the fracas that ensued—probably just harsh words, but even possibly a little pushing and shoving. These twelve men were frequently together twenty-four hours a day, and often the pace was exhausting. Daily the crowds following Jesus grew and the blind, the lame and the halt flocked to him for healing.

At this point of growing tempers and tensions, Jesus stepped in and, as a great leader is wont to do, used the opportunity to give his ambitious disciples an invaluable teachable lesson on leadership. The men knew only too well the harshness of the Roman leadership to which Jesus was referring. For rebellious Jews, a public crucifixion could easily be on the docket for them, many times having the Roman leadership leaving their dead body upon that cross for several days until the birds were pecking at their flesh—a crystal clear picture for any individual who would dare to resist the heavy-handed Roman rule. Jesus then drew a sharp contrast as he sought to characterize a whole new vision of leadership.

Slaves were common in those days, and such a role was hardly something any free person would aspire to. Yet Jesus, in his startling portrayal of this revolutionary leadership, told his flock, "Whoever wants to become great among you must be your servant." No doubt the disciples were listening in stunned silence to this hitherto unheard-of view of leadership. Jesus concluded with another howitzer: "And whoever wants to be first must be slave of all."

This was quite a radical departure from the self-serving request of James and John! The use of the word "slave" was an obvious attention-getter. The Greek word is *doulos.* The term *doulos* came to be used to describe those who had previously been enslaved, but who had received their freedom, and later chose to become slaves out of the motivation of love. These "love slaves" were known for their joy and dedication.

Most certainly, Jesus calls each of us to join this happy band of servants who were once slaves to sin, were set free by his blood shed on the cross on their behalf, and finally chose to spend the rest of their lives as his love slaves. Jesus concluded this lesson on leadership with one final signature claim, "For the Son of Man did not come to be served, but to serve, and to give his life as a ransom for many."

This was another mind-blowing concept Jesus revealed to his followers. So many of the leadership models the disciples had observed (and to this day the majority of the leaders most of us view) issue mandates that they do not practice themselves. But not Jesus.

As I write these words, our society is fighting to emerge from the Covid-19 pandemic lockdown. Some of the harshest rules are being issued by people in leadership roles and are seemingly oblivious and contradictory to the statistics offered by science and even contrary to common sense. One news analyst pondered whether, if those leaders were forced to forfeit their salaries until the lockdown concluded, would they operate by the same set of rigid rules? In other words, they are seeming to tell their audiences: *You must embrace a costly sacrifice that I am not being required, or very likely willing to share.* This radical view of servant leadership, as espoused by Jesus, is to this day in short supply. It is so much easier for a leader to operate by the maxim, "Do as I say," rather than the infinitely more costly guideline of "Do as I do."

Emptied of Self, Ready to Serve

Jesus remains the perfect model of servant leadership two thousand years later. A potent portrait of his costly sacrifice on our behalf is painted in the second chapter of Philippians: "Let your attitude to life be that of Christ Jesus himself. For he, who had always been God by nature, did not cling to his privileges as God's equal, but stripped himself of every advantage by consenting to be a slave by nature and being born a man. And, plainly seen as a human being, he humbled himself by living a life of utter obedience, to the point of death, and the death he died was the death of a common criminal. That is why God has now lifted him to the heights, and has given him the name beyond all names, so that at the name of Jesus, 'every knee shall bow,' whether in Heaven or earth or under the earth. And that is why 'every tongue shall confess' that Jesus Christ is Lord, to the glory of God the Father.'"[72]

As we look closer at this beautiful passage, classically known by theologians as the *kenosis* (meaning the "emptying" of himself), it describes in detail the extent of Jesus' sacrifice for us, and the response of honor the Father bestowed upon him. This is worth a close look. Below I've listed the downward steps Jesus took—the humbling he embraced—and then observed the steps up that resulted from this fragrant sacrifice of love. I've often heard it said, "The way up is the way down"—ironically the polar opposite from the route chosen by most models of leadership. This is a perfect example of that model:

<u>The Way Down</u>

- Though he was God by nature, Jesus didn't cling to his privileges as God's equal.
- He emptied himself (stripped himself of every advantage).
- He consented to be a slave by nature, being born a man.
- He was plainly seen as a human being.
- He humbled himself …
- … even to the point of death …
- … death on a cross (the death of a common criminal)

<u>The Way Up</u>

- God has highly exalted him. (God has lifted him to the heights.)
- God has given him the name beyond all names.

72 Philippians 2:5-11, PHILLIPS

- At the name of Jesus every knee shall bow …
- … knees in Heaven …
- … knees on earth …
- … knees under the earth.
- Every tongue will confess that Jesus is Lord, to the glory of God the Father.

As I reflect on some of the servant leader heroes I have encountered in my life, my dear friend and mentor, the late Bruce Larson, comes to mind. Bruce was the founder of "Faith at Work" and wrote a trove of best-selling books on relational leadership. We first crossed paths when he came to pastor the large Presbyterian church I grew up in, located just adjacent to the University of Washington campus in Seattle. What I came to love about Bruce was he so beautifully modeled the concepts he tirelessly advocated in leadership: affirmation and vulnerability.

I recall the first time he took me to lunch. As the food arrived, he invited us to pray. As I began to bow my head, I noticed Bruce looking straight at me with a big smile. He began, "Lord Jesus, thank you so much for Doug!" And he continued, affirming our growing friendship and expressing thanks for the gifts he saw in me—concluding without ceasing to cast his affectionate gaze upon me. (My nervous head bobbed up and down, trying to understand how to respond to this unusual manner of praying.) In every encounter I had with Bruce, I left knowing I was loved and valued by this encouraging mentor.

Some years later, when I was serving as President of Young Life, I followed up on a brash commitment Bruce had made to me, "Call on me any time to help you any way I can. I am with you, and I believe in you." It was during a difficult, stormy time in my leadership role. I called Bruce and asked him to come to speak at a senior leadership retreat at Trail West, a Young Life resort three hours west of Denver. It turned out to be a very busy week in his schedule, but Bruce, true to his word, carved out two days and joined us to deliver three powerful messages.

What I will never forget is what he did upon my introduction of him after his arrival. He began addressing the seventy-five leaders present by ruminating about the early years of Young Life's history, his admiration and friendship with its founder, Jim Rayburn, and a humorous anecdote or two about those early years. Then he stood erect and softly noted to the crowd, "But that is not why I am here today to speak to you, the leadership of Young Life. I am here today because I love your leader, Doug Burleigh," and he pointed to me. "I have known and worked with him. I love and believe in him." I don't remember a lot of the rest of his words on that occasion, but the gift of his unconditional love, constant encouragement, and sacrificial leadership on my behalf changed my life. When he was promoted to glory, tears of gratitude rolled down my cheeks. Bruce Larson lived what he believed and taught.

I later heard the story of the painful divorce of a longtime member of his staff. As the awful proceedings droned on in an empty local courtroom, there was one solitary figure sitting through the entire difficult debacle—Bruce. He, of a very busy, crowded schedule, always made time to be there for those he loved. But, most important for my life, he was always there for me. I want to be that kind of leader!

The Foot-Washing Leader

> *"It was just before the Passover Feast. Jesus knew that the time had come for him to leave this world and go to the Father. Having loved his own who were in the world, he now showed them the full extent of his love. The evening meal was being served, and the devil had already prompted Judas Iscariot, son of Simon, to betray Jesus. Jesus knew that the Father had put all things under his power, and that he had come from God and was returning to God; so he got up from the meal, took off his outer clothing, and wrapped a towel around his waist. After that, he poured water into a basin and began to wash his disciples' feet, drying them with the towel that was wrapped around him." (John 13:1-4, NIV)*

It was just before the dinner meal in the upper room where Jesus was gathered on this final evening with his disciples. Jesus stunned his followers by his preparations to perform a task that the lowliest servants routinely were assigned. The hot and dusty roads of Galilee made the washing of feet upon arrival as guests at someone's home an absolute necessity. Imagine the shock that gripped his disciples when they realized their master was performing this lowly task for them! It defied all of their previous experiences with this disgusting, menial task.

Peter, in his usual outspoken way, drew back and actually chided the Lord, not understanding the symbolic act of love that was taking place by his leader. As Jesus had done with his disciples on the road, he then used this occasion as a teachable moment on leadership: "'Do you understand what I have done for you?' he asked them. 'You call me Teacher and Lord, and rightly so, for that is what I am. Now that I, your Lord and Teacher, have washed your feet, you also should wash one another's feet. I have set you an example that you should do as I have done for you. I tell you the truth, no servant is greater than his master, nor is a messenger greater than the one who sent him. Now that you know these things, you will be blessed if you do them.'"[73]

I am quite confident that, years after this surprising event, the disciples remembered this humble act of loving service on the eve of Jesus' arrest, trial, and crucifixion. As he encouraged them to understand the important motivation for this loving act, he then challenged them to do likewise unto others. Once again, Jesus' life and actions were the example for his message.

Years ago, I encountered a study, authored by Stanford University, on how learning actually takes place. Even though it has been over forty years since I read it, the message remains indelibly etched in my mind and heart. It affirmed what many of us know intuitively: the greatest method of teaching or learning, by far, is modeling, or example.

For the past fifty-three years I have walked with Jerry. There are few people who have more consistently led by example for me to learn from than him. As we collaborated in Young Life, work in the former Soviet Union and then Israel, and at numerous Prayer Breakfast activities, I observed Jerry as a quiet servant. To this day, he is the first to grab the check for a meal, to take the least desirable place at the table, to honor and bless others, to leave a large tip for the wait staff, and to major in kindness. Ironically, Jerry grew up in a broken home, the oldest of four brothers. Each of his siblings has mightily struggled in their life journeys, but Jerry has quietly loved the Lord, had a loving marriage of fifty years, and raised four great kids.

---

73 John 13:12-17, NIV

I recall many years ago when my wife and I were traveling and my grandmother was at our home caring for our four young children. She called to tell me someone had filled the woodpile outside our house with wood and quickly disappeared as she took notice. I laughed and told her I knew who it was. Jerry is all about Jesus, and it has been my great joy to travel through life with him, learning more about Jesus and servanthood every step of the way by his example.

The second greatest method of learning referenced in the Stanford study was personal experience. Robert Coleman beautifully captures this powerful method of Jesus in his classic book *The Master Plan of Evangelism*. In his analysis of Jesus' strategy of ministry, Dr. Coleman points us to the revolutionary method Jesus employed in his three years of working with the twelve. Dr. Coleman points out that Jesus sent them out by twos (first the twelve, recorded in Luke 9), giving them "power and authority to drive out all demons and to cure diseases, and he sent them out to preach the kingdom of God and to heal the sick."[74] Similarly, he sent out the seventy-two in Luke 10, " … two by two ahead of him to every town and place where he was about to go."[75] Jesus' leadership style valued personal experience.

Even though others might have cautioned him from sending them out so early to minister, Jesus knew they would learn much from doing it themselves. When the seventy-two had triumphantly returned from seeing many miraculous things done in Jesus' name, his loving response speaks volumes: "At that time, Jesus, full of joy through the Holy Spirit, said, 'I praise you, Father, Lord of heaven and earth, because you have hidden these things from the wise and learned, and revealed them to little children. Yes, Father, for this was your good pleasure.'"[76] Jesus, knowing he was to return to the Father, valued giving his disciples personal experience as an important way to learn.

Finally, Stanford's study on teaching and learning gives the third greatest method: didactic (teaching). As we consider Jesus' methods, we begin to realize that we can't separate his teachings from his own personal example and his invitations to his disciples to learn through experience. The teachings of Jesus,

74 Luke 9:1-2, NIV
75 Luke 10:1, NIV
76 John 10:21, NIV

divorced from the context of his life and ministry, would most certainly lack the power and authority that they have because *he lived them*. This is certainly borne out in his words uttered during Luke's writing of the Sermon on the Mount, "A student is not above his teacher, but everyone who is fully trained will be like his teacher."[77] What an observation! We will reproduce who and what we are. What an incredible motivation to keep learning and growing in our journey with Jesus. If he is the one we are learning from and seeking to follow, these words of Jesus can encourage us once again to remember: "As he is, so are we in this world."[78] Jesus changes everything—and everyone who chooses to follow him without reservation.

Jesus' Leadership Method

As we conclude these thoughts on the method of leadership, I would like to share an engaging illustration about Jesus' unique leadership style. I first heard this shared by an esteemed colleague, Tim Kreutter, who has spent much of his life raising up an army of young leaders for Jesus Christ across the continent of Africa. Tim and his wife, Cathy (and now his son and family) lead Cornerstone Academy, which originally started in Kampala, Uganda, and has now spread to a number of other nations in East Africa and beyond. Tim examines the leadership example of Jesus in a most creative way:

R=REVOLUTIONARY MESSAGE It is apparent that the message of Jesus is truly revolutionary. It seems to be a polar opposite from the world's message. For instance, the world says hate your enemies; Jesus says love your enemies. The world says take everything you can; Jesus calls us to be givers—"give and it will be given unto you."[79] The world says to exalt yourself. Jesus says to humble yourself. The world defines leadership as giving orders from the top down. Jesus tells us leadership is servanthood. The world says to save your own life. Jesus tells us the one who loses his life for Jesus' sake will find it. His message is unmistakably revolutionary!

S=STRATEGIC METHOD When we examine the strategy of Jesus' life and ministry, it is strikingly unique. Coming from the right hand of the Father

77 Luke 6:40, NIV
78 1 John 4:17, KJV
79 Luke 6:38

in Heaven, Jesus makes his entrance to the world in a stable, stinking with the aroma of its resident animals because there was no room in the inn. He is then secretly hidden several years in a faraway land for threat of being killed. He serves as a humble carpenter for years in a remote Galilean village. And he dies, nailed to a cross between two thieves. He leaves behind a handful unpaid followers, ordinary fishermen and other commoners to whom he entrusts the future spreading of the revolutionary message. Jesus reveals for us an incredibly unique and strategic method.

G=GODLY CHARACTER He lives a life without sin. He has great compassion for the poor, for widows and orphans. Children flock to him. He is the personification of love and all the fruit of the Spirit. He is utterly selfless, always approachable, genuinely interested and loving toward people, and powerfully driven to listen to and obey whatever his Father tells him, even to enduring a brutal sacrificial death on the cross. Jesus mirrors godly character.

I think we can all agree with this clever illustration: **R+S+G = JESUS' LEADERSHIP METHOD.** Let's see what happens when we remove one of these important components:

R+S= A revolutionary message plus an incredible strategy minus godly character would seem to equal Hitler in Nazi Germany, or Lenin in Soviet Communism, or Mao Tse-Tung in Red China—the message in each case attracted millions. The strategy was to give your all, including your life if necessary, for the cause. However, millions died and were brutalized because of the shocking lack of a moral compass.

R +G= A revolutionary message plus godly character would likely look like the street corner preacher, bellowing out truth to a group of people he does not know, who do not know or respect him. Therefore, the whole spectacle is most likely ineffective and an embarrassment to most of us. A strategy is important.

S+G= Quite likely, this can resemble many of our local churches today. Hard work is done to provide a good facility and an engaging and entertaining program, but lives are often not changed because the message is watered down so as not to offend or discourage the congregation from attending. We can so easily lose the revolutionary message.

When I have two minutes before a large audience anywhere in the world, I love to share the late great John Stott's memorable summary of who Jesus is. The famed British scholar and theologian cogently captured the utter majesty of this one we have been blessed to meet and, hopefully, follow:

> *"More than 2,000 years ago, Jesus was born contrary to the laws of nature. He laid aside his purple robe for a peasant's tunic. He was rich, yet for our sake he became poor. This man lived in poverty and was raised in obscurity. He received no formal education and never possessed wealth or widespread influence. He never traveled extensively. He seldom crossed the boundary of the country in which he lived. But his life has changed the course of history.*
>
> *In infancy, he startled a king. In childhood, he amazed religious scholars. In manhood, he ruled the course of nature—walked on stormy waves and hushed the raging sea to sleep. He healed multitudes without medicine and made no charge for his services. He never practiced psychiatry, yet he healed more broken hearts than all the doctors far and near. He never wrote a book, yet his life has inspired more books than any other man. He never wrote a song, yet he has furnished the theme for more songs than all the songwriters combined. He never founded a college, but all the schools put together cannot boast of having as many students.*
>
> *He never marshaled an army. He never drafted a soldier or fired a gun, but no leader ever had more rebels surrender to him without a shot fired. Herod could not kill him. Satan could not seduce him. His enemies could not destroy him. The grave could not hold him. After three days, he rose from the dead, alive forevermore! He is the ever-perfect one. He is the Christ, the Son of the living God. This man stands forth on the highest pinnacle of Heavenly glory, proclaimed by God, acknowledged by angels, adored by his people, and feared by demons as the risen Lord and Savior, Jesus Christ."*[80]

Hopefully, the takeaway for all of us is—in every activity of life and ministry— to increase our focus upon Jesus: his message, his character, and his method!

---

80 Stott, John R. W. *The Incomparable Christ.* Downers Grove, IL: InterVarsity Press, 2004.

Chapter Seven

The Kingdom of God

"Once, having been asked by the Pharisees when the Kingdom of God would come, Jesus replied, 'The Kingdom of God does not come with your careful observation, nor will people say, 'Here it is,' or 'There it is,' because the Kingdom of God is within you.'" (Luke 17:20-21, NIV)

All of Israel groaned under the stranglehold of the Roman rule, yearning for a return to the times of King David. Then, the armies of the King preserved individual freedoms—liberties long unseen since the downfall of that kingdom. The promised and long-anticipated Messiah would hopefully deliver a new kingdom that many speculated would overthrow the heavy hand of Rome. Hence the question asked by the Pharisees tapped into the hope of the advent of this new kingdom.

Jesus' words suggested a whole new concept of this kingdom—one that was not physical, but that seemed to imply an actual spiritual presence within a person's being. Such an unusual response undoubtedly frustrated and angered the religious leaders whose gaze was irrevocably fixed upon the present-day plight and sufferings of the people of Israel and the constant threat to their well-established religious system.

The Controversial Kingdom

> *The Kingdom of God is the most often-mentioned topic in the four gospels, occurring one hundred and twenty times in the eighty-nine chapters. The importance of this subject is certainly indicated in the accounts of Jesus' final days on Earth, and Luke's writings in the book of Acts: "In my former book, Theophilus, I wrote about all that Jesus began to do and teach until the day he was taken up to heaven, after giving instructions through the Holy Spirit to the apostles he had chosen. After his suffering, he showed himself to these men and gave many convincing proofs that he was alive. He appeared to them over a period of forty days AND SPOKE ABOUT THE KINGDOM OF GOD" … "For two whole years Paul stayed there in his rented house and welcomed all who came to see him. Boldly and without hindrance HE PREACHED THE KINGDOM OF GOD and taught about the Lord Jesus Christ."*[81]

I am often asked by the young friends I mentor to give a characterization of the Kingdom of God. I tell them, "It is the reign and rule of the King, and it needs to start right here," pointing to each of our hearts. I note that as many of the saints throughout history grew in their journey with Jesus, the subject of the Kingdom became more pre-eminent. In other words, as they approached the end of their lives the Kingdom of God vastly grew in importance. May it be so with us as well!

I like to introduce the subject of the Kingdom of God by putting this immense subject in a Scriptural context. That's because most people usually seem to lack any frame of reference, and this context makes it much easier to grasp. With this in mind, I will ask several questions:

---

81 Acts 1:1-3, 28:30-31, NIV (emphasis added)

1. Q: What are the two kingdoms mentioned in the New Testament?
A: The kingdom of God and the kingdom of the world.
2. Q: Who is the king of the Kingdom of God?
A: Scripture reveals that the nature and character of God is revealed to us by Jesus. While God is the king of his Kingdom, Jesus shows us what God is like. He tells us, "No one comes to the Father except by me."[82] When he began his public ministry in Galilee, Jesus proclaimed that the Kingdom of God was at hand.[83]
3. Q: Who is the king of the kingdom of the world?
A: Scripture tells us it is Satan: "The god of this age has blinded the minds of unbelievers, so that they cannot see the light of the gospel of the glory of Christ, who is the image of God."[84] The primary mission of the enemy is to blind people to the powerful person of Jesus.
4. Q: What does the Kingdom of God consist of?
A: Unseen things (excluding demons and the like): "So we fix our eyes not on what is seen, but on what is unseen. For what is seen is temporary, but what is unseen is eternal."[85]
5. Q: What does the kingdom of the world consist of?
A: Everything we can see. Take a folding chair and park yourself at the local landfill. Look around—wrecked cars, discarded appliances, broken toys—all were celebrated when they were new, but over time were worn out, broken and discarded. We take nothing that is seen with us after we die, including these earthly bodies that receive so much attention during our lives.
6. Q: Which kingdom do you live in?
A: Inevitably, this question brings a long pause from my young listeners. The answer, according to God's word is both: we are in the world, but not of the world. In other words, we are temporary residents of this world, but our eternal home is in heaven.[86]

---

82 John 14:6
83 Mark 1:15
84 2 Corinthians 4:4, NIV
85 2 Corinthians 4:18, NIV
86 2 Corinthians 5:1

Living out God's Kingdom Values

This deductive process leads listeners to confront the reality of the fact that, if they are a follower of Jesus, they are only actually citizens of another Kingdom—no matter what their earthly citizenship may be. What a challenge this brings to the followers of Jesus! This brings up all kinds of issues—how do we as citizens of heaven deal with the very present realities of our physical location here on Earth? We have the opportunity to take on God's Kingdom perspective on things like money, sex, and power—driving forces here on Earth. God sees these things very differently from His Kingdom perspective, versus what we often encounter from the world's value system:

Money: Scripture tells us, "The love of money is the root of all kinds of evil."[87] So we use it, but are on guard that its pull does not steal our hearts. We use the monetary system in our daily lives, but at the same time we choose to not overly revere its value.

Sex: God created sex as a precious gift for the expression of love and for the procreation of mankind, but exclusively in the context of a lifelong covenant of marriage between a man and a woman. The enemy has misused this beautiful gift from God in a myriad of ways that bring guilt, shame, untold pain, and condemnation. A Kingdom perspective redeems this misuse of God's gift.

Power: In sharp contrast to the world's definition of power, the Scripture teaches us, "For everyone who exalts himself will be humbled, and he who humbles himself will be exalted."[88] The Kingdom of God calls us to a radical departure from seeking power and adulation through the world system. It is most certainly very fleeting in its gratification.

One of Jesus' most striking conversations about God's Kingdom values was one with the rich, young ruler in Mark 10. Here was a man deemed quite successful in how the world would measure success. He possessed wealth, was young, and had obviously garnered power and influence. Yet something was missing.

---

87 2 Timothy 6:10, NIV

88 Luke 14:11, NIV

He approached Jesus with this all-important question: "What must I do to be sure of eternal life?[89] Jesus initially reminded him of the Ten Commandments, which he audaciously asserted he had kept since his youth. Jesus was unimpressed, and " … looked steadily at him, and his heart warmed towards him, 'There is one thing you still need. Go and sell everything you have, give the money away to the poor—you will have riches in heaven. And then come back and follow me.'"[90]

Years ago, while preparing a Young Life message, I looked up "god" in the dictionary. The definition in *Webster's Collegiate Dictionary* read, "The person or thing of supreme value in one's life." Everyone has one—a thing of supreme value—and we only need to listen to someone for a while to find out who or what it is. It could be self, another person, money, status, sex, or any number of other false idols. In this case, Jesus looked into this young ruler's eyes and saw what was number one in his life—his money. He challenged the young man to relinquish his hold upon it and follow him. But he turned away, and Jesus let him go! We never hear of him again. Most likely some years later he died—a rich, old ruler, quite likely with the same void in his heart that had caused him to initially approach Jesus.

Jesus was not willing to let the rich young rule off the hook with regard to what it cost to enter the Kingdom of God. This reminds me of a story I was told once of a young man who was hired to sell vacuum cleaners.

After being briefly trained by his supervisor, he headed out to peddle the product. After the first day, his boss called him and asked how he had done. To the trainer's amazement, the young man told his boss he had sold fifteen! The trainer was astonished and asked how the new salesman was able to accomplish such an incredible feat. The young man replied, "I sold them for fifty dollars."

After a long silence, the supervisor had to sadly respond, "I'm terribly sorry, but I cannot ratify those sales."

Similarly, Jesus sets the conditions for us and they aren't to be cheapened. He said, "… seek first his kingdom and his righteousness, and all these things

89 Mark 10:17, PHILLIPS
90 Mark 10:21-22, PHILLIPS

will be given to you as well."[91] "All these things" are previously described in the verses leading up to this statement—what we will eat, what we will wear, and all of the rest of our wants and needs in life. We find our fulfillment physically, emotionally and spiritually in the Person of Jesus who invites us to seek first his kingdom and his character. Everything else pales in comparison. Jesus alone fills the void in each of our hearts.

H.G. Wells, the late British author and historian, once wrote, "The doctrine of the Kingdom of Heaven (synonymous with the Kingdom of God), which was the main teaching of Jesus, is certainly one of the most revolutionary doctrines that ever stirred and changed human thought."[92] This is illustrated in two renowned parables Jesus shares in Matthew 13: "The kingdom of heaven is like treasure hidden in a field. When a man found it, he hid it again, and then in his joy went and sold all he had and bought that field."[93] The man, upon finding the treasure, realized this field was far more valuable than it initially appeared. Without a word to anyone else, he joyfully sold all he had and bought the field. The kingdom of heaven is analogous to this story. We are left to conclude that the treasure is a Person—when we encounter Jesus, everything else we have in life falls woefully short of meeting the deepest needs in our life for identity and purpose. We joyfully choose him.

The second parable is similar: "Again, the kingdom of heaven is like a merchant looking for fine pearls. When he found one of great value, he went away and sold everything he had and bought it."[94]

I have probably asked this question a thousand times over the years, "What is the point of this story? Is it the pearl or the price?" About 75 percent of the time the reply is that it is the price. Then I read the verse, strongly emphasizing one must give up *everything* to follow Jesus. The incredible attractiveness and value of the pearl makes the decision a no-brainer—IT IS ALL ABOUT THE PEARL! The correct answer speaks for itself: the pearl is Jesus; the price is irrelevant! These two parables beautifully capture the

91 Matthew 6:33, NIV

92 Wells, H. G., G. P. Wells, and Raymond Postgate. *The Outline of History: The Whole Story of Man*. Garden City, NY: Doubleday, 1961.

93 Matthew 13:44, NIV

94 Matthew 13:45, NIV

majesty of Jesus, the visible manifestation of the Kingdom of God, the pearl absolutely worthy of great price!

The Story of the Rajah

These parables remind me of a story I heard years ago. A poor beggar lived in a remote area in India. He begged for his meager sustenance, but his hopes were lifted when he heard of the upcoming journey of the Rajah, a wealthy ruler, whose caravan was reportedly coming through his village in several weeks. As the days inched closer, the beggar quietly hatched his plan: he would rise long before dawn and position himself at the sharp bend in the road entering his little town. Then he would wait for the arrival of the Rajah.

The day finally came, and a great while before dawn, the beggar arose and took his place. Sunrise came and throngs of people began to line the road, eagerly awaiting the arrival of the much-heralded visitor. The hours crawled by, and the beggar's expectation and anxiety mounted. Finally, approaching the noon hour, one could see the dust of the elephant caravan in the distance. Closer and closer they came, until he could see the elephant with its brightly colored serape on its side, carrying the Rajah. Now they were entering the village … closer and closer they came.

Finally, the beggar stepped out in the path of the large elephant, carrying the Rajah. He nervously beseeched the ruler, "Rajah, give me a gift." The Rajah, a bit surprised, halted the elephant and slowly descended the side of the great beast. He approached the beggar, his large sword glistening on his side in the hot sunlight. The beggar, heart in throat, feared for his life, thinking his ill-timed request could mean an instant end to his life. Then he was astonished by what happened.

The Rajah said, "Beggar man, *you* give *me* a gift." The beggar panicked! He had nothing to give this powerful ruler. Then he remembered the small pouch of rice he had fastened to his belt. With trembling fingers he unsnapped the pouch and carefully selected five grains of rice from it and placed them in the outstretched hand of the Rajah, who, without a word, slowly returned and mounted the side of the elephant. As the caravan slowly moved away, the beggar was overwhelmed with relief and surprise.

Initially, he was just grateful to be alive, but soon he could be heard repeating over and over again, "He asked me for something." After another half hour, the caravan disappeared over the distant horizon. Then something bright and shining caught the eye of the beggar. In his hand that had held the five grains of rice were now five grains of solid gold, shining brightly in the sunlight. His cry could be heard throughout the countryside, "If I had only known, I would have given him everything I had!" As we consider the incredible treasure, the pearl of great price, that is available to us in the Person of Jesus, is it too much to ask that we give him all that we are and have?

The Kingdom of Heaven Is …

My beloved pastor of many years, Dr. Mark Toone, once characterized the Kingdom of Heaven in five succinct ways that might summarize our reflections:

A PLACE—We will go there to be with Jesus for eternity. "Thy Kingdom come … "

A PERSON—The Kingdom of Heaven is God's plan and purpose throughout history, manifested in Jesus Christ.

A PROMISE—He promised he would come back, "Thy Kingdom come … "

A PEOPLE—"The Kingdom of God is within you." We are the keepers of the Kingdom.

A PURPOSE—The Kingdom of Heaven is God's plan and purpose, "Thy kingdom come, Thy will be done on earth as it is in heaven."

The late Bruce Thielemann, a gifted Presbyterian pastor from Pittsburgh, once concluded a message on bearing and sharing one another's burdens with this thought: "We are like islands, separated by waters. Sometimes the waters are calm and silent. Sometimes they are storm-tossed and violent. But when island joins together with island, you have an archipelago. When archipelago joins together with archipelago you have a continent. And when continent joins together with continent, you have a kingdom. And the name of that kingdom … the NAME of that kingdom … the name of that KINGDOM, my brothers and sisters in Jesus Christ is the kingdom of God."

We are joyfully joined with Jesus and one another in this magnificent family that finds its fulness, identity and meaning in being members and inhabitants of the Kingdom of God. My hope, in the years ahead, is that each of us will have our vision and understanding of this wonderful principle, the Kingdom of God, to grow bigger and bigger in our lives and daily experiences.

PART 2

Attributes of a Disciple

Chapter Eight

Jesus before Others, Self, and Possessions

"Then he said to them all, 'If anyone would come after me, he must deny himself and take up his cross daily and follow me. For whoever wants to save his life will lose it, but whoever loses his life for me will save it. What good is it for a man to gain the whole world, and yet lose or forfeit his own very self." (Luke 9:23-25, NIV)

As a graduate student in Political Science at the University of Washington in 1967, there were a number of attractive open doors for me to consider as I finished a Master's Degree. I had spent a week in Washington D.C., interviewing with the C.I.A. over spring break and was subsequently offered a career position with the opportunity to finish a PhD. It would likely be in the area of Russian intelligence, which had been my major field of study in college and graduate school. In addition, after my oral exam, I was offered the chance to continue toward a doctoral degree at the University of Washington, another attractive option given my respect and admiration for my Soviet political systems professor, Dr. John Reshetar. Finally, I had been admitted to the U.W. law school beginning in September.

As I was writing a Master's thesis that summer, I was employed as a Seattle Transit bus driver, usually driving the rush hour "trippers," those being morning and evening four-hour segments. In between, I would study. I was living in the Young Life house basement, two blocks from campus, and serving as a volunteer leader at Lake Washington High School. It was a strategic time in my life.

Long hours of driving, especially when the bus was empty at the end of a route, provided me with valuable time for Scripture memory and meditation, and to process in my heart and spirit what God was teaching me. For some reason, the passage in Luke 9 quoted above kept reverberating back to me as though written in neon lights in my mind's eye. I could not get it out of my thoughts.

Like so many young men in those years, I had grown up in a home where my parents were believers, but my father, a former World War II Navy pilot whom I loved dearly, had never uttered the words, "I am proud of you." I was constantly striving for approval, and this passage seemed to plumb the depths of my need for importance. It was as if God were asking me if I was willing "to lose my life" for him in order to find it. I did have one other job opportunity: I had been offered a position with Young Life at the robust salary of three hundred dollars per month and had never even prayed about it.

God continued to press into me about my source of identity. I had always wanted to "be somebody" of significance. Yet Jesus was quietly beckoning me take a radical step, totally contrary to what seemed to me to be a logical next one, and to follow him. (I would emphasize that this was my particular and unique journey. I am in no way suggesting anyone else would be making the wrong step in choosing the secular paths that appeared to be the wrong choices for me. Each of us has the sacred privilege of seeking to heed the call of Jesus in our lives.)

This was *my* quintessential moment of choice. I remember going to the Law School office and resigning my position in the autumn class. The woman cautioned me that the waiting list was long, and, if I changed my mind, it would be too late. I told her God had told me to work with kids. My professor was surprised. Since the Peace Corps had started a few years before, he cautioned, "Social work? Just be sure you only do it for two years."

And two months later, as I stepped off the bus for the last time, I had the strong sense this was the path Jesus was calling me to take.

Fifty-three years later, after many ups and downs and unexpected twists and turns, I am so grateful that God called me to experience this adventure of letting go of my dreams for his sake in order to find what he had for me. The journey has been amazing. Several years ago, as I noticed fifty years had passed since that unforgettable summer, I decided to go back and reconnect with several hundred of the young people I had worked with in those early years. It was one of the most gratifying experiences of my life.

As I would meet with person after person, so many gratefully shared how God had similarly caused their lives to take a radical and unexpected turn in that adolescent period I often call the "wet cement" years when boys become men and girls become women, and when the trajectory of life can quickly be transformed. I knew that God allowed me the priceless privilege of investing in hundreds of young lives in those critical and formative years. The best part was my getting to know Jesus better as I stepped out of my comfort zone to trust him more and more.

The Call to Commitment

We are beginning to focus on particular attributes of a disciple that Jesus specifically identified, and to which he challenged the twelve who were following him to commit themselves to cultivate. Each of these characteristics is part of a larger life calling.

Fredrick Buechner offered an insightful observation about these original twelve disciples when he said, "The first ministers were the twelve disciples. There is no evidence that Jesus chose them because they were brighter or nicer than other people. In fact, the New Testament record suggests that they were continually missing the point, jockeying for position, and, when the chips were down, interested in nothing so much as in saving their own skins. Their sole qualification seems to have been their initial willingness, when Jesus said, 'Follow me,' to rise to their feet and follow him. As the Apostle Paul said, 'God chose the foolish things of the world to shame the wise; God chose the weak things of the world to shame the strong. He chose the lowly things of this world and the despised things—and the things that are not—to nullify the things that are, so that no one may boast before him.'"[95] For many of us, I would venture that a particular passage of Scripture holds unique significance to us in our respective journeys through life, as does Buechner's observations of the discipleship. Luke 9:23-25 came to become another significant reckoning point for me as well, many years ago. I couldn't get away from the haunting question Jesus asks in Luke 9:25, "What good is it for a man to gain the whole world, and yet lose or forfeit is own very self?" How does a person at the crossroads of life make life-altering commitments, like the career decision that faced me many years ago?

I have often sat with young people who were at such a crossroad. I find the Scriptures so helpful in counseling young friends in this process. While my own personal experience might occasionally be relevant, God's Word is always spot on in helping us navigate the important decisions that face us in these crucial moments of life, especially those decisions that determine to what we will commit our lives, our hearts, our time, and our treasure. In Proverbs 3:5-6, God challenges us to do three specific things in these times of decision, and he promises to accomplish the fourth:

1. **"Trust in the Lord with all your heart."** The first thing I think of when I hear this is to tell the Lord over and over again that I will do whatever he wants me to do. Isaiah 55 says, "My thoughts are not your thoughts, neither are your ways my ways,' declares the Lord. 'As the heavens are higher than the earth, so are my ways higher than your ways and my thoughts higher than your thoughts.'" This tells me I need to be open to options I might never have considered before.
2. **"And lean not on your own understanding."** As the Isaiah passage reminds me, this is far beyond my pay grade. I am truly wanting to be led by the Spirit of God and not my own usual decision-making process.

95 Buechner, Frederick, *Beyond Words: Daily Readings in the ABCs of Faith*, Zondervan: 2009, p.259 (quote includes 1 Corinthians 1:27-29, NIV).

3. **"In all your ways acknowledge him."** The word "acknowledge" means "to accept the truth or existence of." Therefore, in each step of this decision-making process, I choose to tell the Lord I am trusting his sovereignty in this choice. I am asking him to lead me step by step. (Not that he needs reminding, but I know we all surely do.)
4. **"And he will make your paths straight."** This is God's key role—he promises to direct our paths if we follow this previously indicated roadmap of faith.

Bob Mumford, a renowned charismatic teacher, shares a picture for us in his book *Take Another Look at Guidance.* He writes of a perilous harbor in Italy where ships would frequently end up on the rocks as they tried to enter. The residents decided to place three harbor lights that, when exactly lined up, would safely usher a skipper into the harbor. Similarly, the three "harbor lights" Mumford mentions (that can guide our own lives safely) are:

- **Scripture.** As one seeks to receive guidance on an upcoming decision, what are the passages in God's Word that seem to 'jump off the page"? God's Word is indeed a "lamp to our feet and a light to our path."[96]
- **Circumstances.** What events independently transpire that seem to point toward or away from a particular direction? God is the blessed controller of the events in our lives. He often speaks through circumstances.
- **The Peace of the Holy Spirit**. Occasionally, we can sense a direction in Scripture and even in events that take place, but simultaneously feel a strange lack of peace that, as we continue to pray for God's wisdom in making a decision, that lack of peace remains. It can be a subjective roadblock in the face of otherwise objective green lights.

We would all likely agree that navigating these important decisions at crucial crossroads in our lives is often complicated and arduous; however, I would call to mind these encouraging thoughts from the Apostle Paul: "Continue to work out your salvation with fear and trembling, for it is God who works in you to will

96 Psalm 119:105

and to act according to his good purpose."[97] He is our guide in the important decisions that need to be made as we fully answer His call to commitment, and his Spirit and his Word can be trusted.

A second passage in Luke is very important in considering the implications of this attribute of placing Jesus before others, self and possessions: "Large crowds were traveling with Jesus, and turning to them he said, 'If anyone comes to me and does not hate his father and mother, his wife and children, his brothers and sisters—yes, even his own life—he cannot be my disciple. And anyone who does not carry his cross and follow me cannot be my disciple … In the same way, any of you who does not give up everything He has cannot be my disciple.'"[98]

I will often ask my young friends what these two passages in Luke have in common. The obvious answer is they both call for us to carry our cross or to take up our cross and follow Jesus. When we consider for what reason we would take up our cross, it is that we intend to die upon it. The cross is a symbol of death or execution. Both of these passages call for us to follow Jesus, having made the decision that we choose to die to ourselves. The Apostle Paul powerfully summarizes this journey, "I have been crucified with Christ and I no longer live, but Christ lives in me. The life I live in the body I live by faith in the Son of God, who loved me and gave himself for me."[99]

The first vivid picture I remember of envisioning this transformation occurred as a high school student on work crew at a Young Life resort. It was testimony night, and several of us were asked to briefly share our story. Fritz went first. He was a tough wrestler who had several last names—unusual for that day in the early sixties, but his mother had been married multiple times. His life had been radically changed since meeting Jesus. Fritz's testimony was the shortest I had ever heard—probably thirty seconds. I remember almost every word sixty years later.

"Hi, I'm Fritz. I'm the garbage man. (Prolonged laughter since it was the dirtiest, smelliest job in camp.) But I would carry garbage for Jesus any day, because he took all the filthy garbage in my life with him to the cross. And now

---

97 Philippians 2:12-13, NIV
98 Luke 14:25-27, 33, NIV
99 Galatians 2:20, NIV

he lives in my heart, and he is with me everywhere I go, and in everything I do." And he sat down.

Fritz was an example to me of someone who was giving his all to follow Jesus. All the things that had at one time been so valuable, and the object of his affections and pursuits, he had put aside to follow Jesus. They no longer counted as anything to Fritz. Jesus was his all. I have never forgotten that. I believe Jesus wants to live in you and me that same way.

Unpacking Jesus' Call Commitment

We've looked at the positive exhortation Jesus gave to follow him, but we also need to look at something else he said that might not make sense at face value. He told his friends, "If anyone comes to me and does not hate father and mother, wife and children, brothers and sisters—yes, even their own life—such a person cannot be my disciple."[100] The use of the word "hate" is most certainly troubling to any of us who wants to seriously apply this passage to our lives. The Greek word is *miseo,* a rarely used term to indicate that, in comparison to our love for Jesus Christ, our love for all others pales in comparison.

A primary rule of hermeneutics, the study of Biblical interpretation, is that Scripture helps us interpret other Scripture. The next attribute of discipleship we will be considering in the next chapter is the quality of loving our brothers and sisters. We know that "love" is a high-priority characteristic of a follower of Christ. So, obviously, Jesus was not encouraging us to literally hate these important ones in our lives.

Surrender—"Giving It All" to Follow Jesus

Besides our life pursuits and relationships, Jesus calls us to relinquish control of our other assets, like possessions, time, and talents. Throughout the Scriptures, he reminds us that all we possess is a stewardship from God. Only when we surrender it all can we fully appreciate the generosity and abundance of His provision for us.

Perhaps you would know of the only miracle that is in all four Gospels besides the resurrection: it is the feeding of the five thousand. Jesus performed

---

100 Luke 14:26, NIV

this miracle to open his disciples' eyes to the reality of God's provision in their lives. In Matthew's Gospel account of this story, we learn the number of those who were gathered on the shore of the Sea of Galilee to hear Jesus talk was about five thousand men, besides women and children."[101] Let's assume each man had a wife and child—some more, some less—but there were up to fifteen thousand people. It was late in the day, and everyone was hungry.

Jesus initially had his disciples instruct the crowd to sit in groups of fifty—up to three hundred groups. Just imagine three football fields full of groups of hungry people! A young boy graciously gave Andrew his lunch—five barley loaves and two fish—and Andrew took them to Jesus. Jesus gathered the five loaves and the two fish, blessed them, broke them into pieces, and had the disciples distribute them. As we know, the four Gospel accounts agree that everyone ate and was satisfied, and afterwards twelve baskets full of leftover bread and fish were collected.

As we apply this metaphor to the miracle that occurred, there were six important steps that occurred that we can apply to our lives:

- **Bring everything to Jesus.** He asks that we bring all of our time, our talents (abilities), all of our relationships, our possessions—even our future and all of our hopes and dreams—to him.
- **He blesses these offerings.** I believe this is where the miracles take place, but we first need to bring them to him. This is a supreme act of faith and stewardship on our part. Just a reminder—a steward is one who is put in trust of something that belongs to someone else. Have we relinquished all of these precious things to Jesus?
- **He breaks them.** This is called sanctification. He takes my flesh love (my love of self, my need to control, my love of my possessions, etc.), and through the relentless work of the Holy Spirit, Jesus transforms these selfish "loves" into *his* amazing love as described in 1 Corinthians 13. But he can't break these things I'm offering him unless I first am willing to release these areas to his faithful hand. That journey is a large part of our ongoing discipleship process.

---

101 Matthew 14:21

- **He distributes them.** Jesus gives out the loaves and fishes to the hungry masses. His abundance is incredible. Jesus tells us, "Give and it will be given to you. A good measure, pressed down, shaken together and running over, will be poured into your lap. For the measure you use, it will be measured to you."[102]
- **There is enough for everyone.** God is not stingy with his provision. Jesus is still doing miracles. Wouldn't it be a thrill to join him? All he asks is for us to bring everything to him. We don't need to grasp what is ours, for ourselves. Like the boy with his fish and loaves, we just need to surrender all we have to God, and trust that He will provide what we need when we need it.
- **And more is left over.** In this case, twelve baskets of fish and bread were picked up after everyone ate and was satisfied. A boy surrendered his lunch, and Jesus turned it into enough for around fifteen thousand people, with leftovers!

Too often, we think we need to provide for ourselves, to hang onto what we've got or grasp for what others have. We don't trust God to provide for us.

Let's suppose that one of the disciples in the above story was doubting this whole scenario, and chose to quietly snatch one of those fish and place it in his pocket for safekeeping prior to the whole process detailed above. Let's actually become that person for purposes of illustration.

"So, Thomas, you think this whole idea is ridiculous. You think, fifteen thousand men, women, and children are all hungry, and our best plan is to feed them on five small barley loaves and two fish? While no one is looking, Thomas, you have pocketed one of those fish.

They bring the five loaves and one fish to Jesus—he lacks nothing. Remember, Colossians 1:16 tells us "all things were created by him and for him." These fish and loaves are his too! He blesses them, breaks them into pieces, and has the disciples distribute them.

102 Luke 6:38, NIV

That process of passing out and then collecting most likely takes several hours with a crowd of that size. It is a hot day, as is common in Galilee. As dusk falls and you, Thomas, are joining the twelve disciples bringing the twelve baskets of leftovers back to Jesus, what are you thinking about? Undoubtedly, fresh in your mind is the presence and the smell of that fish, now several hours in your pocket.

Just one other question, Thomas: Was that fish part of the miracle that just took place? Obviously, it was not part of the wonderful miracle because it was withheld."

The powerful, clear message to each of us is to bring all of ourselves—abilities, possessions, futures, relationships, time, dreams—to him, and to hold nothing back. I believe the happiest people in life are those who live by such JOY—Jesus, others, you.

The late Mother Teresa of Calcutta famously said, "I am just a pencil in the hand of God." That pencil could write an incredible story, or paint a great masterpiece if placed in the hands of the right person. But a pencil, removed from the hand of a gifted designer, can do nothing itself. Jesus reminded his disciples in that last evening in the upper room, "I am the vine; you are the branches. If a man remains in me and I in him, he will bear much fruit; APART FROM ME YOU CAN DO NOTHING."[103]

I earlier mentioned the word "steward," defining it as one who is put in trust of something that belongs to another. I hope it has occurred to you that the essence of being a person who puts Jesus before others, self, and possessions—"Jesus first"— is one who has clearly recognized that his or her ultimate joy and privilege is to be a *steward* of all of those things the world clings to, not an owner or even possessor. A committed disciple of Jesus has come to recognize that each of those precious commodities are best placed in trust at the feet of Jesus.

In Luke 19:12-27, Jesus shares a marvelous parable that illustrates for us the wisdom of being a good and faithful steward. In this story, a nobleman goes off to a far country. But, before he departs, he gives each of his servants a talent or *mina* with the instruction to put the money to work until he returns.

---

103 John15:5, NIV, emphasis added

Sometime later, he returns and calls for his servants to account for their stewardship. The first one comes and tells him that his *mina* has made ten more. The response of the master is, "Well done, my good servant. Because you have been trustworthy in a very small matter, take charge of ten cities."[104] The second servant informs the master his *mina* has earned five more, and he is rewarded with responsibility for five cities.

Then a third servant approaches his master and says, "Sir, here is your *mina*; I have kept it laid away in a piece of cloth. I was afraid of you, because you are a hard man. You take out what you did not put in and reap what you did not sow."[105]

The response of the master is sudden and shocking, "'I will judge you by your own words, you wicked servant. You knew, did you, that I am a hard man, taking out what I did not put in, and reaping what I did not sow? Why then didn't you put my money on deposit, so that when I came back, I could have collected it with interest?' Then he said to those standing by, 'Take his *mina* away from him and give it to the one who has ten *minas*.'"[106] The crowd reacted to this seemingly harsh decision by the master who reminded them that, in his economy, to everyone who has, more will be given, but to him who has nothing, even that will be taken away.

The takeaway for us from this parable is that God honors our faithfulness in little things, and rewards that faithfulness with more responsibility and blessing. He is telling us the great importance of our stewardship responsibility for what we have been given. As we consider all that the Lord has entrusted to us as stewards—from our physical bodies, to all of our relationships in life, to the twenty-four hours a day each of us has been given, to the abilities and talents each of us possesses, to the possessions that have been given to us—all of these are areas of stewardship for us. As we place Jesus before others, self, and possessions, making him first in our life and affections, we are trusting him to work in and through us to help us faithfully steward these awesome responsibilities entrusted to us in this life. No higher honor could we ever have than to be entrusted with

---

104 Luke 19:17, NIV
105 Luke 19:20, NIV
106 Luke 19:22-24, NIV

such precious responsibilities by the only One we have learned to love and trust with our lives.

"I had walked life's way with an easy tread,
Had followed where comforts and pleasures led,
Until one day in a quiet place
I met the Master face to face.

With station and rank and wealth for my goal,
Much thought for my body, but none for my soul,
I had entered to win in life's mad race
When I met the Master face to face.

I met him and knew him and blushed to see,
That his eyes full of love were fixed on me.
And I faltered and fell at his feet that day
While my castles melted and vanished away.

Melted and vanished and in their place
Naught else did I see but the Master's face.
And I cried aloud, "Oh make me meet
To follow the steps of thy wounded feet."

My thought is now for the hearts of men
I have lost my life to find it again.
E'er since one day in a quiet place
I met the Master face to face.
(Author Unknown)

Chapter Nine

Loving Our Brothers and Sisters

"A new command I give you: love one another. As I have loved you, so you must love one another. By this all men will know that you are my disciples, if you love one another." (John 13:34-35, NIV)

The eleven disciples are huddled together in the Upper Room. Judas has disappeared into the darkness on his ill-fated mission. It is the last night together for this band of followers, having journeyed for three years throughout Galilee with Jesus.

As Jesus prepares to break the news to them that he is going away, he shares this all-important command with them: love one another. One immediately wonders, *Why did he wait so long to share this with them?* It would seem that this should be the quintessential "Discipleship 101" lesson to impart to them! Of course, the answer is that he wanted to show them what this love *looked* like.

As we journey back through those three years they spent together, the faces of so many he touched come to mind:

- the woman at the well who felt so loved and known she brought back her whole town to hear him
- the reviled tax collector Zacchaeus who paid back everyone he cheated four times as much
- Jairus—the synagogue president whose daughter was now alive and well
- the man born blind who could see again
- the woman caught in adultery who was set free from her former life
- the woman with the issue of blood who touched the hem of his garment and he listened to her whole story
- the leper whom Jesus touched despite his sores and was made clean
- … and more.

There were so many portraits of love that Jesus painted in his disciples' presence!

The Essence of Loving One Another

As we consider this crucial command, we observe that it breaks down into three important parts:

1. **The Command:** "A new command I give you: love one another." Five different times in this upper room discourse Jesus reminds them that if they indeed love Him they will keep His commands.[107] It is the clear indication, two thousand years later, that loving Him equals obedience to his commands.
2. **The Example:** "As I have loved you, so you must love one another." Jesus consistently and perfectly models love for us. He is the supreme example of self-giving love. As we spend time with Him, we experience and understand love.
3. **The Effect:** "By this all men will know that you are my disciples, if you love one another." The world is longing to witness living examples of this revolutionary love—self-giving *agape* love. The still-unbelieving world is

107 John 14:15, 21, 23; 15:10, 14, NIV

> watching—will they see Jesus' love in his followers? That is the singular most powerful message that can be given—a daily demonstration.

It was a life-changing revelation to me some years ago to realize that true love is perfectly articulated and illustrated in the life of Jesus. Jesus personifies love. My father-in-law and mentor, Doug Coe, said he believed the greatest truth he had learned over his lifetime was that, "The Gospel is a Person. Love is a Person. Unity is a Person." That person is Jesus.

Conversely, Hollywood tells us love is a *feeling.* As we witness so many gifted and famous movie stars steer through the wreckages of marriage after marriage, it occurs to us that, even though love obviously involves strong feelings, it is so much deeper than the unpredictability of feelings.

I remember when, On July 16, 1999, John Kennedy Jr. and his wife, Carolyn, and her sister, Lauren Bessette, were flying from New York City to the Kennedy family compound in Hyannisport, Massachusetts for a family wedding. He lacked credentials as a pilot to fly by instruments, and the weather was threatening. As they flew north, conditions worsened. In the night's dusky haze, Kennedy's instincts began to lie to him. His mind's eye became blind. Only with experience, which he lacked, can a pilot trust the needles on a dial more than what his feelings were telling him. Black hole vertigo causes a pilot to think he is flying where he is not, and he overcompensates. Tragically, he plunged toward the water at breakneck speed.

Similarly, our feelings are not the most significant barometer in measuring love. Countless lives have been irrevocably broken by similar miscalculations based solely on feelings. For this reason, we must consult the Scriptures to gain an accurate reading of what love is:

> *"Love is patient, love is kind. It does not envy, it does not boast, it is not proud. It is not rude, it is not self-seeking, it is not easily angered, it keeps no record of wrongs. Love does not delight in evil, but rejoices with the truth. It always protects, always trusts, always hopes, always perseveres. Love never fails."*[108]

108 1 Corinthians 13:4-8, NIV

The New Testament writings, originally penned in Greek, had three words for love. *Eros,* so named after the god of love, the son of Aphrodite, signified sexual love or desire. While greatly misused and therefore misunderstood, this love was a gift of God for physical expressions of love and for procreation. *phileo* signifies a kind of friendship love between brothers and sisters. The third word, *agape,* means a unique expression of love not based upon the merit of the person being loved, but rather is unconditional and is actually based upon them as an image-bearer of Jesus Christ.

A well-known conversation recorded in John 21 between Jesus and Peter graphically illustrates the difference between these last two Greek words for love. In their first conversation following the resurrection (which was preceded by Peter's thrice denial of knowing Jesus), the encounter begins by Jesus asking Peter a piercing question: "Simon, son of John, do you truly love (*agape*) me more than these?

"'Yes, Lord,' he said, 'you know that I love (*phileo*) you.'

"Jesus said, 'Feed my lambs.' Again Jesus said, 'Simon, son of John, do you truly love (agape) me?'

"He answered, 'Yes, Lord, you know that I love (*phileo*) you.'

"Jesus said, 'Take care of my sheep.' The third time he said to him, 'Simon, son of John, do you love (*phileo*) me?' Peter was hurt because Jesus asked him the third time, 'Do you love (phileo) me?'

"He said, 'Lord, you know all things; you know that I love (*phileo*) you.'

"Jesus said, 'Feed my sheep.'"[109]

In this passage, we see Jesus is calling Peter to understand a love that is deeper and more costly than a love that is just about companionship and friendship. He wanted Peter to know that true reconciling love required both kinds of love. Jesus goes on to tell Peter in the next sentence, "When you were younger you dressed yourself and went where you wanted; but when you are old you will stretch out your hands, and someone will dress you and lead you where you do not want to go." Here, Jesus is indicating the kind of death that Peter would experience. Historically, he is thought to have been crucified upside down because he felt unworthy to die as Jesus did. Most certainly, Peter

---

109 John 21:15-17, NIV

would come to more deeply understand the *agape* love he witnessed in the life of his master.

Returning to 1 Corinthians 13, this incredible description of *agape* love and its nine characteristics should overwhelm each of us as we consider our own efforts to demonstrate this kind of love toward others. It is gratifying to reflect upon the truism that, indeed, *love is a person.*

The Incomprehensible Love of God

Some years ago I received a couple of startling but helpful pictures (by "picture" I mean a mental image that came to me while in prayer) of the difference between my love and the eternal and overflowing love of God. The picture I received involved two experiences from the third grade—long forgotten over many years since being a nine-year-old—when I was a Cub Scout. For our monthly Cub Pack meetings, we would gather at my local church, University Presbyterian in Seattle, which sponsored this activity.

Before the meetings, we would all scuffle and play. A favorite game was to rub our shoes along the carpet in the meeting room until static electricity collected, and then touch some unsuspecting person on the cheek, often creating a spark and eliciting surprised displeasure. It's what kids do!

The Lord impressed that long-forgotten picture in my mind as representing my fleshly efforts to love: much activity and energy expended, but upon contact with another person, most likely only creating irritation. (So much for me trying to love on my own.)

The second picture, from elementary school, had similarly been long-forgotten. As third graders, occasionally we would be treated to a road trip. On one very special day, we were told this would be a big surprise. We excitedly brought our lunches and arrived early to school and loaded up on two buses. The promised treat was a trip over the Cascade Range mountain pass to visit Grand Coulee Dam in Eastern Washington, which had recently opened.

As we arrived and saw the huge spillway with water roaring down its concrete walls into the Columbia River, we were awestruck. However, the most memorable moment occurred shortly before our departure, as we listened to the guide describe the millions of kilowatts of energy created by the dam. As he pointed to the large power poles, the guide paused and indicated, "The power generated through this pole will light the entire city of Seattle." For a third grader, this was big news!

As the Lord reminded me of this long-forgotten scene, I thought of Jesus' love, was described in his words in John 8:12, "I am the light of the world. Whoever follows me will never walk in darkness, but will have the light of life." His love illuminates the world!

Love Makes the World Go Around

Most certainly, the subject of love captivates the world. Everyone is blessed by great love stories. As I think of a myriad of experiences of working with young people over the years, I am reminded of several glimpses of the incredible, magnetic love of Jesus that draws the lost to him.

It was an all-city Young Life club in my local area—nearly a thousand kids jammed into a hotel meeting room. It was also a parents' night, so I looked forward to greeting the hundred or so parents who were visiting on this evening. My message was on the cross—God's costly gift of love in the person of his son, Jesus, being offered as the ransom payment for our sin, so we might find new life through him.

As I concluded the message, I was eager to meet many of the parents, but I never found my way to them. In my path was Janet, a sixteen-year-old girl with tears in her eyes. I later found out she came from a divorced family and had been using drugs for much of her adolescent years.

As our eyes met, she uttered three words that I will remember the rest of my life: "I need him." That evening, Janet began a journey with Jesus. He came for people like Janet. In Matthew 18:11, we read, "The Son of Man came to save what was LOST," employing the Greek word *apololos.* The noun, translated as "lost" in English, is also used in its verb form, *apolumi.* We see this in Jesus' declaration in John 10:10, "The thief comes only to steal, kill, and DESTROY, but I have come that they may have life, and have it to the full."

This helps us understand that the enemy's mission for folks like Janet (and all the rest of us) is destruction or, capturing this Greek word's essence, for us to lose our way. But, thankfully, we have discovered that THE WAY is a person.

As we seek to communicate to the next generation the winsome message of Jesus, stories or illustrations are often the window through which our listeners can get a better understanding of the message we are sharing. Years ago, I heard the true story of a group of college guys who were traveling around Europe. They happened upon a guide who was leading a tour in a large Roman Catholic cathedral.

As they stood in the back of the sanctuary, the wisecracks and rudeness continued to grow until finally the guide, a young priest, asked the ringleader if he would come with him for a moment. The semi-inebriated young man followed the priest down toward the altar, where they faced a large crucifix, an image of Jesus on the cross. Looking up at the crucifix, the priest asked him to repeat after him these words, "Jesus Christ died for me, and I don't give a damn."

The smirking young man, eager to impress his cronies, nodded and, looking at the cross, loudly repeated, "Jesus Christ died for me, and I don't give a damn." The priest waited a moment, and then asked him to say it again. So he straightened, looked up, and a bit more slowly repeated these words. The priest again waited another moment, and a third time asked him to say those words. As the young college person looked up at that crucifix, for the first time in his life, the words were becoming personal. He slowly spoke, "Jesus Christ died for me…" And he stopped. As he gazed into the eyes of the Savior, it dawned on him that this great act of love had his name on it.

The message for us is incredibly personal. "You see, at just the right time, when we were still powerless, Christ died for the ungodly. Very rarely will anyone die for a righteous man, though for a good man someone might possibly dare to die. But God demonstrates his own love for us in this: While we were STILL sinners, Christ died for us."[110] Yes, even for that inebriated college lad!

As I write these words, America is embroiled in an explosive response to the murder by Minneapolis police of George Floyd, an unarmed black man who was handcuffed and on the ground with the knee of a police officer on his neck for over eight minutes. The initial shock and grief spilled over to rioting in cities across the nation, riots that continue as I write these chapters. I can't get out of my mind the song that, decades ago, Jackie DeShannon famously sang, saying

110 Romans 5:6-8, NIV

that what the world needs now is "love, sweet, love." The song goes on to say that love is the only thing that there is just too little of—not just for some people, but for everyone. Perhaps John 3:16 is the best-known Bible verse on this topic. If we would break it down word by word, it speaks hope to us in the midst of the world's calamities.

I have a dog-eared card that I've been carrying around for years with a poignant reminder of this truth. I don't know the author, but it has been great reminder to me:

For God … the greatest lover
So loved … the greatest power
The world … the greatest company
That He gave … the greatest act
His only begotten Son … the greatest sacrifice
That whosoever … the greatest offer
Believeth … the greatest simplicity
In Him … the greatest attraction
Should not perish … the greatest promise
But … the greatest difference
Have … the greatest certainty
Everlasting life … the greatest possession

Our Response to God's Love

It might be asked what our response as followers of Jesus should be to John 3:16, considering the pain and upheaval that is currently happening in our nation and the world.

Ironically, perhaps 1 John 3:16 and following might give us the best answer: "*We know what love is because Jesus Christ laid down his life for us. We must in turn lay down our lives for our brothers. But as for the well-to-do man who sees his brother in want but shuts his heart against him, how could anyone believe that the love of God lives in him? My children, let us love not merely in theory or in words—let us love in sincerity and in practice!*[111]

111 1 John 3:16-18, PHILLIPS

It would seem so important that our response to his love for us would result in very practical expressions of love, such as these verses call us to. There must be a very direct connection between our love for God and our love for everyone we meet:

> *"Yes, we love because he first loved us. If a man says, 'I love God', and hates his brother, he is a liar. For if he does not love the brother before his eyes how can he love the one beyond his sight? And, in any case, it is his explicit command that the one who loves God must love his brother too."*[112]

In the worldwide family of friends I have worked with for the past twenty-five years, a little brochure has circulated among us called, "A Follower of Jesus." One of my favorite components of it contains reflections on the qualities of a "person who loves the brother and sisters":

> *"Followers of Jesus are from many nations. They care about each other enough to gather together in small groups on a regular basis. They think together, discuss together, pray together, and play together in order to learn, little by little to: love unconditionally, serve God and not money, humble themselves, give without seeking a return, empower, and not control, show mercy, not revenge, seek justice and freedom for all people, encourage and not discourage, spread hope and not despair, believe and not doubt. They have decided to seek to do this together in order to establish throughout the world a 'REVOLUTION OF LOVE' so powerful that the division and animosity separating people and nations will be greatly eliminated or replaced by the spirit of forgiveness and reconciliation as modeled by Jesus of Nazareth.*

Jesus said this can only be accomplished by the transformation of the human heart by the power of God and not man; which is causing them, step by step, to begin to think like Jesus, talk like Jesus, act like Jesus, and love like Jesus."

May it be so!

---

112 John 4:19-21, PHILLIPS

Chapter Ten

Taking the Scriptures Seriously

"To the Jews who had believed him, Jesus said, 'If you hold to my teaching, you are really my disciples. Then you will know the truth, and the truth will set you free.'" (John 8:31-32, NIV)

The mood was tense. A woman had been caught in the act of adultery, and the Pharisees and the teachers of the law had seized her and brought her before Jesus—to humiliate her and to test him. Slyly, they asked, "Teacher, this woman was caught in the act of adultery. In the Law Moses commanded us to stone such women. What do you say?"[113] Once again, they were setting a trap for this one to whom the multitudes were flocking.

Jesus bent down and began writing on the ground, deflecting attention from the condemned woman as the crowd held its collective breath at this curious response. Finally, he stood and said calmly, "If any of you is without sin, let him be the first to throw a stone at her." Not surprisingly, one by one, they each dropped their stones. With the situation defused, Jesus turned to the terrified

113 John 8:5, NIV

woman, saying to her kindly, "Woman, where are they? Has no one condemned you?"

"No one, sir," she said.

"Then neither do I condemn you," Jesus declared. "Go and leave your life of sin."[114]

Jesus under Fire

Following this amazing and loving encounter, the Pharisees verbally attacked Jesus, questioning the validity of his testimony, his heritage, and finally his claims about himself. The explosive interchange ends with this dramatic climax: "'You are not yet fifty years old,' the Jews said to him, 'and you have seen Abraham!

'I tell you the truth,' Jesus answered,' before Abraham was born, I Am!' At this, they picked up stones to stone him, but Jesus hid himself, slipping away from the temple grounds."[115]

It is remarkable how calm and creative Jesus was when under fire. Have *you* ever had a skeptic corner you and send your way a hail of challenging questions about the basis for your beliefs? Inevitably, one of the most fashionable zingers is whether Jesus is really the Son of God or just an historic religious teacher. In the above passage, we see him exercising a position that goes beyond that of teacher to that of savior and judge, a place reserved for God alone. Passages like this serve to help us answer deep questions like this one, if we are willing to examine them carefully.

I avoid getting in religious arguments. They rarely convince anyone, and usually they lead to a growing antagonism between the parties. I do strongly believe we need to base our beliefs on reliable authority. That authority is the Scriptures, the inspired written word of God. I am fully convinced that a primary element in our own growth in Christ is a daily diet of Scripture. Jesus himself mentioned this in John 8:31, where he said, "If you continue on my word, you are truly my disciples" (KJV). Such a daily continuing is an absolute must for anyone who desires to grow in their journey with Jesus, and to be able to understand and apply his truth and wisdom to life.

---

114 See John 8:7

115 John 8:57-58, NIV

The Nature and Value of God's Word

When we talk about "God's Word," we are talking about the three ways, according to Scripture, that God's "words" come to us:

1. **The Spoken Word**— "And God said, 'Let there be light,' and there was light. God saw that the light was good, and he separated the light from the darkness. God called the light 'day' and the darkness he called 'night.' And there was evening, and there was morning—the first day."[116] Merely by speaking, God brought all things into being. His first word was to bring light out of darkness, illuminating his creative work.
2. **The Written Word**—what we commonly refer to as the Scriptures. An eloquent first example is the Ten Commandments, found in Exodus 20:3-17. Much of our consideration will elaborate on the authority and veracity of the written word.
3. **The Living (Incarnate) Word**—Jesus Christ. "In the beginning was the Word, and the Word was with God, and the Word was God…The Word became flesh and made his dwelling among us. We have seen his glory, the glory of the One and Only, who came from the Father, full of grace and truth."[117] The Greek word for "word" in this passage is *logos*, or "living word." Jesus is the living word of God. We don't worship a book, as wonderful as the Scriptures are. We love and worship a *Person,* the living Word, Jesus Christ. The written Word always points us to the living Word—Jesus.

What is the value of Scripture in our daily lives? Why is it unique from the vast array of religious books? We see the Apostle Paul addressed this question when he wrote to Timothy, "All Scripture is God-breathed and is useful for teaching, rebuking, correcting, and training in righteousness, so that the man of God may be thoroughly equipped for every good work."[118] This passage indicates the uniqueness of Scripture: it is "God-breathed" or "inspired by God" (RSV).

---

116 Genesis 1:3-5, NIV
117 John 1:1, 14, NIV
118 2 Timothy 3:16-17, NIV

Unlike all other books, the Scriptures—canonized in what we now know as the Bible, have survived repeated attempts to obliterate them through the centuries, because they comprise the inspired Word of God. I often encounter folks who refuse to believe this truth—that God actually wrote them through giving inspiration to human beings.

It has puzzled me why this is a serious obstacle for some. If we believe the universe and our world and the animal and plant kingdoms are the expression of a Creator, why would it be so difficult to think he couldn't fashion a book that would precisely express his thoughts and design for our lives? Even you and I can write a book expressing our point of view about life and its meaning.

In Paul's comments about the uniqueness of Scripture, he enumerates four specific areas in life that Scripture will prove to be invaluable:

1. **It teaches us.** It informs us about how to navigate our lives. It deals with our thoughts, attitudes, habits, and every aspect of daily living. It is an invaluable daily handbook for dealing with the ups and downs of life.
2. **It rebukes us**. To "rebuke" means to express sharp disapproval or criticism of one's actions. When was the last time Scripture has rebuked you or me? Hopefully, it was quite recently because, if not, we are either approaching perfection or it has been too long since we have been digging into Scripture. It is a good thing, though painful, when we are rebuked by God's Word because it leads us to repentance—an integral part of our growth in Christ.
3. **It corrects us.** Scripture not only tells me when I have gone astray, it beckons me home—it tells me what to do to make it right. An excellent example is in human relationships. When we earlier discussed the ministry of reconciliation, Jesus gave us very specific things to do (Matthew 5: 23-24, 18:15-17) when we are wronged or we perceive we have wronged another. These are not opinions; they are commands to obey. We show our love for Jesus when we obey his commands.
4. **It trains us in righteousness.** Scripture tells us "righteousness" is the character of God, morally right and justifiable. Just as an athlete trains

physically each day, our spiritual training must involve a daily investment in the study of God's word.

I have long admired the ministry of The Navigators in training new believers to develop a lifestyle of being in the Scriptures regularly. Every Navigator staff person I have ever met is a serious student of Scripture. When Debbie and I lived in Colorado Springs, while with Young Life, I loved the opportunities I had to meet regularly with their staff at their beautiful world headquarters, a castle known as "Glen Eyrie." I went away inspired every time.

The Navigators, among the many discipleship tools they have developed, have utilized an illustration to help us understand how to methodically take steps to get deeper into God's Word in practical ways. It is called "The Hand: Five Ways to Gain a Deeper Grasp of Scripture." This five-step process includes:

1. **Hear the Word.** This is the first level. Often it is helpful to listen audibly to God's word. A good way for me to do this is what used to be called (back in the Dark Ages, some might say!) "the Word on tape"—listening to Scripture being read as I drive from place to place. These days, "tapes" are non-existent, but the principle is the same. We can listen to God's Word being read on a number of different apps on our computer or smart phones. In listening to God's Word being read aloud, I begin to recognize it is the opposite from the world's thinking. Hearing it increases my familiarity with God's thoughts. (His thoughts and his voice are always in agreement.)
2. **Read the Word.** Embracing a daily habit of spending time in his Word. God's thoughts and ways are higher than ours in the same way that the heavens are higher than the earth, the prophet Isaiah tells us, and God's Word never returns to us void, but always accomplishes the purpose for which it was sent.[119]
3. **Study the Word.** As I go deeper into Scripture, it illuminates areas of my life. The psalmist said, "Your word is a lamp to my feet and a light to my path."[120]

---

119 Isaiah 55:8-11

120 Psalm 119:105, NIV

4. **Memorize the Word.** I often say that the longest journey in the world is the eighteen inches from my head to my heart. Scripture memory begins the vital process of having God's truth make that all-important journey. Again, the psalmist speaks to the value of God's Word: "I have hidden your word in my heart, that I might not sin against you."[121]
5. **Meditate on the Word.** The "thumb" on the hand in the Hand Illustration represents what is perhaps the most important step in the process. Just as a cow chews its cud, as we meditate upon Scripture, the Holy Spirit quietly transforms it from thoughts to actions in our lives. President John Quincy Adams once said, "I speak as a man to men of the world. And I say to you: search the Scriptures. The Bible is the book of all others to be read at all ages and in all conditions of human life; not to be read once or twice or thrice through and then laid aside; but to read in small portions of one or two chapters a day and never to be omitted by some overwhelming necessity."

In my own journey in life, I can attest to the incredible value of deeply investing in God's Word. I remember when I was a fourth grader, and a memory work program was offered at our church. Our Sunday school teachers gave us each a large card with the three-year program written out on it, and sent it home with us to work on the verses. I was not allowed to go out to play on Saturdays until I had worked on it!

The first year's list included familiar verses such as John 3:16, 2 Corinthians 5:17, and 1 John 1:9. The second year consisted of important passages such as the Beatitudes in Matthew 5 and some shorter psalms such as 1, 23, 46, and 121. The final year was a number of longer psalms, such as 51, 91, 103, and 139, along with key passages like John 1:1-14, 14:1-14, Romans 12:1-14, and concluding with Romans 8:1-39. (These are all classic, significant portions of Scripture; if you are not familiar with them—and even if you are—I hope you will look them up.)

I dutifully prepared each Saturday and before Sunday school, and showed up with my verses ready to recite in the King James translation. Years later, as a

121 Psalm 119:11, NIV

high school student, I first entered into a meaningful personal relationship with Jesus. To my amazement, these Scripture passages I had memorized years before became a major source of blessing, encouragement, and direction for navigating the future shoals of life for me. My experience caused me to continue memorizing, many times doing it with friends to share together our accompanying insights.

In the last twenty-five years as I have spent significant portions of time meeting with and discipling others in their faith journeys, I always ask them to memorize before we meet. I learned the value of this years ago, and even made it a part of the vetting process when determining if someone was really serious about wanting to meet with me for mentoring. Someone would ask me if we could meet together, and I would give them an assignment to memorize a passage and then to give me a call. I was amazed when sometimes I would never hear from that person again to meet. I am not seeking to judge anyone, but all of us have a limited amount of time. I have found the best investment of that time is to meet with folks who are willing to put something into their learning. They always get more out of it as a result! Just as in Jesus' parable of the *minas* or "talents," the person who invested his was given more responsibility, while the one who buried his was chastised. I have been pleasantly surprised that the more I am asking of people I meet with, the more they seem to grow in their journey with Jesus.

God's Word Is Alive

Over the course of my lifetime, one on one and in small groups, I have personally shared with over a thousand people these principles and attributes of a disciple that I am now sharing with you in this book. With these teachings, I seek to capture the essence of what Jesus was communicating to his disciples in the three years of his public ministry. In the Great Commission (which we will explore in the next chapter), he challenged them to teach others, "to obey everything I have commanded you."[122] In the Upper Room, on his last night with them before his death, Jesus told them, "I have called you friends, for everything that I have learned from my Father I have made known to you."[123]

122 Matthew 8:20
123 John 15:15, NIV

We are so privileged to join in on what Jesus imparted to the twelve in reading and studying the Scriptures, in particular the four Gospels. These words are as true and powerful today as they were then, because Jesus' words, the Word of God, is not only relevant and powerful, it is *alive*: "For the word of God is living and active. Sharper than any double-edged sword, it penetrates even to dividing of soul and spirit, joints and marrow; it judges the thoughts and attitudes of the heart. Nothing in all creation is hidden from God's sight. Everything is uncovered and laid bare before the eyes of him to whom we must give account."[124] This passage in Hebrews tells us that God's Word is indeed a living one. It penetrates to the dividing of the soul—our intellect, emotions and our will—the thinking, reasoning, deciding part of us, and our spirit or heart, where we engage God's Spirit.

This imagery employs a medical illustration. Imagine a skilled doctor doing an elaborate surgical procedure. He has around his forehead a plastic band that holds in place a light to illuminate the surgery and a magnifying glass to enlarge the point of contact. He delicately takes the scalpel to separate the joint from the marrow, just as God's Word skillfully locates the exact point where we are choosing whether to follow our fleshly commands, or to listen to the Spirit's still, small voice. It then reminds us that nothing is hidden from God's purview—where every thought and action is laid bare. Only a book that is God-breathed can be so "living and active."

As I have mentioned, for many years I have had the rich privilege of meeting one-on-one or in small groups with friends, most often young friends. When I was younger, I thought my own opinions and convictions would be very helpful to them. I would share them in copious detail. As I have grown older, I have less regard for my personal opinions and experiences as a high priority for teaching others. I am certainly not seeking to diminish the great learning all of us receive through our personal experiences, but I am realizing my experience is not necessarily normative for someone else. What I am increasingly aware of is I am on target one hundred percent of the time when I am giving a person God's Word as they are facing life's challenges, especially when I am quoting it from memory (a nonverbal indication of its importance in my own life).

---

124 Hebrews 4:12-13, NIV

Several times over the past fifty-plus years of meeting with young people, I've had a young man come to me and say, "Doug, I am sensing it is okay with the Lord for me to move in with my girlfriend."

Without appearing surprised, I might respond, "Really! That is the first time this has ever happened in my experience!" (I am avoiding getting into a debate with him about the wisdom of this, especially when it is more and more commonplace in our world, and arguments rarely accomplish anything of value.)

He responds, "What do you mean?"

I explain, "I mean, it is the first time someone has shared with me that God told them to do something he expressly told us not to do in his Word." Then I share God's Word from memory, "Flee from sexual immorality. All other sins a man commits are outside his body, but he who sins sexually sins against his own body. Do you know that your body is a temple of the Holy Spirit, who is in you, whom you have received from God? You are not your own; you were bought at a price. Therefore, honor God with your body."[125] This passage not only clearly commands me to abstain from breaking one of the Ten Commandments, but it gives me clear reasons why.

What happens next is we never get into an argument. He now clearly knows God didn't tell him that; someone else did. I remain his friend, but he has a choice to make: obey the Lord or do his own thing. Either way, I still love him, but he realizes he is not disagreeing with me. He is disagreeing with God. It has been an invaluable lesson that my years of experience have taught me: give God's thoughts first and foremost. Occasionally, my own experiences and thoughts are helpful, but probably not as often as I am thinking they are!

Another important aspect of Scripture is the sharp contrast between what the world's wisdom tells us and what God's Word reveals. For many years I would carry around in my briefcase a list of about a dozen subjects in life which would illustrate this huge contrast.

About twenty years ago, I was meeting with fifty young disciples from a number of different countries from the Youth Core communities in the former Soviet Union. We were at a retreat center outside of Moscow for four days, and early one morning I was to drive into Moscow to meet with a small group of

125 1 Corinthians 6:18-21, NIV

members of the Russian *duma* (parliament), who were gathering at the National Hotel, across from Red Square. This was a group I had been meeting with for the previous five years. A few were believers and others interested friends, and most of us had met at our National Prayer Breakfast some years before.

As I was going to bed the night before our meeting, I had the thought to put the paper that listed these opposites (world's wisdom versus God's Word) in my suit coat pocket. As we met the following morning, toward the end of our meeting I remembered this document. Ironically, we were at a very appropriate moment in our discussions to share this. I pulled it out and asked if I could read it. It went like this:

> *"The world says exalt yourself; Jesus says humble yourself and you will be exalted. The world says take—everything you can, Jesus says give and it will be given unto you. The world says hate your enemies; Jesus says love your enemies and do good to those who hate you. The world says leadership is giving orders to people; Jesus tells us leadership is servanthood. The world says save your own life; Jesus tells us to lose our life for his sake and we will find it. The world says be first; Jesus tells us the last will be first ... "*

... and so on. After I read this, there was a long silence. One of the men asked if he could make a copy. Everyone else in the room asked for one. He headed downstairs to the concierge and made copies for all. This led to fruitful conversations in the months ahead. It was a great reminder of the scriptural truth from Isaiah, " ... So is my word that goes out from my mouth: It will not return to me empty, but will accomplish what I desire and achieve the purpose for which I sent it."[126]

A Lifelong Legacy

As I reflect on over fifty-five years of working with young people (I started leading my first Young Life club in 1964 in tiny Mill City, Oregon, at Santiam High School), I am grateful for many valuable lessons that were learned, often by doing the wrong thing, but God is gracious and always uses us if our hearts are set

126 Isaiah 55:11, NIV

toward honoring him. In the summer several years ago I mentioned revisiting old Young Life kids (who were now at retirement ages!). One thing I heard over and over again: "You taught me to love God's Word, and you gave me responsibility. It helped me gain confidence to lead."

One such person was Judy. She was a very quiet young lady who never missed club or our Bible studies. In those years, we began a group called "Koinonia," borrowing from the Greek word for "fellowship." I decided to have different young people take responsibility to lead the studies. At first, it was up and down—a new experience and intimidating for many. Judy was a part of that group.

When I met up with her a few years ago, she was concluding nearly thirty-five years as an elementary school teacher, the most recent number of years in a faith-based school. Judy beamed as she recounted how those early experiences of risking herself in our Koinonia group contributed to later being willing to step out in faith and lead. I attribute so much of that to the value of studying God's Word.

I only had one brief meeting with Young Life's founder, Jim Rayburn, before he died of cancer in 1970. It was the previous summer, when he had just returned from the hospital from brain cancer surgery. I was invited to meet with him at his home in Colorado Springs. He sat at his desk in his pajamas and bathrobe. It was an unspeakable honor to listen to him. Before it was time to leave, I asked him what he would say to me as a young staff person. In his slow Texas drawl he encouraged me: "Don't ever forget that the kids may not remember the funny skits you did in club or even your clever messages. What they *will* remember—that matters—is what you imparted to them, in word and in action, of the Lord Jesus Christ … They will remember that."

I am so grateful that God's Word, from the beginning, has had such a formative role in my own journey with Jesus and in my relationships with young people. I'm reminded of Paul's words to the Thessalonians, "Our attitude among you was one of tenderness, rather like a nurse caring for her babies. Because we loved you, it was a joy to us to give you not only the gospel of God, but our very hearts—so dear had you become to us."[127] What a powerful combination—God's Word and our very hearts!

127 1 Thessalonians 2:7-8, PHILLIPS

Chapter Eleven

Making Disciples

"Then the eleven disciples went to Galilee to the mountain where Jesus had told them to go. When they saw him, they worshiped him, but some doubted. Then Jesus came to them and said, 'All authority in heaven and on earth has been to me. Therefore, go and make disciples of all nations, baptizing them in the name of the Father and of the Son and of the Holy Spirit, and teaching them to obey everything I have commanded you.

And surely I am with you always, to the very end of the age.'" (Matthew 28:16-20, NIV)

It was forty days after the resurrection. Jesus' disciples—still amazed by the profundity of this miracle—were to rendezvous with Jesus at a designated mountain in Galilee, at his request. When they encountered him there in his transfigured state, worship seemed a natural response. Amazingly, some doubted as well.

As surprising as a doubtful response might strike us, it speaks powerfully to our human condition. Doubt is normative—for all of us. The key question is, *What do we do with our doubts?* If we feed them, they get bigger and bigger. On the other hand, if we expose them to the authority of God's Word, they dwindle and quite possibly disappear.

I will often ask someone, "Who is greater: Jesus or Satan? My young friends most certainly expect the scriptural answer, " … the one who is in you is greater than the one who is in the world."[128] As true as that assurance is, I will also inevitably and truthfully answer my own question, "The one you feed." God has given us free choice, and if I feed my doubts with more doubt, they grow bigger.

James Stewart, in his classic book, *The Life and Teaching of Jesus Christ,* notes, "It is quite certain that the original disciple band was a young men's group. Most of the disciples were probably still in their twenties when they went out after Jesus."[129] The questionings and doubts of these young men were certainly understandable. However, Stewart also beautifully captures Jesus' fondness for the youth of his disciples:

> *"No one has understood the heart of youth in its gaiety and gallantry and generosity and hope, its sudden loneliness and haunting dreams and hidden conflicts and strong temptations, no one understood it nearly as well as Jesus. And no one realized more clearly than Jesus did that the adolescent years of life, when strange dormant thoughts are stirring and the whole world begins to unfold, are God's best chance with the soul. When Jesus and youth come together, deep calls to deep. There is an immediate feeling of kinship, and everything that is fine and noble and pure in youth, bows down in admiration and adoration before him."*[130]

The amazing reality that Jesus invested the majority of his time in those three years of public ministry in twelve young men, as opposed to holding massive evangelistic gatherings, speaks to the heart of the strategy of the Son of God, who

---

128 1 John 4:4, NIV

129 Stewart, James S. *The Life and Teaching of Jesus Christ*. Edinburgh: Saint Andrew Press, 1995, p. 55.

130 Ibid, p. 55-56.

communed closely with his Father. He said, "I tell you the truth, the Son can do nothing by himself; he can do only what he sees his Father doing."[131] Robert Coleman ponders this strategy, asking:

> *"Why did Jesus deliberately concentrate his life upon comparatively so few people? With the glowing announcement of John the Baptist ringing in the ears of multitudes, the Master easily could have had an immediate following of thousands if he wanted them … The answer to this question focuses at once the real purpose of his plan for evangelism. Jesus was not trying to impress the crowd, but to usher in a Kingdom. This meant that he needed good men who could lead the multitudes."*[132]

Matthew's Gospel concludes with this final meeting of Jesus and his disciples on what is now known as the "Mount of Transfiguration." Obviously, these were very important moments as the Master gave his disciples last instructions before he returned to the Father.[133] Jesus made the clear and undeniable claim that all authority in heaven and on earth had been given to him by the Father, and that he was passing that authority on to them (and to us). In considering the all-inclusive power of this majestic proclamation, it should embolden all of us who believe on his name to stand against any opposition we might face. In other words, Jesus isn't waiting for the upstate votes to come in to determine whether he is Lord of all!

Therefore …

> *Then Jesus came to them and said, "All authority in heaven and on earth has been given to me. Therefore go and make disciples of all nations, baptizing them in the name of the Father and of the Son and of the Holy Spirit, and*

---

131 John 5:19, NIV

132 Coleman, Robert E., and Billy Graham. *The Master Plan of Evangelism*. Grand Rapids, MI, MI: Revell, 2006, p. 31.

133 Acts 1:6-9 records a gathering of Jesus and the eleven when he promises the Holy Spirit and is taken up to heaven, but this passage, known as "the Great Commission" to many signifies Jesus' final instructions and challenge to them.

teaching them to obey everything I have commanded you. And surely I am with you always, to the very end of the age."[134]

The word following Jesus' amazing declaration is "therefore." Whenever we see this word in Scripture we have to ask why it is there. On the basis of the fact that all authority in heaven and on earth is given to Jesus, he is in turn giving his disciples (and, in turn, us) four commands:

1. **"Go."** Jesus is challenging each of us to go in his name and with his power and authority. So often we think it is the role of the pastor or church leader to go forth in his name, but the clarion call is to all of us. If we love him, we keep his commands—this is one of them!
2. **"Make disciples of all nations."** The Greek is best translated, "as you are going, make disciples." In other words, Jesus is calling each of us to a lifestyle of reproducing disciples. It isn't a special project we endeavor to practice on occasion. It is an integral part of who we are—disciple-makers—because Jesus called us to be.

We so often think in terms of the division into "sacred" and "secular." To Jesus, all things are sacred. There are no part-time folks in his Kingdom. Each of us is privileged to partner with Jesus in fulfilling this blessed command. Ironically, those of us who are working in the secular world actually might have an advantage in fulfilling this challenge: we can more easily "sneak up on people." That is, we build relationships at work, in the gym, in the classroom, in the neighborhood—where regular people are. And we have the opportunity to build relationships and love those regular people into the Kingdom.

One of the greatest adventures of my life was in such an endeavor many years ago. We had just moved to a beautiful home in a small community in Washington State. Our kids were approaching their teens. It was a wonderful time of life—except we had next door neighbors that were a real challenge. If you caught them by afternoon, there was a good chance Bob and Alice were inebriated. In their late 80's, he was a retired truck driver. They were estranged

---

134 Matthew 28:18-20, NIV

from their grown kids, one of whom who had tragically committed suicide. They were not happy people—or friendly neighbors. When our boys were playing ball, if it rolled into their yard, they would get an epithet-laced tongue-lashing from Bob. When our dog would poop in their yard, Alice would show up with the evidence in a cup at our front door.

We awkwardly tried to be friendly, but one day, my world changed. As I was weeding in the back yard, Bob and I engaged in small talk until he said abruptly, "You don't like me, do you?" I don't remember my feeble answer, but that day, I felt a gentle nudging from Jesus, "You travel the world to tell people about me, but when I put you next door to some difficult people, you abhor them." He was right.

Debbie and I resolved that day to be different. We began to pray regularly for Bob and Alice and for ourselves to see them through the eyes of Jesus. I began to pick up their mail down at the end of the street and bring it by each afternoon. That was when I discovered that he would often fall and be on the ground for hours. I asked Alice to call me—day or night to help. Their sixtieth wedding anniversary came, and our whole family baked a cake, brought a gift, and serenaded them.

Soon, it was apparent they needed additional care. I called their son, and they were subsequently moved to a local assisted living community. I would visit them at least weekly, and one day I asked if I could read them a story. I read a Gospel account about Jesus. They listened attentively, though they had never been church-goers, and this soon became a regular part of our frequent times together. One very special day, as Bob and I talked about life, he said to me, "Doug, you're my best friend in the world." That was a great day for me!

Some months later, I read them the story of the four friends[135] who, from the rooftop of a house where Jesus was teaching, lowered their paralyzed buddy to the feet of Jesus. Jesus first forgave the man's sins and then healed his body. I told Bob and Alice that Jesus would forgive them, too, if they asked him and would come to live in their hearts. That day, in the senior care center, the three of us joined hands and prayed, and Jesus entered their hearts—absolutely one of the best days of my life!

---

135 See Mark 2

Some months later, as Debbie picked me up at the airport from a trip to Russia, she told me Alice had died. We headed to the senior center, and as I walked into the room, Bob pointed to heaven. I was honored to do her memorial service. Six months later, Bob graduated too. I was thrilled to also lead his service.

After the memorial, his son came up to me and said, "I don't know what you did with my parents, but I wanted to thank you."

With moist eyes, I looked at him and replied, "Becoming friends with your mom and dad was one of the greatest experiences of my life." The takeaway for me is, remembering Francis Schaeffer's renowned book title, there are, in his poignant words, *No Little People.* Everyone is created in the image of God, and our Lord's challenge to each of us is to see each of them through the eyes of Jesus and share the greatest news the world's ears will ever hear: Love is a Person … Life is a Person … Jesus came for the whole world!

3. **"Baptizing them in the name of the Father and of the Son and of the Holy Spirit."** Perhaps Jesus was also encouraging us to baptize these friends, but more importantly, his challenge to us is to walk closely alongside them as their lives change, and they experience Jesus Christ living in and through them. Isn't that what baptism is all about? It is following Jesus in his death, burial, and resurrection. Among our greatest joys in life must be the inexpressible delight of seeing Jesus transform lives. And he allows us to play a part in that holy process.
4. **"Teaching them to obey everything I have commanded you."** The incredible reality that Jesus would choose you and me to partner with him has to be one of the supreme blessings in our lives. As I am writing this today, I have just finished a two-hour zoom call with ten of our Youth Core communities in six cities in Russia, Ukraine, Armenia, Kazakhstan, and several cities in America where some have emigrated. As each team shared the ups and downs of living through this difficult pandemic, stories of hope and new life in Christ brightened each of our days. When we obey Jesus by teaching others to obey Jesus, we get to share in the joy of the fruitfulness and influence that obedience generates in their lives.

As we face challenging times in our world two thousand years after Jesus' scintillating pronouncement to the disciples, we may still draw hope from his Word: "But we also rejoice in our sufferings, because we know that suffering produces perseverance; perseverance, character; and character, hope. And hope does not disappoint us, because God has poured out his love into our hearts by the Holy Spirit, whom he has given us."[136] I remember a visit to The Cedars a few years ago by the pastoral leadership of Bethel Church in Redding, California, known worldwide for the abundance of signs, wonders, healings and other miracles taking place on a regular basis. Listening to them, I could not miss the spirit of joy, humility, and optimism that surrounded them. The senior pastor, Bill Johnson, made a comment that has stayed with me, "He who has the most hope has the most influence."

The Multiplication of Our Faith

Undoubtedly, the resurrection of Jesus Christ is the supreme miracle that defines the hope that the Scriptures impart to us. Coleman observes, "Interestingly enough, every one of the ten post-resurrection appearances of Christ was to his followers, particularly the chosen apostles. So far as the Bible shows, not a single unbelieving person was permitted to see the glorified Lord. Yet it is not so strange. There was no need to excite the multitudes with his spectacular revelation … He actually spent more time with his disciples than with everybody else in the world put together. He ate with them, slept with them, and talked with them for the most part of his entire active ministry."[137] Thus, the disciples were getting the benefit of everything he said and did to others plus their own personal explanation and counsel. The amazing result is two thousand years later, the message is still being passed on from life to life.

As the Apostle Paul was speaking in his final written letter to Timothy, his young son in the faith, he exemplified this passing along to generations of others: "You then, my son, be strong in the grace that is in Christ Jesus. And the things you have heard me say in the presence of many witnesses entrust to reliable

136 Romans 5:3-5

137 Coleman, Robert E., and Billy Graham. *The Master Plan of Evangelism*. Grand Rapids, MI, MI: Revell, 2006, p. 42-43.

men who will also be qualified to teach others."[138] I will often ask, "How many generations of disciples are mentioned in verse two?" Of course, the answer is four: Paul to Timothy to reliable men to others.

Then I might ask if Timothy discipled ten and each of them in turn discipled ten more, how many total disciples would you have? The answer is one hundred twelve, including Paul and Timothy.

Perhaps the most important question then could be asked, "If you continued that process and everyone did their part, how soon would the whole world be reached? The answer is about a dozen successive multiplications would touch every person on the planet!

The final question I might ask is, "Using the scriptural language of 2 Timothy 2:2, what is your role in all of this?" Most certainly, it is to be a "reliable man or woman" who will be qualified to teach others. (Hopefully each of us will do our part as reliable people taking seriously Jesus' command to make disciples!)

Perhaps one of the greatest motivations for each of us to keep growing in our own personal journeys with Jesus is found in a comment he made to his followers: "He also told them this parable: 'Can a blind man lead a blind man? Will they not both fall into a pit? A student is not above his teacher, but everyone who is fully trained will be like his teacher.'"[139] What a great motivation to continue our discipleship journey! Obviously, first and foremost, it is because we love him. But we also are modeling discipleship to those we are seeking to teach—both positively and negatively. Over the years, I would be stunned and sometimes grieved to see where my own sarcasm, bad habits, unkindness, or other flaws were reproduced in those around me. It is truly a powerful statement that Paul makes to the church at Corinth, "Copy me, my brothers, as I copy Christ himself."[140]

Many years ago, I heard an arresting story that beautifully frames this exhortation to continue growing in our own journey with Jesus in discipleship. A female lion or lioness was pregnant and about to give birth to lion cubs. The father lion had departed and was nowhere to be found. Upon delivering two

138 2 Timothy 2:1-2, NIV
139 Luke 6:39-40, NIV
140 1 Corinthians 11:1, PHILLIPS

baby cubs, the mother died, leaving the lion cubs as orphans. After two days, one of the cubs died.

The second one was on the point of death when a herd of goats appeared. One of the female goats came to the lion cub and nursed him, saving his life. The little lion cub followed the goat herd. Each day, he grew stronger, drinking milk from the mother goats and beginning to eat the grass they grazed upon. The days became weeks, and the lion cub had become part of the herd of goats. He noticed they would hippity-hop along, and he would try to do that, but it felt awkward. He liked to spring through the air, but he was slowly learning to hop. Despite drinking the milk and eating much grass, he always felt a gnawing hunger—never feeling fully satisfied.

One day, he was down at the pond drinking water and saw his reflection—so surprising! He was most unlike the other goats—much bigger, with flowing hair! Then another goat came to drink, stirring up the water, and he soon forgot about what he had seen. The weeks turned into months, and the lion cub was now an integral part of the goat family. But one day, something very strange changed everything for this young lion cub.

The birds overhead flew away; the goat family ran quickly from the meadow where they lived. The lion cub looked up and standing above him was a huge lion. The great beast roared. The lion cub responded as he only knew how, "Baa, baa! The huge animal scowled at this lion cub and dropped a piece of meat at his feet. The cub sniffed at it, munched on nearby grass, came back for another whiff, then a nibble, then a bite … and soon he had devoured the whole piece of meat. For the first time in his life those ever-present hunger pangs were gone.

Now the huge lion began to amble across the meadow. He looked behind him to see the cub hippity-hopping behind. As the cub watched this large, tawny beast leaping through the air, he decided to try. He soared through air like he had springs! The last time the goat herd saw their friend, the lion cub, he was following the lion, springing through the woods. As the days went by, the lion cub followed the big lion, and gradually he became who he was created to be.

What is the connection here? Jesus is called "the lion of the tribe of Judah.[141] As we follow him, we mystically become the one we were created to be. Once

141 Revelation 5:5

again, Scripture uses the Greek word *teleios,* meaning "perfect "or "fully mature," to indicate the thrilling journey Jesus has in mind for us as we follow him: "And we, who with unveiled faces all reflect the Lord's glory, are being transformed into his likeness with ever-increasing glory, which comes from the Lord, who is the Spirit."[142]

And the Lion of Judah then allows us to participate with him in the extraordinary privilege of helping others become the ones they were created to be. The making of disciples is most certainly what we were created for—to know him and to make him known by our lives and witness. As we do, may we never forget his striking final words: "Surely I am with you always, to the very end of the age."

> *"Jesus … the Man … the bronzed Galilean who spoke with such thunderous authority and loved with such childlike humility … the God. The One who claimed to be older than time and greater than death. Gone is the pomp of religion; dissipated is the fog of theology. Momentarily lifted is the opaque curtain of controversy and opinion. Erased are our own blinding errors and egotism. And there he stands. Jesus. Have you seen him? Those who first did were never the same." (Max Lucado)*[143]

142 2 Corinthians 3:18, NIV

143 Lucado, Max. *God Came near: God's Perfect Gift*. Nashville, TN: Thomas Nelson, 2013, p. 15.

Chapter Twelve

Being Led by the Holy Spirit

"He said to them, 'It is not for you to know the times or dates the Father has set by his own authority. But you will receive power when the Holy Spirit comes on you; and you will be my witnesses in Jerusalem, and in all Judea and Samaria, and to the ends of the earth'. After he said this, he was taken up before their very eyes, and a cloud hid him from their sight." (Acts 1:7-9, NIV)

Following Jesus' ascension into heaven, as the eleven disciples continue to look up in the sky in astonishment, two angels suddenly stood before them and assured them that Jesus would someday return in the same manner.[144] Forty days later, the Holy Spirit fell upon them in Jerusalem, and the New Testament church was born. "Don't go anywhere, don't do anything, until I send you a helper," Jesus had told them.[145] Clearly, the person of the Holy Spirit is foundational to the work of the Church. Yet, surprisingly, I have discovered over

144 See Acts 1:11
145 See Acts 1:4-5

the years that many believers lack even basic understanding of what it meant that Jesus promised the Holy Spirit to his followers.

It would be so easy to look at these troubled times we are living in and conclude, "If only Jesus were here today!" Upon careful reflection, that would mean he could only be in one place at one time. In that case, you might be able see him on worldwide television, but he had a better idea: to live in each of our hearts!

I frequently use the following object lesson to illustrate this point. If I am speaking to a group, I will ask for one of them to go get a toaster. Eyebrows raise and there is a snicker or two from the crowd. I place the toaster on my lap and proceed to extol the benefits of a toaster in quickly heating pop tarts, frozen waffles, cinnamon bread, etc. Then to illustrate, I push down the button to start the toaster.

Nothing happens. I try again, slapping the side. Nervous laughter begins. I try one more time. Finally, someone says, "Doug, you have to plug it in." And Jesus told his disciples basically the same thing while they were in the Upper Room: "Apart from me, you can do nothing."[146] So often we are ignorant about plugging into the power source!

Over the years, I have come to realize the importance of talking about the person and work of the Holy Spirit in very practical terms. Here's another way I explain it: Someone very close to me has died, someone with great resources. After the memorial service, I receive a message from his attorney's office—meet next Friday at the law office for the reading of the will. I will find out what I am receiving! As I arrive, I find myself with others who were also close to the departed one. We all eagerly listen to find out what has been willed to us.

In a similar gathering, on the night before he died, Jesus spoke to his disciples in the Upper Room about the promised Holy Spirit. In a mere fifteen verses, he told them about the blessed and powerful benefits they would receive as he left behind the Comforter.[147] As we sit in on this conversation around the table, with believers from throughout the ages, let's discover from John chapter 14 what we will receive as the promised Holy Spirit comes to live in us:

146 John 15:5, NIV
147 John 14:16-17, 26-27; 15:26-27;16:7-15

1. He is a Counselor to be with me forever. (14:16)
2. He lives with me and in me. (14:17)
3. He teaches me all things. (14:26)
4. He reminds me of the words of Jesus. (14:26)
5. He gives me his peace, unlike the world's peace. (14:27)
6. He testifies about Jesus. (15:26)
7. He enables me to testify as well. (15:27)
8. He convicts me of sin, which leads me to repent. (16:8-11)
9. He guides me into the truth (16:13)
10. He tells me what is to come. (16:13)
11. He always glorifies Jesus, not himself. (16:14)
12. He always takes from Jesus to make known to me. (16:15)

As we slide our chairs back from that imaginary table, we are very blessed people! What a treasure trove of gifts we have been given by Jesus as he goes to be with the Father! Let me highlight several. Have you ever prepared a message, and when you stood to give it, the Holy Spirit gave you words that were most certainly not in your notes? As you spoke, you felt his power working through you, and the effect was that all who listened were blessed and encouraged?

I am certain that Peter, as he stood to address the crowd at Pentecost in Acts 2, was not speaking from prepared notes. The Holy Spirit, who knows the hearts of those listeners, is so well-prepared to speak truth to the deepest recesses of our hearts. (This is not to discourage careful and prayerful preparation, but rather to gratefully acknowledge the promise that the Holy Spirit will continue to testify through us.) Similarly, it almost sounds like bad news to hear that the Holy Spirit convicts us of sin. But how else will we repent[148] and turn back toward following Jesus?

The world is currently reeling in fear, anxiety, and uncertainty as the horrendous fruits of hatred, division, and strife manifest their presence. Jesus promises us an inward peace through the Holy Spirit that transcends this world's understanding of it. God's people can find themselves in the midst of all of this chaos, and have a peace that only the Spirit of Jesus can impart.

148 from the Greek word *metanoia,* meaning "a change of mind and heart"

Two Kinds of Wisdom

The Apostle Paul shares an amazing comparison between the wisdom of the world and the wisdom of God, as revealed by the Holy Spirit, beginning with 1 Corinthians 1:18 and continuing through the second chapter: "For since, in the wisdom of God, the world through its wisdom did not know him, God was pleased through the foolishness of what was preached to save those who believe."[149] Paul, formerly a leading Pharisee and esteemed teacher of the Law, testifies, "My message and my preaching were not with wise and persuasive words, but with a demonstration of the Spirit's power, so that your faith might not rest on man's wisdom, but on God's power."[150] Then Paul describes the powerful work of the Holy Spirit, the wisdom of God:

> *"'No eye has seen, no ear has heard, no mind has conceived what God has prepared for those who love him'—but God has revealed it to us by his Spirit. The Spirit searches all things, even the deep things of God. For who among men knows the thoughts of a man except the man's spirit within him? In the same way no one knows the thoughts of God except the Spirit of God. We have not received the spirit of the world, but the Spirit who is from God that we may understand what God has freely given us. This is what we speak, not in words taught us by human wisdom but in words taught by the Spirit, expressing spiritual truths in spiritual words."*[151]

Here Paul presents the work of the Holy Spirit in very practical terms, beginning by quoting the prophet Isaiah[152] and contrasting it from the spirit of the world. He tells us the great news that a primary work of the Holy Spirit is to impart to us those things God has freely given to us. He goes on in verse fourteen to note that the unbeliever will not understand these things—they are actually foolishness to him, because they can only be understood as revealed by the Holy Spirit.

---

149 1 Corinthians 1:21, NIV
150 1 Corinthians 2:4-5, NIV
151 1 Corinthians 2:9-13, NIV
152 Isaiah 64:4

As we reflect upon our experience with non-believing friends, this is very helpful to us. It should cause us to realize that argument or pressure seldom is helpful in convincing them. Most certainly, unconditional love and a life of grace and kindness go a long way in imparting the truth of God's wisdom. The contrast between the two wisdoms concludes in verse sixteen with a final question from Isaiah, "For who has known the mind of the Lord that he may instruct him? But we have the mind of Christ."[153] What a fabulous promise!

As I walk in the Spirit, he increasingly gives me his mind and his thoughts. The Phillips translation of the Bible concludes this passage with, "… we who are spiritual have the very thoughts of Christ." In other words, Jesus gives me a new set of eyes and ears that correspond to his heart when I see lost people doing foolish things. I can respond with his love so that, rather than imparting criticism or condemnation, I can exude his love and compassion.

Overcoming the World's Enmity

As we consider the fragile condition of our world, the great need of the hour is for the work of the Holy Spirit, the one who brings peace to shine through the followers of Jesus Christ:

> *"For Christ is our living peace. He has made us both one by breaking down the barrier and enmity which lay between us. By his sacrifice he removed the hostility of the Law, with all of its commandments and rules, and made in himself out of the two, Jew and Gentile, one new man, thus producing peace. For he reconciled both to God by the sacrifice of one body on the cross, and by his act killed the enmity between them. Then he came and brought the good news of peace to you who were far from God and to us who were near. And it is through him that both of us can now approach the Father in the one Spirit."*[154]

In this case, the division and enmity was between Jew and Gentile. Simply fill in the blank to indicate the division that is being perpetrated by the enemy, the father of lies, throughout the world today.

153 Isaiah 40:13
154 Ephesians 2:13-18, PHILLIPS

As racial tensions have recently spiked in America, we see riots, anger, and hatred at a boiling point. The political divisions in America seem to be escalating at a frightening speed. I often travel to Russia and Ukraine, two nations that have been at war for years. Across the world, the enormous and obvious need is for a peace than is unlike the peace of the world.

Some years ago, I heard the story of a father and a young son who were sitting together in the living room before supper. Dad was reading the evening newspaper after a long day at work while his eight-year-old, having eagerly awaited his father's arrival, wanted to play.

As he repeatedly sought his father's attention, finally, Dad, seeing a sheet of paper containing a map of the world, carefully tore it into thirty pieces, and placed them on the floor. He challenged his son to put together this hastily-made jigsaw puzzle. Barely two minutes later, the boy had completed the arduous task. Putting down his newspaper, his astonished father asked how he had put the world together so quickly? His young son replied, "I knew on the other side of the world map was a man's picture. I turned the pieces over and assembled the man's face, and then the whole world fit together."

As we consider the division and enmity in the world today, God's solution is to continue to make "in himself … one new man, thus producing peace." Jesus, in his Sermon on the Mount[155], gives us a picture of how that one new person lives his or her life through the power of the Holy Spirit in these turbulent times:

1. **Blessed are the poor in spirit.** When we know our true spiritual poverty, we recognize the need to live our lives in humility before man and God.
2. **Blessed are they that mourn.** Most certainly we mourn for the carnage of the world, but we are comforted by Jesus as he sends us out to lovingly minister to the wounded and oppressed. We have his heart for the world.
3. **Blessed are the meek.** Meekness is not weakness! It means bridled strength, being able to be molded into his likeness. The meek will inherit the earth.

155 See Matthew 5

4. **Blessed are they who hunger and thirst after righteousness.** God longs for a people who delight in his ways. They will be filled by their Master.
5. **Blessed are the merciful.** People who are givers, not takers, are often in short supply. These people obtain mercy from the Lord, so they have much to give. The Lord blesses those who are concerned for others.
6. **Blessed are the pure in heart.** Scripture tells us such people will "see God." These are people whose yes is a yes, and their no is a no[156] They walk their talk.
7. **Blessed are the peacemakers.** These people, referred to as the children of God, are able to see through difficult issues and situations. They are problem solvers and bring divided factions together. They exude love, acceptance, and forgiveness.
8. **Blessed are those who are persecuted for righteousness' sake.** These people give themselves for the poor and oppressed, for the hurts of the world regardless of the cost. Jesus notes that "theirs is the Kingdom of heaven."

Jesus is painting a beautiful word picture for us: the character of a person reformed in Christ, which is crafted only by the beautiful, quiet, mystical work of the Holy Spirit. Two thousand years ago, as Jesus prepared to return to the Father, he promised the disciples the coming of the Holy Spirit after his departure. He knew this was the greatest gift he could give them. We too are in need of this precious gift! As we look at our present-day challenges, it is helpful to look back at the purposeful plan of Jesus to assist the disciples in their enormous future endeavor:

> *"This was no theory, no creed, no makeshift arrangement that Jesus was talking about. It was the promise of a real compensation for the loss which the disciples were to sustain. 'Another Comforter' just like Jesus was to fill them with the very Presence of the Master. Indeed, the privileges which the disciples were to enjoy in this deeper relationship to the Spirit were greater*

156 Matthew 5:37

than they had known as Jesus walked with them along the roads of Galilee. After all, in his flesh, Jesus was confined to one body and one place, but in the Spirit these limitations were all removed. NOW HE COULD BE WITH THEM ALWAYS, and literally be enabled never to leave them or forsake them. Looking at it from this perspective, it was better for Jesus, having finished his work, to return to the Father and send the blessed Comforter to come and take his place."[157]

I think of many, many times over the years when I have experienced the presence and work of the Holy Spirit in my life, starting when I was very young, even before I knew I needed it! Like the time I was at Malibu, as a camper, when I was sixteen years old.

Now, you need to know that many of my cherished memories working with young people took place at Malibu, a Young Life resort on the Princess Louisa Inlet, one hundred water miles from Vancouver, British Columbia. I estimate I have been privileged to spend over two years of my life at that sacred place, beginning in 1961 when, as a teenager, I was actually sent there against my will!

I was sixteen, had my driver's license, and was most excited about my first dating relationship. My parents, who had been to Malibu several years before at an Adult Week, came home raving about the place. As a teenager, I naturally assumed it had to be the last place I wanted to go. When they announced to me I was already signed up, my dissenting pleas went unheard.

As the only guy from my high school going with twenty girls, I was placed in a cabin with the wildest guys in camp from Riverside, California. These guys had no idea what this week was about because they had their agenda—girls, party, girls. As we sat in cabin time at the end of each evening, one by one the staff would search for them out on the golf course with the opposite sex. Cabin discussions were chaotic—lots of coarse talk and wild laughter—until the night of the cross message. As we returned to our cabin, I was immediately surprised by everyone's presence, but most shocked by seeing Mike, the ringleader, standing with our counselor outside the door, with tears in his eyes.

---

157 Coleman, Robert E., and Billy Graham. *The Master Plan of Evangelism*. Grand Rapids, MI: Revell, 2006, p. 68-69.

Cabin time that evening was a different story—everyone listening, honest dialogue, and our leader offering anyone to join him in closing prayer. Breaking the silence, Mike prayed. I remember thinking, as a regular churchgoer, his was the worst prayer I had ever heard! He didn't pray anything like the people did on Sunday morning. Then they turned off the lights, and I began to reflect more about his prayer. The more I thought about it, I realized it was THE BEST PRAYER I had ever heard, because it was genuine, vulnerable, and from the heart in front of all of his buddies. Mike was talking to Jesus, the one he just realized had died for him. I certainly knew how to pray, but mine were practiced and routine religious prayers. The more I thought about it, I realized rebellious Mike actually had received a gift I didn't know existed—a love relationship with Jesus instead of a religious practice.

The next day, I asked Jesus to give me what Mike had found—a love relationship with him. In the nearly sixty years since that wonderful discovery, it never gets old to watch the incredible work of the Holy Spirit in changing lives. The late Episcopalian priest Sam Shoemaker, a founder of Alcoholics Anonymous, once said, "We are merely one beggar telling another beggar where to find the bread." And we realize "the Bread" is a Person: "Then Jesus declared, 'I am the bread of life. He who comes to me will never go hungry, and he who believes in me will never be thirsty.'"[158]

The hunger and thirst of our hurting world screams for a Savior, for one who will fill the deepest needs for meaning. The Holy Spirit continues his sole purpose through the ages—to point us to Jesus, the only one who can lift the wearisome burdens of life from off our shoulders and onto his—urging us, "Come to me, all you who are weary and burdened, and I will give you rest. Take my yoke upon you and learn from me, for I am gentle and humble in heart, and you will find rest for your souls. For my yoke is easy and my burden is light."[159]

---

158 John 6:35, NIV
159 Matthew 11:28-30, NIV

Chapter Thirteen

Bearing Fruit

"If you remain in me, and my words remain in you, ask whatever you wish, and it will be given you. This is to my Father's glory, that you bear much fruit, showing yourselves to be my disciples." (John 15:7-8, NIV)

If I were asked for one chapter in the Scriptures that would best highlight the importance of our daily walk with Jesus, I would point to John 15. Here we see the eleven disciples, circled around Jesus in the Upper Room, listening in rapt attention as he gives them a beautiful word picture, painted in the rural agricultural language of their day, about the all-important relationship they would have with the Father and him. It is framed in terminology they are very familiar with, and spoken to them by their beloved Teacher in those final hours before his arrest and crucifixion: "I am the true vine, and my Father is the gardener. He cuts off every branch in me that bears no fruit, while every branch that does bear fruit he prunes, so that it will be even more fruitful."[160]

160 John 15:1-2, NIV

I confess that I am not a gardener. However, I have spent much of my life, beginning at age twelve, mowing, trimming, edging, and weeding my own lawn and garden and, as a teenager, at least a dozen others. I would willingly do the weekly maintenance, while scrupulously avoiding the planting, nurturing, and the pruning! However, my sole experience with pruning is a very vivid one.

It was the last year that we were living in our waterfront home in Washington State, the house in which we raised our kids. There was a large apple tree in the front yard of this house that had never yielded much fruit. However, it did grow bigger and bigger, with willow shoots and other nonessential paraphernalia clogging its branches.

One morning, Debbie mentioned a gardener had stopped by with an unrequested three-hundred dollar bid to prune the tree and haul away the branches. Since the kids had exited the house for college and then marriage, we jumped on this offer. I will never forget returning home that evening. Our apple tree looked like a sheared poodle dog! All that remained was the large trunk and a handful of main branches.

As I entered the house, I learned that we had stumbled upon quite a bargain—three truckloads went to the dump that day! As the months went by, we forgot about the apple tree until harvest time. Four times as many apples appeared—big, juicy ripe apples!

It was my happy lesson on pruning. So, now as I meet with the young friends I'm teaching or discipling, this is the imagery I have in mind when I'm talking with them about John chapter fifteen.

Submitting Ourselves to the Master Gardner

I believe it is always important to ask what pruning project our Lord would want to undertake in each of our lives. What habit or character flaw would we submit to his loving spiritual pruning shears to cut away from our lives in order that we, like the apple tree, could bear more fruit—fruit that would remain? Jesus said, "Remain in me, and I will remain in you. No branch can bear fruit by itself; it must remain in the vine. Neither can you bear fruit unless you remain in me."[161]

161 John 15:4, NIV

Many translations of the Bible use the word "abide" instead of "remain." Either word would signify "to live or dwell" with someone. A second rendition is "to continue without fading or being lost." The clear and unmistakable essence of the term is "presence."

Four centuries ago, a Carmelite monk, known as Brother Lawrence, had an experience, as an eighteen-year-old, of seeing a tree in winter that had been stripped of its leaves, with only barren branches. He caught a vision of that same tree being renewed in the coming spring. The rest of his life, Brother Lawrence was preoccupied with cultivating a keen sensitivity to the presence of God in everyday life. Whether he was washing the dishes or doing any other common chores, he basked in the glory of communion with Jesus.

Would that it be so with each of us four hundred years later! The late Oswald Chambers, in his classic devotional, *My Utmost for His Highest*, challenges us to stand against all the distractions that take us away from abiding in Christ: "Think of the things that take you out of abiding in Christ—Yes, Lord, just a minute, I have got this to do; Yes, I will abide when once this is finished; when this week is over, it will be all right, I will abide then. Get a move on! Begin to abide now. In the initial stages it is a continual effort until it becomes so much the law of life that you abide in him continually. Determine to abide in Jesus wherever you are placed."[162]

My Argentinian friend, Juan Carlos Ortiz, whom I mentioned earlier, was always a model for me of one who, moment by moment, practiced the presence of Jesus in his life. I recall one conference in the late '70's when we had asked him to speak at a discipleship conference held at a retreat center on a small island in Washington State. It necessitated taking a speed boat to the island early in the morning and staying until late evening.

After several days of this torturous schedule, we were walking up to the car from the boat dock in the late evening. I, feeling guilty for allowing such an unreasonable schedule for my friend, asked, "How are you doing, Juan Carlos?"

His answer shocked and challenged me, "I'm walking and leaping and praising God," he responded, jumping for joy into the air! I instantly realized

---

162 Chambers, Oswald, and James Reimann. *My Utmost for His Highest: Selections for Every Day*. Grand Rapids, MI, MI: Discovery House Publishers, 1995, p. 66.

my dear brother was communing with Jesus all day long. He still had energy to spare!

In the first chapter of this book, I mentioned my dear friend Connie. Several weeks before his graduation from this life, he and his wife and Debbie and I were driving to an annual pre-Christmas dinner that our longtime small group of four had held each year with our spouses. Debbie, knowing that Connie had been dealing with stage four pancreatic cancer, asked him what he was currently excited about in God's Word. He instantly responded with Philippians 1:21, "For me to live is Christ, to die is gain." He went on to share that, while he longed to remain with his loving wife and family, he had not one ounce of fear of death, which meant being with Jesus face to face.

Having walked with Connie for over forty years, he was a model for me of someone who lived his life out of a center of communion with Jesus Christ. His quiet discipline of beginning each day with Jesus and abiding in him showed itself in the fruit of his life. He was one of the most kind and thoughtful people I have ever known. He exuded godliness! And he exuded the strength that comes from being rightly connected to the Vine.

The Perils of Going without Pruning

If I failed to take up that gardener on his offer to prune my apple tree, it would have continued in its condition of being overgrown, diseased, unfruitful. This is what happens to a neglected tree. Jesus pointed this out when he said, "I am the vine; you are the branches. If a man remains in me and I in him, he will bear much fruit; apart from me you can do nothing. If anyone does not remain in me, he is like a branch that is thrown away and withers; such branches are picked up, thrown into the fire and burned."[163]

The Apostle Paul carried this teaching further when he actually described to the Galatian church what such a "branch" might look like in real life: "The acts of the sinful nature are obvious: sexual immorality, impurity and debauchery; idolatry and witchcraft; hatred, discord, jealousy, fits of rage, selfish ambition, dissensions, factions and envy; drunkenness, orgies and the

163 John 15:5-6, NIV

like. I warn you, as I did before, that those who live like this will not inherit the kingdom of God."[164]

Here Paul lists fifteen different kinds of fruit that are produced by the flesh. Earlier in his treatise in Romans 8, on life in the Spirit, he concludes, "The sinful mind is hostile to God. It does not submit to God's law, nor can it do so. Those controlled by the sinful nature cannot please God."[165] I am frequently asked by my young friends why I include this torturous list of fruits of the carnal nature in their memory work assignment. I respond by asking if perhaps we might discover that some of these qualities are a bit too familiar to us in our daily lives. If so, their presence is a warning to us of the enemy's desire to sow seeds of his poisonous fruit in our attitudes and habits, and to steer us away from submitting to the pruning touch of the Master's hand.

We examined in an earlier chapter of one of the quintessential questions in our lives: "Who is more powerful in us—the flesh or the Spirit? The answer, of course, is the one we feed! Romans 8:6 summarizes this truth: "The former attitude (the flesh) means, bluntly, death: the latter (the Spirit) means life and peace." (Phillips) Jesus often talked about the difference between good and bad trees, "No good tree bears bad fruit, nor does a bad tree bear good fruit. Each tree is recognized by its own fruit.[166] That's why it is so important for us to be spiritual "fruit inspectors" in our own lives. It means keeping a close lookout for bad fruit appearing in our lives, and remembering Jesus' words to his disciples, "By their fruit you will recognize them."[167]

Bearing Good Fruit

In sharp contrast to the fruit of the lower nature, Paul gives us nine character qualities that emanate from the Holy Spirit: "But the fruit of the Spirit is love, joy, peace, patience, kindness, goodness, faithfulness, gentleness, and self-control. Against such things there is no law."[168] By our own efforts, we cannot produce any of these. They only come through abiding in Jesus.

---

164 Galatians 5:19-21, NIV
165 Romans 8:7-8, NIV
166 Luke 6:43-44, NIV
167 Matthew 7:20, NIV
168 Galatians 5:22-23, NIV

Over the years I have heard many messages on the fruit of the Spirit, but by far the most powerful and down to earth one was shared a decade ago by Dr. Earl Palmer, a beloved pastor and Bible teacher I was fortunate to encounter sixty-five years ago at my local Presbyterian church in Seattle. Then, fresh out of Princeton Seminary, he came to the church as the college minister. (I recently came across a picture of the two of us in 1957 when he was awarding me the Boy Scout God and Country award!)

At the time he delivered the message I am about to share with you, Earl and his wife, Shirley, were in Washington D.C. for some months while he served as an interim pastor at National Presbyterian Church. I took advantage of his presence to ask him to share with about fifty single young adults that Debbie and I were meeting with every Thursday night at The Cedars. These young people were just out of college and many were serving on the Hill. They were a delightful group to engage with on issues of faith.

Earl's assignment was to talk about the fruit of the Spirit, listed in Galatians chapter five. I will never forget his words. Sitting next to him, I immediately noticed he had no notes. He knew by heart the Greek word for each character quality. He made each of them come alive. Allow me to borrow a few of his observations that remain with me ten years later.

Earl noted that self-control was last and not first in the list. In other words, we don't lead with it, but it tempers our appetites in life. He graphically illustrated that these nine qualities are not cookie cutter traits that look the same with each branding; rather, each person's love is unique, unlike anyone else's in the world.

I immediately thought about my dear wife's love, which I get to experience daily. But, in particular, I now observe its effect upon each of our sixteen grandchildren. She has bonded with each one. They recognize that unique flavor of love oozing from her, and they want as much of it as possible. God has specially designed each of these character qualities that flow from those disciples who abide in him to be special and absolutely unique.

A third unforgettable takeaway from Earl was how he described the crisis that Eastern Washington apple growers had been going through, when Fuji apples from Japan were taking over the market and threatening to close down the orchard fields that had been leaders in that industry for decades. The orchard owners discovered they could actually graft onto a yellow delicious apple tree Fuji branches that would yield this tasty brand of apples. The message, of course, is relevant for us: from the same vine can be grown many different kinds of apples just as from the vine, Jesus, many diverse branches yielding unique, tasty, spectacular fruit can be grown. Each one is special in its own way.

As the evening with Earl continued, the room was electric with the realization that the fruit of the Spirit is the incredible evidence of the quiet work of Jesus Christ in each of our lives two thousand years later. Most certainly, "by their fruit, you shall know them!"

Growing Certain Fruits

Reflecting over the many years of ministry, certain experiences stand out to me as amazing learning opportunities about fruit-bearing. It never ceases to amaze me how God works so intimately and personally with us, to both prune and cultivate us, to produce his desired results in our lives. He has an individual plan for each of us.

One such experience for me occurred in 1973 when, as a single young area director for Young Life, I contracted with a California travel company to take twenty-seven young people from Tacoma, Washington to spend a month traveling in three Volkswagen vans through Eastern Europe and into the Soviet Union from Ukraine all the way to Leningrad (now St. Petersburg). Many of these were young disciples I had in my Young Life club, and others were college or young adult volunteers.

The trip was so significant that we have had twenty, thirty, and forty-year reunions, and hope to celebrate fifty in a few years. The group, now in their mid-sixties, cannot understand how their parents allowed them to make such a trip led by a twenty-seven- year-old bachelor! (Actually, I agree with them!) What stands out about that trip is I secretly asked the Lord to build in me the quality of steadfastness. It is defined as the quality of being resolute or unwavering. I had no idea how our Lord would go to such effort to answer that prayer! It is used a number of times in Scripture, but notably in I Peter 5:10, "And the God of all grace, who called you to his eternal glory in Christ, after you have suffered a little while, will himself restore you and make you strong, firm and steadfast."

To add a bit of adventure, I encouraged each participant to secretly carry one Russian Bible with them, and pray for the right person to give it to during the trip. Hearing the stories afterward brought tears to my eyes! Bibles were scarce at that time in the U.S.S.R.; at that time over a half century into godless Communism. The trip was going famously as we traveled through Czechoslovakia (now Czech Republic) and Poland, but we hit a snag in Prague, the Czech capital, when Bill Taylor, a Vice President of Young Life who had joined us in route, had to wait twelve hours to find out he was sadly denied a Russian visa. All of us were disappointed, and we departed twelve hours behind schedule.

In those days, Intourist, the Communist travel service, was absolutely inflexible. You had a hotel to get to—no changes allowed. So, the next few days we played catch-up, driving until three or four in the morning to arrive at our designated hotel. Over a day into this rigorous schedule, one of the young leaders, Bill, a college senior football player and dedicated follower of Jesus, had a mental breakdown. Bill, having lost both parents in high school, visibly tightened as we entered Communist countries. I didn't pick up on the seriousness of his anxiety that we were being followed until it boiled over. Late one evening, while he was driving a van near the Russian border, I saw him suddenly pull over, and the kids jumped out. Bill was incoherent.

The next two weeks, we loved on Bill, but he was like a child, drifting in and out of reality. Late that night, we arrived at our hotel in eastern Poland. I had Bill staying with me. Several hours later, I awoke to see him loudly talking to a surprised Pole, but standing on the ledge of the eighth story. From then on, I slept across the doorway. Bill would get up numerous times, and I would send him back to bed. He was obedient, never violent, but obviously divorced from reality.

In Kiev, the authorities demanded he be hospitalized in a mental facility. When it was time to leave, I came to get him. The conditions were frightful—delirious people roaming the dark halls. They wouldn't release him, and I wouldn't go without him. Finally, I prevailed, and a week later from Leningrad my female team partner, Bev, was able to take him on the train to friends in Germany. They were able to transport him back to America where, after a hospital stay, he recovered.

That was the hardest month of my life. Making sure we could keep Bill safe plus twenty-six others, all first-timers in a Communist nation, made for long days and short, often nearly sleepless nights. Upon arrival in Amsterdam, I collapsed on my hotel bed and thanked the Lord for getting us through the month—and I then thought about steadfastness. *If that was the 101 course, I'm not sure I am ready for 201!*

I look back on that month, and I know God heard and answered my often desperate prayers. And in the process, a whole group of kids had an unforgettable month. Almost fifty years later, we still talk about that adventure. And I learned a bit about steadfastness! The Lord helped me realize that I can't produce it in my own strength. It comes as a precious gift from the Lord.

I reflected many times during those challenging days that I was anything but "resolute or unwavering." The Lord helped me to see this very clearly, and he guided us through a maze of challenges. As I look back on that experience nearly fifty years later, it is a wonderful reminder of the truth of John 15:5, "Apart from me you can do nothing at all." It was perhaps one of the most important lessons in my life about fruit-bearing. I look back with gratefulness that in the midst of my shortcomings as a leader, my young friends had a wonderful month of learning and growth that we return over and over again to reminisce over and celebrate. God is doing a work in each of us. He isn't finished yet!

MAN-MAKING

Edwin Markham (1852-1940)

We are all blind until we see
That in the human plan
Nothing is worth the making if
It does not make the man.

Why build these cities glorious
If man unbuilded goes?
In vain we build the work, unless
The builder also grows.

Chapter Fourteen

Being a Person of Unity

"My prayer is not for them alone. I pray also for those who will believe in me through their message, that all of them may be one, Father, just as you are in me and I am in you. May they also be in us so that the world might believe that you have sent me." (John 17:20-21, NIV)

The dinner party in the Upper Room had disbanded. Judas, long before, had disappeared into the night. Jesus knew what would soon take place and headed to one of his favorite places of retreat, the Garden of Gethsemane, where he prayed his longest recorded prayer in the four Gospels.[169]

Initially, he prayed for himself as he prepared for the horrendous upcoming ordeal. Then he prayed for the eleven disciples who would soon be carrying the message of God's love for the world without his physical presence. Finally, HE PRAYED FOR US! This is not a misprint. Jesus prayed for you and me—and all the spiritual grandchildren of Peter, James, John, Andrew, Philip, Nathanael, etc.—for all the generations to come. Would it not be beneficial for each of us to

169 See John 17

take careful heed of his prayer, and to seek to answer it lovingly and affirmatively by the way we live and the way we love?

Jesus' Priority on Unity

What kinds of things did Jesus pray for us? What were his priorities? I believe we should take careful note of his passion expressed in verses 20-23 of John 17. Here, he repeatedly prays for "oneness" among his disciples, with the measure of that oneness being the love relationship of Jesus and the Father. He also mentions several times the profound effect this oneness will have upon the world.

We are currently as divided in our world as I can remember in my seventy-five years of life. There is a desperate need, both in America and around the world, for men and women who, because of their love for Jesus, are flesh and blood answers to Jesus' prayer for oneness. His prayer for us continues, repeating these main themes in the final hour before his arrest and crucifixion:

> *"I have given them the glory that you gave me, that they may be one as we are one:*
>
> *I in them and you in me. May they be brought to complete unity to let the world know that you sent me and have loved them even as you have loved me."*[170]

The world is searching for "glory" in all the wrong places. Most of what they think they have found quickly loses its glitter and attraction: Money. Fame. Success. Sports. Entertainment. Possessions. Conversely, Jesus makes the astounding claim that he is imparting *his* glory in and through these humble men that he will empower and grant his trust. The Greek word used here for glory is *doxa,* literally translated "a weight." Glory connotes radiance and splendor. It is shining and bright, dazzling like a diamond. And it is meant to be seen! Our Lord actually prayed that, perhaps two thousand years later, this glory would be manifested in the love and unity of the followers of Jesus Christ.

The world is not yearning for religion. What people are longing for is reality, and Jesus is praying for them to see his glorious reality reflected in the ones

170 John 17:22-23, NIV

naming Jesus as their Source. Once again, Jesus affirms that when this happens, the world will ultimately recognize that the Father sent the Son to shower his love upon each and every person. What a prayer! May we dare to believe for God to answer it through ordinary people like you and me, living in and with an extraordinary Savior.

I mentioned previously one of my spiritual heroes, Juan Carlos Ortiz. During the 70s and 80s, when he frequented Young Life conferences, the other attendees and I clamored to participate in his Q&A sessions. It was during the time of the Charismatic Renewal, and there were many emerging groups who gathered great followings, but raised numerous questions for the Body of Christ.

As a younger person with a freshly obtained seminary degree, I was "much wiser" in those days—I was quick to give answers that would come much more measured today, if you know what I mean. We would frequently pepper Juan Carlos with terse questions about a particular organization or church, asking, "What about this group?"

Invariably, Juan Carlos would smile broadly and reply, "They are wonderful friends. We love them." He seemed disinclined to disparage any of these brothers and sisters. Decades later, in the Washington Hilton lobby following a National Prayer Breakfast, I saw Juan Carlos through the crowd and inched my way toward him. As we embraced, I drew back and spoke to him, "Juan Carlos, I think I get it—what you were telling us about all those far-out friends in the Body of Christ. We love them—John 17." We both wept. It took me a long time to see it—despite our differences, we are called to love one another first and foremost. And when we do, we are beginning to answer Jesus' prayer in John 17.

One other picture my brother Juan Carlos painted for many of us is found in his book *Disciple.* In it, he talks about the kind of love to which Jesus has called us. He uses the odd analogy of a sack of potatoes:

> *"When the harvest comes, all the potatoes are dug up and put into one sack. So they are regrouped. But they are not yet united. They may say, 'Oh, praise the Lord! Now we are all in the same sack.' But they are not yet one. They must be washed and peeled. They think they are closer yet. 'How nice is this love among us!' they say. But that's not all. They must be cut in pieces*

and mixed. They really think they are ready for the Master now. But what God wants is mashed potatoes. Not many potatoes—one mashed potato. No potato can stand up and say, 'Here I am! I'm a potato.' The word must be WE. That's why the Lord's Prayer begins, 'OUR Father which art in Heaven'... 'not' MY Father which art in Heaven.

"With all the reverence possible, I say to you that the Father, Son, and Holy Spirit are three potatoes made into mashed potatoes. And Jesus is hungry for mashed potatoes. He is going to have them. He is already doing something very profound in his church."[171]

This odd analogy is not saying that we should forfeit our own respective and blessed uniqueness, but that our unity and love for one another would appear before the world in such a powerful way that it would validate the message we proclaim. The Apostle Paul summarized this when he wrote to the Roman church, "Just as each of us has one body with many members, and these members do not all have the same function, so in Christ we who are many form one body, and each member BELONGS to all the others."[172] Similarly, this theme is echoed in his letter to the Corinthians: "... so that there should be no division in the body, but that its parts should have equal concern for each other. If one part suffers, every part suffers with it; if one part is honored, every part rejoices with it."[173]

Our Unity Validates Our Testimony

The second chapter of Philippians is perhaps the best-known description of the extent to which Jesus went in emptying himself of all privilege he would naturally have as the Son of God, by dying the death of a common criminal for our sake. Immediately prior to verses 6-11, describing that sacrificial journey of love, Paul exhorts each of us:

"Now if you have known anything of Christ's encouragement and of his reassuring love; if you have known something of the fellowship of his Spirit, and of compassion and deep sympathy, do make my joy complete—live

171 Ortiz, Juan Carlos. *Disciple.* Creation House: 1975, pg. 62-63.

172 Romans 12:4-5, emphasis added

173 1 Corinthians 12: 25-26, NIV

together in harmony, live together in love, as though you had only one mind and one spirit between you. Never act from motives of rivalry or personal vanity, but in humility think more of each other than you do of yourselves. None of you should think only of his own affairs, but consider other people's interests also. Let your attitude to life be that of Christ Jesus himself."[174]

In these five beautiful verses, we are given a snapshot of exactly what it looks like to be a twenty-first century person of unity. How do we best live this challenging passage out in our individual lives? I believe one powerful way is by embracing long-term committed relationships of trust and accountability.

Forty-seven years ago from this writing, I became part of such a group. There were six of us, at the time all on Young Life staff. We perhaps unconsciously thought this was part of the bonding. However, as we left one by one to pursue other callings, it became apparent Young Life was merely a common catalyst to initially bring us together.

As the years went by and we continued to meet, the challenges got bigger. We married, had children, and moved around the country from one another. This is the point most groups quietly disintegrate—too many other things crowd out such a formerly meaningful connection. We had the bright idea of socializing the costs—meaning we would pool the travel and food and lodging expenses and divide by six. I recall flying from Moscow to see my brothers and receiving significant checks from them for the expense. I remember later hosting them in our home and writing checks to the others. When they met at our house, our kids all happily piled into one bedroom because "their uncles" were in the house! Each summer, we decided to devote a week together as families to meet, pray, and play together. Surprisingly, our wives bonded, and our collective gaggle of kids seemed to become "common property."

I recall one summer in the mountains of Idaho, I was playing ping pong with my middle son, James. Being a competitor by nature, I gave it my all, trouncing him in several games. Afterward, Tom, one of my brothers, appeared alongside me and observed what a good ping pong player I was! He paused, and then noted that, in his purview, James hadn't enjoyed that experience as much as I obviously

---

174 Philippians 2:1-5, PHILLIPS

did. Then he went further, candidly speculating that James hadn't enjoyed it at all, and that it might have been more important for my ego to win than to have fun with my son. Then he hugged me and left.

A few minutes later, I went and found James. I looked him in the eye and asked his forgiveness for giving him the strong impression that winning at ping pong was more important than having fun between father and son. I told him I didn't like that person he sometimes saw in me and I wanted to be the kind of dad he loved to play with.

I could give story after story of being helped in my life through these friends. At times, I have revealed my own shortcomings to my brothers over the course of walking together through the years. I believe the Scriptures challenge us to adopt this as a part of our lives, as we read in James: "You should get into the habit of admitting your sins to one another, and praying for each other, so that you may be healed."[175] This verse suggests to us that corporate confession is important in bringing healing and authenticity to our relationships with God and with one another. Many years later, as we continue to meet, I know that my friends know me and love me—for better or for worse! And best of all, they know me and love me *truly*, having seen me at my worst.

I share this in the hopes that it might be an encouragement to each of us to go deeper with a few, and to stay together over the long haul of life in order to discover more of the beauty of the oneness Jesus is calling us to embody. I don't know of a better way to discover it except through committed relationships. Certainly, marriage is the best example, but it is wise to deeply invest in committed, long term non-romantic relationships as well.

It is interesting to note that each of my kids has put a high value on such committed relationships. I didn't have to tell them how valuable they were—they could just watch and learn for themselves. Incidentally, I have met with a number of my brothers' kids over the principles of Jesus I'm sharing with you in this book, and count many of them good lifelong friends. My own offspring feel the same way about their "uncles and aunts." As we think about answering Jesus' prayer in John 17 for unity, these committed relationships are a veritable gold mine of investment value!

175 James 5:16, PHILLIPS

Friends in Good Times and Bad

Some of the greatest experiences of my life have come through what I would call "burden-sharing" encounters. Whether it has been a friend being sentenced to prison, a painful divorce, or a tragedy such as the loss of a child, the privilege of bearing each other's burdens is a blessed gift that enriches the bearer, and, hopefully the one who is hurting. We get this verbiage from the Apostle Paul, who wrote to the Galatians, *"Brothers, if someone is caught in a sin, you who are spiritual should restore him gently. But watch yourself, or you also may be tempted. Carry each other's burdens, and in this way you will fulfill the law of Christ."*[176]

Paul calls us to bear each other's difficulties and challenges, and in so doing, we live out his law of love. But in order for someone to bear them, they must first be shared. In our world of division and short-term relationships, this may often seem dangerous and intimidating.

In addition, God often uses the heartbreaking events in our lives to further enable us to meaningfully empathize with and share the pain of others. Many examples flood through my mind as I think of this holy means of healing and comfort. One picture stands out from recent memory. Thirty-five years ago, my wife's youngest brother, Jonathan, died of cancer at the age of twenty-seven, leaving a wife and a three-month-old daughter. It was a crushing blow for a close family.

Jonathan was an amazing young man with a vivacious smile and an engaging and winsome personality, who was a dedicated follower of Jesus Christ. We all mourned his too-early graduation. I watched as my wife's parents joined the undesired fraternity of parents who had buried a son or daughter. I observed as they grieved honestly and openly. The years went by and, perhaps contrary to the old maxim, "Time heals all wounds," the feelings of loss remained strong.

Many years later, as I hosted many of my Ukrainian brothers and sisters at the National Prayer Breakfast, I met with a close friend, and discovered she had recently lost a son to a tragic automobile accident. I brought her up to meet with my father-in-law, who knew her and had previously established a strong bond of love and trust with her. He took her hand and looked into her eyes and asked how she was doing. She then poured out her story of grief and heartbreak.

---

176 Galatians 6:1-2, NIV

He empathetically listened for what seemed like hours. As he did, I realized he understood her agony so much more than the rest of us in the room. He had walked long years through that painful valley.

It must have been close to a half hour before he mentioned Jonathan. By then, I had tears running down my cheeks. In that moment, I realized God never wastes anything! He takes some of the greatest hurts and heartaches in our lives and, if we keep our trust in his unfailing love, uses them in incredible and unusual ways years later. Sharing and bearing each other's burdens is another wonderful way he brings us together as one family of brothers and sisters. In so doing, Jesus sows unity in costly and indescribable ways.

Jesus' Finished Work

Before we conclude our reflections on unity, let's return to Jesus' prayer in John 17. He begins by praying for himself:

> *"Father, the time has come. Glorify your Son, that your Son may glorify you. For you have granted him authority over all people that he might give eternal life to all those you have given him. Now this is eternal life: that they may know you, the only true God, and Jesus Christ, whom you have sent."*[177]

In these final hours, facing a humiliating arrest, a sham trial, and a brutal execution, Jesus pauses to commune with his Father, and to offer to us a beautiful definition of eternal life: knowing God and his Son, Jesus. What a liberating word to each of us who so often get our attention caught up in things. Eternal life is relationship with a Person!

Jesus, in his darkest hour, calls us to himself in loving relationship. He defines eternal life in the context of such a loving relationship. He points out to his Father, "I have brought you honor upon earth, I have completed the task you gave me to do."[178] According to Scripture, the finished work of Jesus Christ, the Son of God, was giving his life as an eternal sacrifice for our sins. None of us could ever do that. However, what was the finished work of *Jesus the man*? In

---

177 John 17:1-3, NIV
178 John17:4, PHILLIPS

verse eight, Jesus tells his Father he has told the disciples everything the Father has told him. Therefore, **the finished work of Jesus the man was to share with a motley band of young men all that the Father had entrusted to him.**

Friends, we can do that! And it is a significant reason for my writing this book. What Jesus taught the twelve in those years are things we want to learn ourselves—and then savor and share with others. These principles of Jesus and attributes of his disciples are the essential truths that Jesus imparted to his followers. What an exciting thought to partner with Jesus in what he gave himself to do in those years on the dusty roads of Galilee!

So, what does it look like for us to answer Jesus' prayer for us, over 2,000 years later? I believe it means we choose to meet people in a spirit of love, genuinely seek to understand where they are in their journey of faith, and then join them at that sacred place. Winning or losing arguments never accomplishes God's purposes in bringing us together.

As I grow older, it has become more important for me to see people through the eyes of Jesus and to be an eager listener in knowing and understanding the ups and downs of their lives of faith. I get very excited about answering Jesus' prayer for unity as I encounter a wide variety of his followers around the world. I always seek to remember the truth of the exhortation I heard years ago, "Don't convert others; convert yourself." I find that the Lord will do amazing things in and through us if our deepest longings are to answer that prayer that we would be one, even as he and the Father are one. Our deeply divided planet will take notice of that unusual kind of love and unity. It is perhaps the most-needed message the followers of Jesus can display to the watching world.

Chapter Fifteen

Being a Person of Prayer

"One day Jesus was praying in a certain place. When he finished, one of his disciples said to him, 'Lord, teach us to pray, just as John taught his disciples.' He said to them, 'When you pray, say: Father, hallowed be your name, your kingdom come. Give us each day our daily bread. Forgive us our sins, for we also forgive everyone who sins against us. And lead us not into temptation.'" (Luke 11:1-4, NIV)

This final attribute of discipleship is embodied through the way the disciples observed Jesus' life of communion with his Father. He spent most of his life apart from the flurry of activity that the crowds constantly demanded. Yet Jesus did not appear consumed by a need or desire for such activity. He drew strength from his time with the Father.

Saints throughout history have drawn strength from Jesus' example of choosing to step away from the tyranny of the urgent to quietly commune with his Father. Hundreds of years ago, Madame Jeanne Guyon, a French mystic, challenged us and our busy environment:

> *"Forget about yourself and all your household and occupational interests. Simply listen and be attentive to God. These passive actions will permit God to communicate his love to you. You should repeat the process of becoming internally quiet as often as distractions occur. It is really not much to ask of ourselves to take an hour or even a half hour from our day to quiet our spirits in order for the spirit of prayer to remain with us the entire day."*[179]

As we reflect on those three years Jesus was with his disciples, we can imagine it would have been easy for Jesus to feel pressed by the small amount of time he had to prepare his followers to carry on the message of God's love. But rather than adopting a frenetic pace, Jesus always seemed to have time to reach out to those around him in need, or to share for hours with groups small and large, using parables and stories and colorful yet common language.

Before he teaches the disciples on prayer in Luke 11, Jesus shares the story of a man going to his friend at midnight, seeking to borrow three loaves of bread because an acquaintance has stopped by while on a journey, and he has no food to give him. The friend declines, having already gone to bed with his family. However, the persistence of his friend, continuing to knock, finally forces him to give his friend what he asks for. This is the example Jesus uses to challenge the disciples as he taught them how to pray.

My friend, Pastor Mark Batterson, calls this "shameless audacity." He writes:

"I love this depiction of prayer. There are times when you need to do what it takes. You need to grab hold of the horns of the altar and not let go. You need to dare demonic forces to a duel. You need to do something crazy, something risky, something different."[180] This is a great commentary on Jesus' words to his disciples:

> *"So I say to you: Ask and it shall be given to you; seek and you will find; knock and the door will be opened to you. For everyone who asks receives; he who seeks finds, and to him who knocks, the door will be opened." Which*

---

179 Guyon, Madame. *Experiencing God through Prayer.* Cedar Lake, MI: Read A Classic, 2009, pp. 52-53.

180 Batterson, Mark. *The Circle Maker: Praying Circles around Your Biggest Dreams and Greatest Fears.* Grand Rapids, MI: Zondervan, 2016, p. 44

of you fathers, if your son asks for a fish, will give him a snake instead? Or if he asks for an egg will give him a scorpion? If you then, though you are evil, know how to give good gifts to your children, how much more will your Father in heaven give the Holy Spirit to those who ask him!"[181]

In this oft-quoted passage, the Greek is best translated as, "Ask and keep on asking, seek and keep on seeking, and knock and keep on knocking …" Jesus' previous story emphasizing persistence is now impressed upon the disciples as they are instructed how to pray.

One might wonder why our Lord, who knows what we need before we ever ask, would place this emphasis on persistence in asking, seeking, and knocking. Years ago, I read Greg Boyd's great book, *Letters From a Skeptic*, in which he, a seminary apologetics professor, responds to his father's multitude of questions about issues of faith. One such question involved his father asking precisely this question.

I loved the son's winsome answer to his skeptical, inquiring dad in which he told him that our Lord desires a relationship with us, and good relationships involve lots of communication. What a great answer! The God who created the universe wants a love relationship with each of us, and he delights in our communication with him through prayer!

Jesus uses the love relationship between a father and a son to further highlight how much our Father in Heaven wants to give the Holy Spirit—his loving presence—to those who ask him. Isn't that the greatest gift our Heavenly Father could ever give us—a closer and more loving relationship with himself! Isn't it interesting how relational Jesus' focus is as he teaches his disciples about prayer—communication with a God who loves his creation and who delights in knowing and being known by each of us?

Talking to God

When we think of prayer, it might be better understood and practiced if we break it down into several components under the three categories of "talking to God," "listening to God," and "God listening while several of us talk together."

181 Luke 11:9-13, NIV

The Scriptures indicate at least five aspects of talking to God. Let's consider them:

1. **Praise.** "Great is the Lord and most worthy of praise; his greatness no one can fathom. One generation will commend your works to another; they will tell of your mighty acts."[182] Praise is acknowledging who God is. It is not about God somehow needing our praise, but, rather, it lifts us up above our common lives and circumstances as we recognize who He is. Scripture tells us the Lord dwells in the praises of the saints.
2. **Thanksgiving**. "Enter into his gates with thanksgiving ..."[183] As we give thanks to the Lord for all he has done, we develop an attitude of gratitude. A grateful heart is not only a blessing to the Lord, but truly lifts and blesses everyone around us, most significantly—ourselves!
3. **Confession.** "If we confess our sins, he is faithful and just and will forgive us our sins and purify us from all unrighteousness."[184] Keeping a clear conscience with our Lord is the path to a healthy and growing relationship. This passage is written for the followers of Jesus to practice this important discipline.
4. **Intercession.** "After Job had prayed for his friends, the Lord made him prosperous again."[185] We have the great privilege to pray for one another. There are many "one anothers" in God's Word. One of my favorites is in the Book of James, "You should get in the habit of admitting your sins to one another and praying for each other, so that you might be healed."[186]
5. **Petition.** James also tells us, "You do not have because you do not ask God. When you ask you do not receive because you ask with the wrong motives, that you may spend what you get on your pleasures."[187] We are repeatedly invited to "ask for anything in my name and I will do it."[188]

182 Psalms 145:3-4, NIV
183 Psalms 100:4
184 I John 1:9, NIV
185 Job 42:10, NIV
186 James 5:16, PHILLIPS
187 James 4:2-3
188 John 14:13-14

> As a matter of fact, Jesus spells out the incredible opportunity available for us to ask in his name three separate times during the upper room discourse.[189]

It is an incredible privilege that Jesus invites us to come before him on a regular basis. The above five aspects of prayer are merely a part of that communion. One of the most exciting opportunities we have is to expand our knowledge of how to not only talk with God, but to listen to him as well.

Listening to God

> *"God is our refuge and strength, an ever-present help in trouble. Therefore, we will not fear, though the earth give way and the mountains fall into the heart of the sea …"*[190]

Culminating a psalm that aptly describes our current day upheavals, the psalmist concludes with this comforting assurance, "Be still and know that I am God."[191] As I reflect about listening to God, I realize that some of the greatest and most important moments of my life have been when God whispered something to me.

One of God's whispers to me occurred late at night on a deserted Main Street at Malibu, Young Life's resort in Canada, while on staff with that organization. I had been told earlier in the day that I was being moved from an area I had joyfully served for five years to a place that was in deficit and disarray. As the program director at an Adult Weekend, I had the untimely task of being the funny man. However, as I sat on the boardwalk alone well after midnight, I contemplated resigning. I felt like a pawn being moved at will—against *my* will.

The next day, the office administrator called to tell me that there were seven letters waiting for me, from people who had been at camp during the four-week assignment I was just completing. I read each one—encouraging, affirming, loving—from kids who had met the Lord, adults who had been moved by their

189 John 14:13-14, 15:7-8, 16:23-24
190 Psalm 46:1-2
191 Psalm 46:10, NIV

week, and a few volunteer leaders from my area. As I finished the last letter, the quiet whisper of the Lord spoke to me, "Trust me. The best is yet to come." I was strengthened, and hope arose in my heart. The next years were among the most joyful and productive of my life. Almost fifty years later, I count many of the friends I made in those years as lifelong companions. The Lord kept his promise, spoken to me as a whisper in the quietness of my own heart.

Jesus reminds us of his voice as he calls himself the good shepherd: "It is his voice the sheep recognize. He calls his own sheep by name and leads them out of the fold...and the sheep follow him because they know his voice."[192] How do we recognize his voice from the cacophony of voices shouting at us for attention?

For one, the Spirit and God's Word always agree. As we are filling our minds with the Scriptures, we more easily recognize his still, small voice from all of the others. My longtime friend Ted Thwing, in his book *So You Want to Grow Spiritually*, muses:

> *"We grow spiritually when we listen to God and what he is trying to say to us. But often we are not good at listening. Sometimes we think the problem in communicating with God is to get his attention when we have something to say to him or ask him ... It turns out the real challenge is not how we can get God's attention, it is how he can get our attention."*[193]

Ted's observation strikes at the heart of a pervasive issue that plagues many Christians today: seldom do we take time away from our busy and noisy lives on earth to spend quality time in silence, listening for the voice of our Father. It can be difficult to unplug oneself from society when unaccustomed to doing so, but it is a necessary component of living out a true love relationship with God. Another of my longtime friends, Barry, a corporate executive, has frequently taken eight- day silent retreats at monasteries. He greatly anticipates those times of solitude because he goes in great expectation of hearing from Jesus in those days.

---

192 John 10:3-4, PHILLIPS

193 Thwing, Ted, *So You Want to Grow Spiritually?*, Mount View Press, Edmonds, WA: 2017, p. 45.

My own experience, even in shorter times of silent retreat, is that the single greatest difficulty is to slow down the whirring rotors of thinking, decision-making, and remembering the many things I need to do. I have a holy hunch that the enemy hates it when any of us spend extended time alone with Jesus. When our family lived in Colorado Springs, Young Life's headquarters, our home looked down on a beautiful nunnery, Mount St. Francis. I would occasionally take three-day retreats there, and the sisters were so gracious and welcoming. I found that some of the best and unexpected decisions came from being alone with Jesus.

I have loved the story in Mark 1, when Jesus and his disciples were in Capernaum at Peter's mother-in-law's house. The Scripture tells us that, after sunset, "the whole town gathered at the door, and Jesus healed many who had diseases."[194] So, it was a late night. Then, "very early in the morning, while it was still dark, Jesus got up, left the house and went off to a solitary place, where he prayed."[195] Hours later, his baffled disciples looked everywhere for him. The disciples were anticipating days of very productive ministry ahead in Capernaum. To their great surprise, Jesus told them they were headed to the nearby villages. He had received his instructions listening to the Father in the pre-dawn hours when everyone else slept.

As I reflect on my experiences of listening to God over the years, one stands out as a pivotal learning opportunity. Early in my work with young people, I started a Young Life club in a middle-class suburban area. It took off immediately, largely because of the influence of one family where all three daughters came to Jesus and the mother was a bedrock of support. The father, Bob, though appreciative of the positive influence in his daughters' lives, was a seasoned skeptic. Occasionally we would meet for lunch. Bob always thought of me and my ideas about Jesus as an oddity.

As Bob's daughters graduated from high school and I moved away, our paths did not cross for many years. After over twenty years, I heard he had leukemia. I called him and we met together. He maintained his skepticism, but because of our long history, the time together was warm. Then, about six months later, I was

194 Mark 1:33-34
195 Mark 1:35

driving on the freeway, and I had this impression, "Call Bob." This was before cell phones were in everyone's pockets, and I soon forgot about this prompting. A week later, one of his daughters called me and told me he had died. A few days later, I attended the memorial service.

Afterwards, one of the daughters came up to me and told me of an amazing time she had with her father the day before he died. As they talked about dying, she told him how much she wanted to be with him in Heaven. As they talked, Bob gave his life to Jesus Christ. I was thrilled, but lurking in my mind was the prompting from Jesus to call him. I'm so glad Jesus doesn't need me to do the work he is doing in people's hearts and lives! But I did wonder if I missed a golden and blessed opportunity to connect with my longtime friend before he graduated from this life.

The lesson learned from that experience is I try to act on those promptings. It has been an interesting phenomenon in my life. Sometimes, I will call a person, and there is nothing particularly urgent. Other times, I will hear, "I can't believe you called! Let me tell what just happened …" Either way, I am blessed to initiate with friends whether there is an impending crisis or not! Remember: "My sheep hear my voice!"

My father-in-law, Doug Coe, was always someone who encouraged everyone around him to experiment in prayer and to learn more. I recall a number of friends he would ask to embrace a "forty-day prayer challenge," in which a person might pray every day for Africa, or something/someone/somewhere God had somehow placed on his or her heart, and see what God would do. The stories of amazing encounters with people in that part of the world or unforeseen events that incredibly lined up with what they were daily asking the Lord to reveal, would quite often result in lifelong commitments to a needy cause or a region of the world.

As a physics major in college, Doug loved to offer a challenge to the Lord to show himself strong in answering these repeated prayers for guidance. One of my many experiences with him over the years has been life-changing. As Debbie and I were preparing to commit ourselves to working full-time with this worldwide family of friends twenty-five years ago, Doug came to me and asked, "Will you make me a promise?" Then he waited. It slowly occurred to me that he wanted me to answer before I knew what I was promising. I thought I should trust him—I had been married to his daughter for over twenty years at the time ...I finally said I would. Then he stunned me by saying, "Promise me you will never ask anyone to help with your personal ministry support."

I was shocked! We owned a home with a sizable mortgage. Our oldest son was less than a year away from college, and three more were close behind. In Young Life, we were never required to raise personal support, though as the President of Young Life, a major part of my role was fund-raising. I think Doug instinctively knew this. He just wanted me to experience trusting the Lord to do it, rather than to rely on my own experience in raising money. A quarter of a century later, I can say that was one of the greatest gifts anyone has ever given my wife and me. We discovered the generosity of the Lord in ways we never would have if "I was in charge."

Ten years after this promise was made, Debbie and I were having dinner with a good pastor friend and his wife. He observed, "You two are people of faith. Tell us some stories of what God did in providing your support all these years." An hour later, I was still regaling them with story after story of God's abundant faithfulness, many times at the eleventh or twelfth hour, but always a rich blessing. On one occasion, I was out on the West Coast several weeks before Christmas, and I noted our support account had dipped pretty low. I would come to Seattle every year before Christmas, attend a number of gatherings, and often would be handed a check by friends. This year that happened less frequently for some reason, and as I went to my bank to deposit several checks, I asked the teller, who was a friend, to let me know how much was in the account. Thinking she would tell me something like $2,500, she instead read from the computer, $27,500. My stunned response embarrasses me to this day, "I think there must be some mistake."

She looked again and reiterated the same amount. Infrequently, people send checks to the office in Seattle. Almost all the others are mailed to me. So, I asked if there had been any deposits during the week I was out there. "Yes, one for $25,000 came just last Friday." I went to my car and called the office. A young man answered and apologized for not letting me know, but acknowledged the gift and the donor. I sat in my car and wept. I thought, "After all these years of seeing your faithfulness, Lord, I'm still in the 101 class of trusting you!" By the way, that is a great place for all of us to be—in a front row seat in the 101 class with Jesus as our teacher!

God Listening as Several of Us Talk Together

About a dozen years ago, I came in touch with a third way of experiencing prayer. Each Tuesday afternoon at The Cedars, a group of my associates and I would meet together for several hours. One Tuesday, we had come to the end of our sharing about what the Lord is doing around the world, and someone noted that we had forgotten to pray. One of the participants shared this verse:

> *"Then those who feared the Lord talked with each other, and the Lord listened and heard. A scroll of remembrance was written in his presence concerning those who feared the Lord and honored his name."*[196]

The person challenged us to consider that our whole meeting could be a prayer together for the world. Pointing to an empty chair in the circle of a dozen or so colleagues, he asked us to envision Jesus sitting in that chair listening to the amazing reports of the Spirit's work all over the planet.

The first thought I had in response to this was it would certainly give me pause before I uttered a critical word or disparaging comment against someone! To have a meeting with Jesus as one of the participants and to consider all of our offerings in that time as prayers to him was a captivating thought! I will frequently share the same thought as friends gather to share about the work of Jesus around the world—he listens and answers our prayers. As a fifth grader, I recall memorizing Psalms 24:

"The earth is the Lord's and everything in it, the world and all who live in it … Who may ascend the hill of the Lord? Who may stand in his holy place? He who has clean hands and a pure heart, and who does not lift up his soul to an idol or swear by what is false."[197]

Certainly our Lord is blessed to join us in our discussions and prayers for his world! Let's keep an empty chair for him at every such meeting!

---

196 Malachi 3:16, NIV
197 Psalms 24:1, 3-4, NIV

The Lord's Prayer

One of the best books I have encountered in many years is *The Secret Message of Jesus* by Brian McLaren. His observations about the Lord's Prayer are riveting:

> *"The average person—committed Christian or non-Christian, Catholic, or Orthodox or Protestant—most often encounters the secret message of Jesus in a line of what we call 'The Lord's Prayer.' Sadly, the prayer has been recited in such a bland, thoughtless, autopilot monotone that few people realize what a revolutionary, challenging, and well-crafted work of art it is. How many millions of people have mouthed the words, 'Thy Kingdom come,' with little or no idea what they were saying? The prayer, you'll remember, comes in the section of Jesus' kingdom manifesto (Matthew 5-7, Sermon on the Mount) dealing with three spiritual practices: right between giving to the poor and fasting. Jesus' emphasis is on the secrecy needed for these practices to have their full impact. Don't do them for show, Jesus says, to be seen as pious by other people. Instead, do them secretly with God as your only audience."*[198]

I like to use this to break down the Lord's Prayer and apply its oft-uttered words to the everyday challenges that we face in our journey through life. I borrow these words from a well-traveled handout on the principles and attributes that has circled amongst many friends:

> I cannot say **OUR** if my life has no room for others and their needs.
>
> I cannot say **FATHER** if I don't live out that relationship in my daily life.
>
> I cannot say **WHO ART IN HEAVEN** if my interests and commitments are on earthly things.
>
> I cannot say **HALLOWED BE THY NAME** if my life does not honor and glorify Him.
>
> I cannot say **THY KINGDOM COME** if I do not have his kingdom growing in my heart, my life, and in my home, country, and world.

---

198 McLaren, Brian D. *The Secret Message of Jesus: Uncovering the Truth That Could Change Everything.* Nashville, TN: Thomas Nelson, 2007, pp. 209-210.

I cannot say **THY WILL BE DONE** if I am unwilling to have it manifested in my life.

I cannot say **ON EARTH AS IT IS IN HEAVEN** unless I am truly willing to bring him everything in my life today.

I cannot say **GIVE US THIS DAY OUR DAILY BREAD** when I am ignoring the needs of my brothers and sisters.

I cannot say **FORGIVE US OUR TRESPASSES AS WE FORGIVE THOSE WHO TRESPASS AGAINST US** if I harbor a grudge toward anyone.

I cannot say **LEAD US INTO TEMPTATION** if I deliberately choose to remain in a situation that is tempting me.

I cannot say **DELIVER US FROM EVIL** if I am not willing to fight with the weapons of the Word and prayer.

I cannot say **THINE IS THE KINGDOM** if I am not willing to be the King's loyal subject.

I cannot say **THINE IS THE POWER** if I fear what those around me will say or do.

I cannot say **THINE IS THE GLORY** if I seek my own glory above his.

I cannot say **FOREVER AND EVER** if I am anxious about the affairs of each day.

I cannot say **AMEN** unless I can agree that, whatever the cost to my life, this is my prayer.

As we pray the Lord's Prayer in the years ahead, may it be a true and genuine reflection of the daily practices of our lives. If that is so, it truly becomes an act of worship before our Lord.

Isn't it incredible that the God of the Universe highly values communication with each of us, his loving creation? And he desires to listen to us as we bring our requests, our hurts, our praises, and our problems to him.

The late Dr. Vernon Grounds, former President of Denver Seminary and a beloved mentor in my life, once gave a powerful message on "The Curse of Prayerlessness." I remember reflecting upon hearing that if there were ever reason for sadness in Heaven, it would be when we realized how much our Lord desired consistent and constant communication with each of us. When Genesis 1:27 notes that we are created in his image and likeness, it really means that, unlike the rest of creation, we are designed to delight in a living and loving relationship with Jesus Christ.

The enemy would love to have us think of such communication with God through prayer as a chore or a duty. Our Lord views it as the loving lifeline he has with each of us to guide us through the dangerous shoals and snares that our lives inevitably experience. Perhaps the beautiful words of an old hymn say it best: "What a friend we have in Jesus. All our sins and griefs to bear. What a privilege to carry everything to God in prayer. Oh, what peace we often forfeit. Oh, what needless pain we bear. All because we do not carry everything to God in prayer."

PART 3

Thoughts and Afterthoughts

Chapter Sixteen

Spiritual Warfare

"Oh, Simon, Simon, do you know that Satan has asked to have you all to sift like wheat?—but I have prayed for you that you may not lose your faith. Yes, when you have turned back to me, you must strengthen these brothers of yours. Peter said to him, 'Lord, I am ready to go to prison, or even to die with you!' 'I tell you, Peter,' returned Jesus, 'before the cock crows today you will deny three times that you know me.'" (Luke 22:31-34, PHILLIPS)

Jesus was very open with his disciples about the reality of their enemy—the devil—and the need for spiritual warfare against him. When he sent out the twelve in Luke 9, he "gave them authority over all evil spirits and the ability to heal disease."[199] Jesus knew what they were up against, and that they would need his authority and power in them to defeat all the onslaughts and resistance of Satan against them.

At the same time, Jesus was also aware that his friends were subject to personal temptations, and knew that Satan had already entered the heart of Judas. In the

199 Luke 9:1, PHILLIPS

passage above, he warns Peter of the enemy's intended assault upon him and prays for him.

Over two thousand years later, things haven't changed. We, as modern-day disciples, are subject to the same enemy attacks and temptations as Jesus' first-century followers. As we consider in this chapter how we, as followers of Jesus, should view this warfare, it is helpful to consider the words of C.S. Lewis in his preface to *The Screwtape Letters* (his classic novel containing letters from a senior devil to a junior devil named Wormwood). Lewis penned:

> *"There are two equal and opposite errors into which our race can fall about devils. One is to disbelieve their existence. The other is to believe and feel an excessive and unhealthy interest in them. They themselves are equally pleased by both errors and hail a materialist or a magician with the same delight."*

I heartily agree. The devil is content for us to either think he is a fictional cartoon with a pitchfork, or that he is ever present in our lives—behind every tree, hidden under every rock. Our challenge is to live with recognition of his existence, but with the faith to believe in the power of the name of Jesus over him.

Frankly, I think to mock or minimize the existence of Satan and the need for spiritual warfare against him on the part of believers is sheer arrogance. I think of the time some friends and I were meeting with five student body officers at a prominent Christian university. As we queried them about the challenges they were facing, the conversation remained superficial until one of my brothers asked the young men about pornography. It was as if the dam had broken and a waterfall ensued. This was clearly a bigger issue than anyone had realized or was willing to admit—and the enemy had obviously gained a foothold. I think we talked and prayed until 1:30 in the morning, and the result was the breaking of bondages and new freedom through Jesus!

There is an all-out assault against sexual purity in our culture that has been building for many years. When I was a teenager in the late fifties and early sixties, *Playboy* magazine was what tempted guys my age. Today, with unlimited amounts of pornography easily available on the internet, the challenge is daunting. Sexual purity is only one issue in a vast arsenal of the enemy's weaponry against us.

With this in mind, I will frequently offer several passages in the New Testament to my young friends to ponder. Both are preceded by the Old Testament proverb, "God is opposed to the proud, but gives grace to the humble."[200] Note the similarity in these two exhortations from James and Peter:

- *"Submit yourselves, then, to God. Resist the devil, and he will flee from you. Come near to God and he will come near to you."201*
- *"Be self-controlled and alert. Your enemy the devil prowls around like a roaring lion looking for someone to devour. Resist him, standing firm in the faith, because you know that your brothers throughout the world are undergoing the same kind of sufferings."*[202]

The unmistakable similarity in these passages, besides the caution to be humble, is the word "resist," which means "to succeed in ignoring the attraction of" and "to struggle against someone or something." This word seems to indicate an aggressive choice on our behalf. In other words, I am not a victim of the enemy's schemes and devices; I *choose* to resist his influence in my life. This reminds me of the promise God made to Moses and the Israelites: "This day I call heaven and earth as witnesses against you that I have set before you life and death, blessings and curses. Now choose life, so that you and your children may live and that you may love the Lord your God, listen to his voice, and hold fast to him."[203] As followers of Jesus, we have the power to resist the enemy and to choose life.

Knowing Our Resources

Let's consider what tools and weapons we have as followers of Jesus to help us in this spiritual battle going on in our lives. Perhaps the most complete list of

---

200 Proverbs 3:34, NIV
201 James 4:7-8, NIV
202 1 Peter 5:8-9, NIV
203 Deuteronomy 30:19-20, NIV

spiritual resources is contained in the final chapter of Paul's letter to the church at Ephesus:

> *"Finally, be strong in the Lord and in his mighty power. Put on the full armor of God so that you can take your stand against the devil's schemes. For our struggle is not against flesh and blood, but against the rulers, against the authorities, against the powers of this dark world and against the spiritual forces of evil in the heavenly realms."*[204]

Here, Paul challenges us to actually put on "the armor of God" so we can combat the schemes of the devil. It might be helpful to ponder what exactly are those schemes. Paul mentions in his letter to the Corinthian church that he will choose to forgive anyone, "in order that Satan might not outwit us. For we are not ignorant of his schemes."[205]

When I first read this passage years ago, I wondered, *How aware am I actually of the devil's schemes?* This is a good self-check for all of us. Remembering C.S. Lewis' earlier warning, we don't want to give the enemy too much credit. We do want to be wary of him and his tricks and traps.

When I think about Satan's schemes, I think of two very effective and oft-repeated ones. One is that he attacks each of us at the level of our identity. Either this little voice tells us we are a loser and not as good as others (inferiority), or, even worse, that we are better than all of them and it is all about us (narcissism) The second scheme is that he is a divider—he loves to divide us and to sow discord. Satan is very effective at both.

In Paul's letter to the Ephesians, he reminds us that this common struggle, unlike all the others we will face, is against an *unseen* enemy. It's not against people, although the battle may *feel* like it's coming through people. Where our struggle really is, Paul tells us, is against rulers, authorities, powers, and spiritual forces deployed in "the heavenly realms." This term, used five times in Ephesians, refers to the place where spiritual warfare is taking place. It is not heaven, nor

---

204 Ephesians 6:10-12, NIV
205 2 Corinthians 2:11, NIV

hell, nor earth, but in spiritual realms where the battle for the lives, hearts, and souls of humans is happening.

Some readers may remember the book that author Frank Peretti wrote years ago, *This Present Darkness,* describing the epic battle between angelic forces and demonic powers in the heavenly realms.[206] For many of us, this book was our first and most vivid realization of that battle's existence. It awakened many of the reality of this warfare and the need to be equipped to resist the enemy and his evil intentions. (It's a compelling read and if you've not read it, I recommend it.)

Book's like Lewis' *The Screwtape Letters* and Peretti's *This Present Darkness* may be fiction, but they raise our awareness of the hidden reality of spiritual warfare, and give context to us for Paul's exhortation to us in Ephesians 6. This classic passage, which is well worth memorizing, provides us with some very practical helps in how we can be prepared for the enemy's schemes in our lives:

> *"Therefore, put on the full armor of God, so that when the day of evil comes, you may be able to stand your ground, and after you have done everything, to stand. Stand firm then ... "*[207]

On the basis of the enormity of the spiritual battle against an unseen foe, we need to do two things: (1) to put on the full armor of God, and (2) to stand. For the former, Paul gives us some specific pieces of that armor to equip us. Then he challenges us to stand—an absolutely essential position of aggressive readiness to do battle. No one does battle sitting or lying down. This is so important that Paul calls us to stand *four* times in this passage. Passivity does not cut it in this epic battle!

Our Spiritual Armor

So, what are these specific pieces of armor that God gives us? Note them highlighted below:

> *"Stand firm then, with the **belt of truth** buckled around your waist, with the **breastplate of righteousness** in place, and with your **feet fitted with***

206 Peretti, Frank, *This Present Darkness,* Crossway Books, Wheaton, IL: 2003.
207 Ephesians 6:13, NIV

***the readiness** that comes from the gospel of peace. In addition to all this, take up the **shield of faith**, with which you can extinguish all the flaming arrows of the evil one. Take the **helmet of salvation** and the **sword of the Spirit**, which is the word of God. And **pray in the Spirit** on all occasions with all kinds of prayers and requests. With this in mind, be alert and always keep on praying for all the saints."*[208]

1. **Belt of Truth.** The belt of truth protects us from the enemy's relentless and all-out assault against God's plumbline of righteousness and truth in our lives. Years ago, I heard someone say that we don't break the commandments; we break *ourselves* on the commandments. I think that means God designed his commandments to be important guidelines for how we live. When I choose to violate them, it not only frequently hurts others, it always hurts me, and most of all it hurts God. Take sexual purity, for example. What I am doing when I dedicate myself to sexual purity, I am honoring God who designed my body, myself who dwells in it, and others who are affected by my choices. That's how wearing the belt of truth helps us stand firm in keeping God's commandments.
2. **Breastplate of Righteousness.** "Above all else, guard your heart, for it is the wellspring of life."[209] This breastplate covers my heart. The Great Commandment begins by exhorting us to love God with all of our heart. In Scripture, the terms "heart" and "Spirit" are interchangeable. They connote the essence of who we are. Righteousness is the character of God, which he freely imparts to us in Jesus Christ: "God made him who had no sin to be sin for us, so that in him we might become the righteousness of God."[210] As we abide in Jesus, he protects our hearts!
3. **Feet Fitted with the Readiness of the Gospel of Peace.** Scripture frequently refers to feet as connoting ministry: "How beautiful on the mountains are the feet of those who bring good news."[211] Our feet transport us places. I recall years ago, while playing basketball, tearing

208 Ephesians 6:14-19, NIV
209 Proverbs 4:23, NIV
210 2 Corinthians 5:21, NIV
211 Isaiah 52:7, NIV

ligaments in my ankle. I was laid up with crutches for weeks! The enemy would love to disable us from effectively living out our lives for Jesus. Our healthy feet bring the good news! Jesus guards our feet.

4. **Shield of Faith.** This shield extinguishes the flaming arrows of the enemy—so often it is a random thought, lusting or demeaning or criticizing someone else or even ourselves. It seems to appear out of nowhere: "You are a loser ...," "I hate him ... ," etc. When those unwelcome thoughts appear, the Holy Spirit gives us the shield of faith to quench those arrows so they miss their intended mark—our hearts and minds!
5. **Helmet of Salvation.** This helmet protects our head. Romans 12:2 tells us, "Don't let the world around you squeeze you into its own mold, but let God remake you so that your whole attitude of mind is changed."[212] This armor doesn't just protect our heart, but also helps us to think more like Jesus—so important, because, "As a man thinketh in his heart, so is he."[213]
6. **Sword of the Spirit.** This is the one offensive weapon. It is the Word of God—and Jesus showed us how to use it in his temptation by the devil in the desert, responding to the enemy with Scripture.[214] Hebrews tells us God's Word is "living and active, sharper than any double-edged sword...and judges the thoughts and attitudes of the heart."[215] It is our always-reliable resource in doing battle with the enemy.
7. **Prayer in the Spirit.** I add this one to the list because it is an indispensable part of our spiritual armor. We have a direct line to the One whom Scripture tells us has "all authority in heaven and on earth," the One who assures us, "Surely I am with you always, even to the end of the age."[216] As we stand against the enemy, we can commune with Jesus, the overcomer. We are never alone! With this in mind, I love how James Stewart, in *The Life and Teaching of Jesus Christ,*

---

212 PHILLIPS
213 Proverbs 23:7, KJV
214 Matthew 4:4
215 Hebrews 4:12, NIV
216 Matthew 28:18-20

beautifully concludes why the early disciples were able to overcome the temptations of the world:

> *"As time went on, they found they could conquer the love of the world in themselves and indeed every low love, not by crushing it down by sheer force of will, but by having a better love to set against it, the love of Jesus, who had gone the same hard road himself. Contact with his radiant, dynamic personality achieved the impossible. God's own victorious power was coming across into their weak lives, not through any moral code, impersonal and cold and uninspiring, but through this splendid, magnificent, adorable Lover of their souls; not by any strained or difficult obedience, but by 'Christ in them the hope of glory!'"*[217]

My longtime friend, John, a former Marine sent to Vietnam and then to Washington D.C., has helped me understand spiritual warfare in a new and deeper way. He talks about other weapons that we have in doing spiritual warfare that I had never considered to be part of our arsenal. One of them is forgiveness. There is nothing like unforgiveness to leave the door wide open for the enemy to gain valuable territory in our lives. Paul called this scheme out when he wrote: "'In your anger do not sin': Do not let the sun go down while you are still angry, and do not give the devil a foothold."[218] We slam that door and lock it—denying the enemy a foothold in our life and thinking—when we forgive. The power of Jesus Christ in our lives that is released by true forgiveness and unconditional love is amazing.

I can recall many profound pictures of forgiveness over the years, but one that sticks out is at a Washington State Governor's Prayer Breakfast in the late 90's. The keynote speaker was a young Vietnamese woman who had been the poster child of a brutal napalming attack by American jet pilots in the war with Vietnam in the late 60's. She was seen in a video running terrified on a road in rural Vietnam with napalm aflame on her body.

---

217 Stewart, James S. *The Life and Teaching of Jesus Christ*, Edinburgh: Saint Andrew Press, 1995, p. 45.

218 Ephesians 4:26-27, NIV

After multiple surgeries and being used as a poster child against American imperialism, this woman came to know Jesus Christ. She showed us a video of her forgiving the American pilot who released the napalm and the two of them embracing. The Governor had to follow her profound message of forgiveness. He, Gary Locke, of Asian descent, was so moved by her message of forgiveness and reconciliation that he could not speak until finally composing himself. It was a most powerful demonstration of the freedom that comes through forgiveness and unconditional love.

Our Other Divinely Powerful Weapons

Another weapon is generosity. Whether I am giving my time, my finances, my friends, or my possessions, the power of Christ is released in generosity. It frustrates the enemy who delights in my selfishness. When I am a generous giver to all, it negates the devil's schemes and plans.

I would count these weapons—among others—in the group of weapons Paul may have been referring to when we wrote,

> *"For though we live in the world, we do not wage war as the world does. The weapons we fight with are not the weapons of the world. On the contrary, they have divine power to demolish strongholds. 5 We demolish arguments and every pretension that sets itself up against the knowledge of God, and we take captive every thought to make it obedient to Christ."*[219]

Here Paul speaks directly to the incredible power of God that is released in spiritual warfare. As we have earlier noted, our battle is against an unseen foe. Therefore, we do not use traditional earthly weapons. They are far more powerful than the world's traditional weapons. These divinely powerful weapons are all easily accessible to all of us who name Jesus as our Lord, and who have God's Spirit living in us. In fact, they are so accessible, I had never thought of them as "weapons" to directly and effectively counteract the devil's scheme! But they are. And, obviously, the greatest weapon of them all is unconditional love. As the

219 2 Corinthians 10:3-5, NIV

Scriptures tell us, it is the one thing that stands when all else has fallen: "Love never fails."[220]

I believe this would include a very strong corporate or "crew-served" weapon available to us in this offensive arsenal: a band of brothers and/or sisters committed together. As we have earlier discussed, the power of a team, knit together over the years, is a potent force in overcoming the schemes of the enemy.

In the 2 Corinthians 10 passage cited above, we see another area of spiritual warfare we can mount against the enemy—right thinking and a clear conscience: "We demolish arguments and every pretension that sets itself up against the knowledge of God, and we take captive every thought to make it obedient to Christ."[221]

I believe Satan and his army do some of their most effective work in the context of shame, guilt, and broken relationships. When we practice confession and repentance, we take away the territory of wrong thinking, damaged emotions, and broken relationships he attempts to claim in our lives.

I remember when, a number of years ago, my wife and I were leading a Bible study with about eight other couples. We had been meeting for several years, when I stopped one day by the office of one of the men in the group, whom I will call Dan. I would pretty regularly come by his office, but this time he was looking at the want ads in the newspaper.

When I asked him what he was looking for, he went over and closed the door, and in soft tones confided in me that he was seeing another woman and was thinking about separating from his wife. I listened and asked a few questions, but it seemed his mind was made up. Shortly after that, I headed to Russia and other countries for several weeks.

It was an Easter Sunday morning, and I was headed from the capital of Armenia, Yerevan, to the capital of the nation of Georgia, Tbilisi. No planes flew this route, so I boarded a fifteen-passenger van, and because I was tall, I was given the front seat. That was the good news; the bad news was the driver was a chain smoker, so I unfortunately shared his smoke for four hours before we stopped for lunch! It was at a beautiful wooded area on a raging river.

---

220 1 Corinthians 13:8

221 2 Corinthians 10:3-5, NIV

Since I had no Armenian money, I was going to go sit by the river for an hour, but a very kind Armenian handed me a *shashlik*—a stick of tasty meat. As I sat by the river, suddenly a video went through my mind. It was my friend, Dan, five years later, at Christmas time. He was having dinner with his new wife and her three kids. It was strained—the kids liked their real dad and missed him. My friend, after an awkward meal, went to call his two kids and that, too, didn't go very well. They were still upset about the marriage breakup. He thought about how much he had lost. Then the video ended.

I sat by the river, a bit stunned by the reality of what had just happened. As I returned home the following week, I resolved to meet with my friend and share the story without saying that I believed that the Lord had given it to me. We set a meeting several days after I returned, and I met with Dan at the local golf club coffee shop. We talked about a number of things, and after a half hour, I told Dan I had a picture I wanted to share with him. I left out any spiritual language, but just shared the story as I saw it. He didn't react in any way to it, and I thought that was the end of it.

Several days later, Dan called and asked to meet again. We had hardly sat down before he turned to me and asked, "How did you know she had three kids?" I was surprised at the speed and bluntness of his question. I told him I believed the Lord had given me this picture, not to condemn or criticize him, but to keep him from making a decision that would hurt and destroy his family. He ended the relationship, stayed with his wife, and the years ahead were wonderful—the kids got married, grandkids showed up, and joy abounded.

These kind of miracles are in the list of spiritual gifts described in 1 Corinthians 12 and 14. They are also some of the "divinely powerful weapons" mentioned in 2 Corinthians 10:3-5. When Dan responded with repentance and turned the opposite way from the temptation in his life, the scheme of the enemy was defeated.

God is mightily at work in our world today, and his power is revealed in the ordinary and in the extraordinary. I firmly believe that, just as the Holy Spirit did miracles throughout the Book of Acts in the early church, he still is doing them today all over the world—and you and I have the incredible privilege of joining him.

Chapter Seventeen

Authority

"... Jesus went with them; but just before arriving at the house, the captain sent some friends to say, 'Sir, don't inconvenience yourself by coming to my home, for I am not worthy of any such honor or even to come and meet you. Just speak a word from where you are and my servant boy will be healed. I know because I am under the authority of my superior officers, and I have authority over my men. I only need to say, 'Go!' And they go; or, 'Come!' And they come; and to my slave, 'Do this or that,' and he does it. So just say 'Be healed!' and my servant will be well again. Jesus was amazed. Turning to the crowd he said, 'Never among all the Jews in Israel have I met a man with faith like this.' And when the captain's friends returned to his house, they found the slave completely healed!" (Luke 7:6-10, NLT)

There is a popular bumper sticker I often notice while driving that reads: "RESIST AUTHORITY!" In our contemporary society it seems this theme is gaining popularity. Ironically, in God's economy, such a view is considered disastrous.

In chapter two, we reflected on the incredible account of the Roman centurion who amazed Jesus because of his outrageous faith. Let's return to this story as we consider the (currently) very controversial subject of authority.

In the previous chapter, I pointed out how our enemy, Satan—described in Scripture as "the father of lies"[222]—delights when we disregard authority. In the Old Testament, King Saul was rebuked for this offense by the prophet Samuel:

> *"Does the Lord delight in burnt offerings and sacrifices as much as obeying the voice of the Lord? To obey is better than sacrifice, and to heed is better than the fat of rams. For rebellion is as the sin of divination, and arrogance like the evil of idolatry. Because you have rejected the word of the Lord, he has rejected you as king."*[223]

I could point to a number of passages that highlight the same principle. The theme of honoring authority runs throughout the Scriptures. We want to explore it in this chapter to better understand how (and why) we as followers of Jesus can and should honor him with humble and obedient hearts. The account of the faith of the Roman centurion is an indicator of the importance of pursuing this subject of authority.

Over twenty years ago, my longtime friend, Morrie, handed me a book called *Under Cover* by John Bevere. He noted that reading this book had made a profound impact upon his life. As I read this book, I understood how the enemy tricks us by distorting our ability to recognize God's *inherent* authority and his *delegated* authority. God makes it very clear that living under the umbrella of authority will provide for us a place of experiencing God's provision and his protection.

Several weeks after I read Bevere's book, I was traveling to Chico, California, to speak at a college weekend. It happened to be President's Day the following Monday, and my good friend and colleague, Gil, asked me if I would stay over to get some time with the students Monday evening at his home. I decided I would make the topic of authority an area of discussion. We began our interaction

---

222 John 8:44, NIV
223 1 Samuel 15:22-23, NIV

about 7:30 that evening. The last students left the house around 1:00 a.m. I realized we were mining for gold that evening! The relevancy to each of their lives, family histories, and relational challenges was amazing.

A week later, I was speaking to 150 college students living in Vision 16 fellowship houses at the University of Washington on a Friday evening. In the question-and-answer time following my message on authority, a young woman became unhinged in what felt like a demonic display of rage as we discussed this topic. It obviously evoked some very strong reactions in her. Who knew that this topic would arouse such interest—and such visceral reactions?

In the years following these experiences, I have had many more like it. It has repeatedly been demonstrated to me how interrelated our views on having a submissive heart and experiencing a growing peace and joy in our lives are (and conversely how disregarding authority leads to growing turbulence and conflict in our lives). For this reason, I have added this topic to my list of favorites when meeting with young friends wanting to grow in their journeys with Jesus Christ.

What Submission to Authority Looks Like

I want to point out four specific areas of relating to authorities in our lives. But, before I do, I want to mention how important it is to establish an overall attitude of heart. As Paul urged us: "Submit to one another out of reverence for Christ."[224]

The context of this passage helps us to understand how important it is. In verse 18, Paul exhorts the church at Ephesus to not be drunk with wine, but to be filled with the Spirit. In the following three verses he tells them what it looks like to be filled with the Spirit:

1. **"Speaking to yourselves in psalms and hymns and spiritual songs, singing and making melody in your heart to the Lord."**[225] One key indication of the infilling of the Holy Spirit is a life of praise and worship—making melody in our hearts to our Lord!

---

224 Ephesians 5:21, NIV
225 Ephesians 5:19, KJV

2. **"Giving thanks for all things unto God and Father in the name of our Lord Jesus Christ."**[226] We choose to give thanks in all things, even in our trials. We have thankful hearts! This is an unmistakable sign of the infilling of God's Spirit.
3. **"Submitting yourselves one to another in the fear of God."**[227] We choose to have submissive hearts toward one another because of our love for Christ.

Following on from looking at what being filled with the Spirit looks like, the scriptures indicate four areas of practicing the discipline of a submissive heart. Each one is important, because it provides a specific area to practice this challenging opportunity:

1. Parents

> *"Children, obey your parents in the Lord, for this is right. 'Honor your father and mother,'—which is the first commandment with a promise—that it may go well with you and that you may enjoy long life on the earth."*[228]

I would suspect that most of us have long since passed through childhood, during which the authority of parents is most vital in our lives. However, as the years go by, the counsel of parents remains very important.

My wife Debbie and I had a very abbreviated courtship. We were together less than four days over a several-week period when we both knew we wanted to get married. I was the camp speaker at Malibu for four weeks. After this assignment, when I returned home, I was entering a new role as regional director for Young Life in the Northwest. The fall calendar was packed.

At the news of our courtship and knowing our desires, my father, whom I had taken to an "Institute in Basic Youth Conflicts" seminar (some of you may remember that ministry by Bill Gothard) several years before, called me on the radio phone at Malibu. This was a little embarrassing, as all the loggers in the

226 Ephesians 5:20, KJV
227 Ephesians 5:21, KJV
228 Ephesians 6:1-3, NIV

logging camps could overhear! My dad strongly advised me to cancel my other plans so I could go to meet Debbie's family on the East Coast. He had never done anything like this before, but he cited the lecture we'd heard at IBYC on "Chain of Command and Counsel." I listened to him, and I am forever grateful that I did!

Obviously, not everyone has believing parents. Some may understandably ask, "What do we do when our unbelieving parents tell us to do something unlawful or immoral?" Thankfully, that is not a common occurrence. However, when it does happen, even in our unwillingness to obey them, we choose to honor them by our attitudes and actions. We can show respect and love even when we cannot accede to their counsel. In the vast majority of instances, our parents, whether they are believers or not, sincerely want our welfare and are important voices in our lives. There is Scriptural promise that goes along with the commandment to honor our parents—"that it may go well with you and that you may enjoy long life on the earth."[229] All of us would want both of those precious blessings!

2. Employers

> *"Whatever you do, work at it with all your heart, as working for the Lord, not for men, since you know that you will receive an inheritance from the Lord as a reward. It is the Lord Christ you are serving."*[230]

In high school, college, and graduate school, I always had at least a part-time job. I graded Chiquita bananas, unloaded boxcars and bagged potatoes, cleaned offices at night, washed dishes at multiple places, worked at a flour mill, mowed hundreds of lawns, sold return address stickers, delivered newspapers, painted houses, drove buses, was the campus mailman, and many more diverse jobs. In every one of these jobs there was an employer.

Some employers were delightful to work for; others were demanding and unpleasant. Regardless of the quality of the employer, much of the outcome was

229 Ephesians 6:3
230 Colossians 3:23-24, NIV

based on my heart attitude, not theirs. If I was diligent and hardworking, I could expect a positive recommendation.

The message to all of us is that we are solely responsible for OUR attitude and integrity in the workplace. We want to be the same person whether or not anyone is looking, and whether or not we have an agreeable employer. Keeping an attitude of excellence is a worthy habit to adopt for life. In actuality, we are working for the Lord, not for human beings.

Then, in the same way I experience various attitudes from employers, I also have the opportunity as an employer myself to demonstrate the kind of leadership that values the people working for me. When I am under authority, I should honor that authority. When I am in authority, I should view it as delegated from God and make it easy for people to submit to it.

Ken Blanchard, in his book, *Lead Like Jesus*, observes in his introduction: "We want you to change not only your knowledge, but your attitudes, actions, and behaviors—your very life! Do you know how long it took Jesus to change his disciples' attitudes and behaviors related to servant leadership? Three years of daily interactions!"[231] When I truly understand that I'm ultimately working for Jesus, I can embrace excellence in attitude and action toward my employer, and also become the kind of caring employer for whom I would want to work.

3. Government

> *"Everyone must submit themselves to the governing authorities, for there is no authority except that which God has established. The authorities that exist have been established by God. Consequently, he who rebels against the authority is rebelling against what God has instituted, and those who do so will bring judgment on themselves ... "*[232]

In our modern day of deep divisions in society, this passage becomes very controversial—and very relevant. I think it is important that we first consider the spirit of the message so we can appropriately respond to the letter.

231 Blanchard, Kenneth H., and Phil Hodges. *Lead like Jesus: Lessons for Everyone from the Greatest Leadership Role Model of All Time.* Nashville, TN: Thomas Nelson, 2008, p. 14.

232 Romans 13:1-2, NIV

In his letter to his young charge, Paul urges Timothy (and ultimately us) to "pray for those in authority, that we may live peaceful and quiet lives in all godliness and holiness. This is good and pleases God our Savior…"[233] So, with this scripture in mind, my attitude can most certainly NOT be one of resistance!

Several important indicators would be whether we obey the speed limit as we drive, and do we attempt to illegally cut corners in paying our taxes? My attitude toward those who are in authority over me in government must be one of prayer for them and a genuine desire to obey the spirit and the letter of the law. Once again, we need to remember we are living our life for an audience of one.

Eric Metaxas, in his classic biography, *Bonhoeffer*, introduces the important question of what we do when those in authority over us are pursuing means and ends that are utterly inconsistent with God's laws.[234] Certainly, around the world today this is a very relevant question.

I do believe that we often are asking it long before it is actually requiring us to do something contrary to our God-given convictions, which should trump everything else. For instance, I am a very ardent pro-life advocate. I cannot imagine how, except in extremely rare circumstances, the life of an unborn infant should be terminated. The scriptures—and science, for that matter—clearly indicate life begins at conception.[235] I believe the responsible options for me are certainly to pray for the leaders to see this truth, peacefully protest or demonstrate, and to pursue any legal means, including communicating with my representatives in Congress.

In the case of Dietrich Bonhoeffer, he realized the Nazi government leadership had reached such ungodly extremes that the only responsible decision was to join the forces opposing them. This decision cost him his life, and seventy-five years later we respect and honor his costly commitment. I thought it was made so clear in the writings of Metaxas that, even in his opposition to the evils perpetrated by the Nazi leadership, Bonhoeffer maintained a Christlike spirit—even in the end—toward those who executed him. The message here is, even when our

233 1 Timothy 2:2-3, NIV

234 Metaxas, Eric. *Bonhoeffer: Pastor, Martyr, Prophet, Spy*. Nashville, TN: Thomas Nelson, 2015.

235 Psalm 139:13-16, NIV

opposition to the actions and decisions of government are clearly warranted, our attitude and course of action should be honoring to the Lord and consistent with Jesus' command to love our enemies. In other words, while we are told to "hate what is evil,"[236] we are also reminded, "As for those who make your life a misery, bless them. Don't curse, bless."[237] As controversial as these verses in Romans 13 can be today, it would seem they are calling us to a submissive, respectful heart toward those who lead us in the vast majority of circumstances.

4. Spiritual Leaders

> *"Obey your leaders and submit to their authority. They keep watch over you as men who must give an account. Obey them so that their work will be a joy, not a burden, for that would be of no advantage to you."*[238]

I sincerely wish I had realized the importance of this one many years ago. I think I became "high maintenance" in some early years for those who supervised me in ministry. Years later, I actually went to several who had been in authority over me and asked their forgiveness for the times I thought I knew better than they did. The irony is, even if that were actually true in the letter, it was violated in the spirit.

One picture that comes back to me almost fifty years later was, when, as a twenty-seven-year-old, I was experiencing significant growth in our ministry. I was in a meeting with several older brothers who were shepherds in the community. We had been meeting together for a year or two, and both of them were experiencing financial support challenges and smaller numbers in their ministries. They shared openly and vulnerably. When it came my turn—I am embarrassed to admit—I was far too full of myself.

As I shared all the great things that were happening, one brother finally turned and smiling, said to me, "That's okay, brother. The Lord has a cross just your size." I remember thinking that maybe he was just having a bad day. The amazing and wonderful thing is that fifteen years later, when I was experiencing

---

236 See Proverbs 8:13
237 Romans 12:14, PHILLIPS
238 Hebrews 13:17, NIV

some significant challenges in ministry, this friend's words came back to me. Suddenly, they were spot on! What I had been unable to understand in those earlier days made perfect sense that day.

It is an awesome privilege to have a submissive heart toward those God has placed over us in authority. Much of what I have learned over the years has been because of those God placed in authority over me. I truly believe I became a better supervisor in direct proportion to my own willingness to have a submissive heart toward spiritual leaders over me. When I encounter someone over whom I am in a position of leadership, my prayer is that, when our time together is over, both of us will have a deeper love for Jesus and for one another than when we started.

Years ago, I heard a cassette tape message by Bob Mumford, the charismatic Bible teacher. It was on firing pots. I'm not much for artistic endeavors, but in high school shop class, we did make a few clay pots. Mumford notes that once pots are shaped on the lathe, you put them in the oven and turn up the heat. After a while, it is important to check on them. With a small instrument you can tap the side to find out if they are done. If you hear a "kerthunk!" it goes back in the oven and you turn up the heat! Then, when more time has passed, you pull out the pot and try again. This time it sings! That's how you know it's done. I think the point is that the measurement of our own growth and maturity is, when adversity hits, is our response a "kerthunk," or do we sing? I believe the relationships we have—both as mentor and mentee—are splendid opportunities for us to grow in having a submissive heart.

One final picture of spiritual leadership comes to mind. In my fifteen years of working with hundreds of young men who came to live at Ivanwald, the young men's discipleship house at The Cedars, I have worked with young friends from every continent in the world. The vast majority have been a great delight. There are always a few who become a significant challenge.

A few years ago, there was such a young man from a nation in Asia. He tended to have the answer for everything—how to do a work project, how to solve any problem, and how we should run the house. I think I was unconsciously steeling myself against his know-it-all demeanor. In other words, my responses to him were more often an exercise in endurance than helpfulness.

In one of our sessions discussing the principles of Jesus, he asked a question totally unrelated to the subject. I recall my response was dismissive, and I quickly returned us to the subject. The next day, one of the young men stopped by my office and told me that this brother had felt offended by my actions. As I reflected upon this incident and the nine other young men who were observing in the circle, I realized this was a golden opportunity to practice what I am sharing today. The next time we were all together, I began by publicly singling him out, briefly reviewing the incident, and then asking his forgiveness for my insensitivity to his question. Ironically, that was the beginning of a sea change in our relationship together.

It was very important to me because I truly believe in having a submissive heart because of my reverence for Jesus Christ, and that this principle is equally applicable in all of my relationships. I think that quite often the five most important words that any of us—leaders or followers—can utter are, "Forgive me. I was wrong." I also believe that my own attitude toward this young man changed when I realized I was actually part of the problem rather than part of the answer! The rocky start to my relationship with this man taught me of the incredible privilege that each of us has to serve under the authority of leadership and to seek to give leadership ourselves.

Our ultimate example of this is Jesus. He provides the perfect model of a servant leader who loves us unconditionally, fervently believes in us, and promises to use even our failures to build character in us. I do believe that the very best textbook we have for both leading and following is the scriptures, and in particular, the four Gospels that reveal in great detail the method and spirit of Jesus as he addresses a needy and hurting world.

British theologian N.T. Wright, in his treatise, *Simply Jesus*, reflects on what the world might look like if Jesus were running it:

> *"This is, after all, what he told us to expect. The poor in spirit will be making the kingdom of God happen. The meek will be taking over the earth, so gently that the powerful won't notice until it's too late. The peacemakers will be putting the arms manufacturers out of business. Those who are hungry and thirsty for God's justice will be analyzing government policy and legal*

> *rulings and speaking up on behalf of those at the bottom of the pile. The merciful will be surprising everybody by showing that there is a different way to do human relations other than being judgmental, eager to put everyone else down. 'You are the light of the world,' said Jesus. 'You are the salt of the earth.' He was announcing a program yet to be completed. He was inviting his hearers then and now, to join him in making it happen. This is, quite simply, what it looks like when Jesus is enthroned."*[239]

Basically, Wright is saying that if we take literally Jesus' Sermon on the Mount, this is what the world would look like. When we operate in and under God's authority, everything falls into place.

Let's not forget some of his last words to the disciples, "ALL AUTHORITY in heaven and on earth has been given to me. Therefore go and make disciples of all nations…"[240]

---

239 Wright, N. T. *Simply Jesus: a New Version of Who He Was, What He Did, Why It Matters.* New York, NY: HarperOne, an imprint of HarperCollins Publishers, 2018, p. 240.

240 Matthew 28:18-19, NIV

Chapter Eighteen

Presenting the Gospel Message

"Don't forget to pray for us too, that God will give us many chances to preach the Good News of Christ for which I am here in jail. Pray that I will be bold enough to tell it freely and fully, and make it plain, as, of course, I should. Make the most of your chances to tell others the Good News. Be wise in all your contacts with them. Let your conversation be gracious as well as sensible, for then you will have the right answer for everyone." (Colossians 4:3-6, NLT)

Jim Rayburn, the founder of Young Life, famously said, "It is a sin to bore a kid with the Gospel." Before he started this outreach mission to teenagers, he looked across from the Presbyterian Church where he was interning and saw the local high school. God spoke to him, "There is your mission field."

Jim's favorite verses were Colossians 4:5-6, in the King James version, "Walk in wisdom toward them that are without, redeeming the time. Let your speech be always with grace, seasoned with salt, that you may know how to answer every man." For the past eighty years, Young Life has sought, in this hallowed tradition, to communicate the gospel message to young people. In this chapter, I hope to communicate some of the order, clarity, and substance of this precious message of Good News as I was taught many years ago. This is not to say Young Life has a corner on communicating the gospel of Jesus Christ, but they certainly got through to me sixty years ago—and to many millions more.

Getting to Know Jesus

I mentioned in an earlier chapter my lone encounter with Jim Rayburn, then recovering from brain cancer surgery but sitting behind his desk at his home in Colorado Springs. What lingers in my mind and heart from that encounter was the majestic way Jim talked about Jesus. I have listened to many of his messages to kids given at Frontier Ranch in Colorado, and in each one he speaks about Jesus with his homespun Texas drawl, espousing a combination of wonder, awe, and familiarity.

Throughout Jim's lessons, reproduced thousands if not millions of time across the country and over the years, the practice he emphasizes the most is to clarify who Jesus is, and perhaps even before that, what God is like. Obviously, in the crowds of young people sitting on the floor listening, there are a wide variety of views. For some, he is "the heavenly highway patrolman"; that is, he is rigidly keeping track of your good and bad deeds to determine your eternal fate—heaven or hell. For others, he is the hoary old grandfather who has lost control of this world and is wringing his hands as he sees it flying wildly out of control. For some, he is the effeminate, sad-eyed carpenter, holding a little lamb, who couldn't beat his way out of a wet-paper sack. And, of course, for some he is a fairy tale spun by people who need a crutch to help them through life's challenges. What we want to tell them, regardless of their current views is, "If you want to know what God is like, take a long look at Jesus." That's why the first step in Jim's teaching is to look closely at Jesus—how he walks, how he talks, how he lives, how he loves. He claimed to be fully man and yet fully God. It is important to present both aspects of his person.

One person whom I have appreciated reading is a Wall Street businessman who wrote a book a century ago about Jesus, the man. Bruce Barton, in his best-selling book *The Man Nobody Knows* (published in 1924), wrote concerning the manliness of Jesus:

> *"… there are those to whom it will seem almost irreverent to suggest Jesus was physically strong … Look for a minute at those first thirty years … See him bending his strong clean shoulders to deliver heavy blows … trudging away in the woods, his ax over his shoulder, and return at nightfall with a rough-hewn beam. He walked constantly from village to village; his face was tanned by sun and wind. Even at night he slept outdoors when he could. He was the type of outdoor man whom our modern thought most admires; and the vigorous activities of his days gave his nerves the strength of steel. Almost all painters have misled us. They have shown us a frail man, under-muscled, with a soft face—a woman's face covered by a beard—and a benign but baffled look, as though the problems of living were so grievous that death would be a welcome release. This is not the Jesus at whose word the disciples left their business to enlist in an unknown cause."*[241]

I love Barton's unique perspective of the person of Jesus. I have also been drawn to study the questions Jesus asked people—so many were penetrating and personal—such as his somewhat rhetorical question to the paralyzed man who lay by the Bethesda pool for thirty-eight years, "Do you want to get well again?"[242] Or to the blind beggar Bartimaeus, "What do you want me to do for you?"[243] Or to the demon-possessed man controlled by "Legion," "What is your name?"[244]

Jesus, the man, was not only a healer and preacher, but a profound listener. As the disciples were nervously pushing him toward the house of Jairus, the synagogue president, to heal his dying daughter, a woman touched his garment. John's gospel account tells us she "flung herself before him and told him the whole story."[245] Jesus was a man who listened and deeply felt people's pain. At

241 Barton, Bruce. *The Man Nobody Knows: a Discovery of the Real Jesus*. Chicago, IL: I.R. Dee, 2000. (originally published in 1924)

242 John 5:6, PHILLIPS

243 Mark 10:51, PHILLIPS

244 Mark 5:9, NIV

245 Mark 5:34, PHILLIPS

the raising of his dear friend Lazarus from death, he listened and loved those who mourned his passing: "When Jesus saw Mary weep and noticed the tears of the Jews who came with her, he was deeply moved and visibly distressed…'Lord, come and see,' they replied, and at this Jesus himself wept."[246]

As God in the flesh, Jesus was born in a stable stinking of animal droppings. He died on a Roman cross, sentenced as a common criminal between two thieves. A century ago, Dr. James Allan Francis, summarizes the life of Jesus in his book *One Solitary Life*:

> *"He was born in an obscure village. He worked in a carpenter's shop until he was thirty. He then became an itinerant preacher. He never held an office. He never had a family or owned a house. He didn't go to college. He had no credentials but himself…Nineteen centuries (now twenty) have come and gone and today he is the central figure of the human race. All the armies that ever marched, and all the navies that ever sailed, all the parliaments that ever sat, and all the kings that ever reigned have not affected the life of man on earth so much as that one solitary life."*[247]

But, while Jesus was fully man and fully observable and relatable in that manhood, he was also fully God. We picture him turning water into the finest wine, calming the wind and the waves, walking atop those waves, healing the sick, raising the dead, forgiving sins, knowing the very thoughts of those who antagonized him, expelling evil spirits, and ultimately bearing upon himself the sin of mankind and overcoming it by his resurrection from the dead. He closely communed with his Father, and his mission and message were precisely what his Father revealed to him. There are many passages in Scripture that describe Jesus as fully God. My longtime favorite is:

> *"Now Christ is the visible expression of the invisible God. He was born before creation began, for it was through him that everything was made, whether earthly or heavenly, seen or unseen. Through him, and for him,*

246 John 11:33,35, PHILIPS

247 Francis, James Allan, Kenneth H. Blanchard, Mac Anderson, and Gandalf. *One Solitary Life*. Naperville, IL: Inspired Faith, 2007.

also, were created power and dominion, ownership and authority. In fact, all things were created through, and for, him. He is both the first principle and the upholding principle of the whole scheme of creation. And now he is the head of the body which is the church. He is the beginning, the first to be born from the dead, which give him pre-eminence over all things. IT WAS IN HIM THAT THE FULL NATURE OF GOD CHOSE TO LIVE, and through him God planned to reconcile to his own person everything on earth and everything in heaven, making peace by virtue of Christ's death on the cross."[248]

What an incredible summary of Jesus as fully God!

Our Need for Jesus

Why did Jesus come to Earth? Knowing the limitation of his human frame, the way he would be rejected, and the impending torture and excruciating death that awaited him, why would he submit to such a plan? Simply put, he came and endured all this to serve as the remedy for mankind's sin problem.

I have found that most people, when asked to define sin, are more prone to emphasize its symptoms rather than the problem itself. The symptoms are everywhere—

hatred, murder, lying, stealing, cheating, etc.—the list goes on endlessly. But, the problem is not simply a material one; it is a relational one—a broken relationship with God. The challenge is to deeply understand that, while I can't address and solve all these horrible problems in the world, I *can* seek forgiveness and healing for myself through Jesus.

Years ago, I heard and memorized this poem, written as a cry of our world (I don't remember who wrote it):

WHY GOD, WHY?

I walked today through the slums of life—down the dark streets of wretchedness and pain.

I trod today where few have trod, and as I walked I challenged God.

248 Colossians 1:15-20, PHILLIPS, emphasis mine

I walked along the lonely streets and saw the prostitutes selling themselves,
the drunk passed out in his own vomit, saw the thieves as they picked pockets,
men and women, devoid of life, living in worlds of sin.
And above the din I whispered, "Why God, Why?"
*I walked today down the lanes of hate—I heard the cries of bitter men as they cursed and spat: 'D*go, n****r, k*ke, J*p!' And I saw the dejected men they stoned.*
Snarling, growling were these fiends of Hell... these God called his sons??
And I stopped and shouted, "Why God, Why?"
I walked today through war's grim dregs—in my mind's eye I saw the headless, the limbless, I heard the pleading and the crying.
I smelled the odor of rotted flesh, the baby trying to nurse from a dead mother.
Disaster! Disaster all around! The world is in disaster!
Blinded with tears, I fled down these streets. I finally stopped and shouted,
"Why God, Why? Why do you make man sin, hate, suffer?
Unmerciful Father, are you wicked and cruel? Can you watch all this and do nothing?"
I waited a long time for an answer. The echo of my cries was still ringing in my ears.
I was still waiting, half rebuking and half fearing
when I heard a voice close beside me, "Why Man, Why?"

This painful poem, written in the turbulent sixties, is still supremely relevant to describe the disastrous symptoms of sin and our personal culpability. Someone once told me that, in order to appreciate how *good* the Good News is, you must first recognize how *bad* the bad news is. The challenge in communicating the problem of sin is to recognize my own personal responsibility. Until I deal with my own personal moral and spiritual bankruptcy and repent, I am still part of the problem.

The prophet Isaiah wrote:

"'Come now, let us reason together,' says the Lord. 'Though your sins are like scarlet, they shall be as white as snow; though they are as red as crimson, they shall be like wool. If you are willing and obedient, you will eat the best from the land; but if you resist and rebel, you will be devoured by the sword. For the mouth of the Lord has spoken.'"[249]

That promise was fulfilled in the sacrifice of Jesus, the lamb of God. We must deeply discover that sin is a broken relationship with God. Jesus, in one of his parables aptly summarizes true recognition of sin and a contrite response:

"To some who were confident of their own righteousness and looked down on everybody else, Jesus told this parable: two men went up to the temple to pray, one a Pharisee and the other a tax collector. The Pharisee stood up and prayed about himself, 'God, I thank you that I am not like other men—robbers, evildoers, adulterers—or even like this tax collector. I fast twice a week and give a tenth of all I get. But the tax collector stood at a distance. He would not even look up to heaven, but beat his breast and said, 'God have mercy on me, a sinner.' I tell you that this man, rather than the other, went home justified before God. For everyone who exalts himself will be humbled, and he who humbles himself will be exalted."[250]

Once we have thoroughly understood the bad news, the good news is truly the best news we have ever heard.

Good News: Jesus Paid It All

"And we can see that it was at the very time we were powerless to help ourselves that Christ died for sinful men. In human experience it is a rare thing for one man to give his life for another, even if the latter be a good man, though there have been a few who have had the courage to do it. Yet

249 Isaiah 1:18-20, NIV
250 Luke 18:9-14, NIV

> *the proof of God's amazing love is this: that it was while we were sinners that Christ died for us. Moreover, if he did that for us while we were sinners, now that we are men justified by the shedding of his blood, what reason have we to fear the wrath of God?"*[251]

The formal theological term for this monumental act of sacrificial love is "substitutionary atonement." That's rather a mouthful, but basically it means: HE DIED FOR ME. It is best understood as always being intensely personal. Jesus took *my* place.

Over the years, I have often had the unspeakable privilege of sharing a message on the cross to hundreds of young people. One of my favorite stories to share in these talks, illustrating the cost of such a gift, is that of a father who worked with a railroad company. His job was to switch the tracks at a key junction where there was a steep trestle, and multiple trains would come within minutes to cross a single track towering hundreds of feet above a roaring river below. Staying on schedule became a matter of life and death.

After working this for some time, he knew the schedule by heart. One day, he brought along his young son for companionship. They were having a great day together—father and son. During a lull in the schedule, the son was playing by the tracks. As he was stepping between the tracks, his foot became firmly wedged where the tracks converged. He worked to wrestle his foot free, but it was hopelessly jammed in the crack. His father, seeing the dilemma, rushed to his aid and could not free him as the shrill whistle of an oncoming train broke the silence. Despite herculean efforts to free him, the father was faced with a tragic choice—immediately switch the track or send the train hurtling over the trestle. He made the most heartbreaking choice a parent can make, and as the train cars passed, the people waved and had no idea of the enormous cost of their safety.

As horrific as this imaginary story is, there is one big difference to note: rather than a tragic accident, God's choice to sacrifice his son was deliberate, supremely loving, and very costly. Indeed, it is true, "For God so loved the world, he gave his one and only Son, that whosoever believes in him shall not perish but

---

251 Romans 5:6-9, PHILLIPS

have eternal life."[252] It is truly life-changing for each of us when we realize that this supreme act of love has our name written all over it. The familiar acronym summarizes the enormity of this gift: GRACE=God's riches at Christ's expense.

The Necessity of Our Response

If I am sharing the gospel message over a week at camp, I love to use a visual illustration to review the content of the previous days. I begin by asking the campers to really use their imaginations and have me represent God. Then I walk into the center of the room. I ask them to all turn and face me, and I review my messages on the person of Jesus—how he shows us what God is like—and reminding them of a few of the stories I used about him. It is a great chance to be sure they all understand Jesus' claims, and his love for each of us.

Then we review the problem of sin. I ask them to turn their backs to me as I remind them how sin not only separates us from God, but, as they can obviously see, it separates us from one another—they can only see the back of other people's heads or the wall. Then I review the previous evening's message on what Jesus did to solve that problem of sin.

As I conclude this brief review, I am standing in the middle of the room looking at hundreds of backs turned away from me. It is quite a picture. I conclude with telling them it appears that, despite the great act of love by Jesus in dying for each of us, we still have a problem. "If anyone can figure out how to solve this problem, please do that right now!" One by one they begin to make a one hundred and eighty degree turn from having their backs to me—representing God—to turning and facing me/him. Then I return to the stage and talk about that wonderful word repentance or *metanoia*, as it appears in the Greek: a change of mind and heart. It literally means an "about face" from living life with myself at the center to asking Jesus to take that hallowed place as Lord of my life.

Jesus calls us to such a response in Revelation 3:20, "Here I am! I stand at the door and knock. If anyone hears my voice and opens the door, I will come in and eat with him, and he with me."[253] The late Episcopalian priest,

252 John 3:16, NIV
253 (NIV)

Dr. Sam Shoemaker, graphically captures this supreme invitation in his beautiful poem:

> *I stand by the door. I neither go too far in nor stay too far out.*
> *The door is the most important door in the world.*
> *It is the door through which men walk when they find God.*
> *There is no use my going way inside and staying there,*
> *When so many are still outside and they, as much as I,*
> *Crave to know where the door is.*
> *And all that so many find is only the wall where a door ought to be.*
> *They creep along the wall like blind men, with outstretched, groping hands,*
> *Feeling for a door, knowing there must be a door, yet they never find it*
> *So I stand by the door.*
>
> *The most tremendous thing in the world*
> *Is for men to find that door—the door to God.*
> *The most important thing any man can do*
> *Is to take hold of one of those blind, groping hands*
> *And put it on the latch—the latch that only clicks*
> *And opens to the man's own touch.*
> *Men die outside that door, as starving beggars die*
> *On cold nights in cruel cities in the dead of winter.*
> *Die for want of what is within their grasp,*
> *They live on the other side of it—live because they have found Him.*
> *Nothing else matters compared to helping them find it,*
> *And open it, and walk in, and find Him. So I stand by the door.*

The great news is the door is a Person.[254] It is also tremendous news that the Lord gives us the enormous privilege of joining him in sharing the only message in the world that can change the human heart. It is the theme of this chapter that we would be diligent stewards of that gospel message, both in communicating the message and having our lives bear witness to it as well.

---

254 John 10:8

The above poem does go on to offer a few final thoughts for you and me to receive and ponder:

As for me, I shall take my accustomed place,
Near enough to God to hear him and to know he is there,
But not so far from people as not to be able to hear them
And to remember that they are there, too.
Where? Outside the door—thousands of them … millions of them!
But—more important for me—
One of them, two of them, ten of them
Whose hands I am intended to put on the latch.
So I shall stand by the door and wait for those who seek it.
I had rather be a doorkeeper …
So I stand by the door.

Chapter Nineteen

Things I Know for Certain

It seems appropriate to conclude my reflections on the teachings of Jesus with a handful of strong convictions I have gathered over my seventy-five years of living, that didn't fit neatly into any of the other chapters. These are "Jesus principles" I have garnered over the years and now hold as precious cornerstones to my life that I seek to live out and understand even better as the years go by. It is a short list, but each continues to grow in my life as I spend time with Jesus and family and friends around the world.

Relationships Matter

Early in this book, I shared what my father-in-law told me when I married his daughter, "Invest your life in things that are eternal. I can think of two: a relationship with Jesus Christ, and relationships with family and friends in Christ. Ten thousand years from now, these things matter." I have no desire to become wealthy in material assets. Perhaps in years gone by that was a greater interest, but I am convinced what makes all of us truly happy and fulfilled are meaningful relationships.

I find that many of the decades-old friendships get sweeter and sweeter, like a fine-aged wine. The tragic result of a lack of emphasis on nurturing relationships is the pox of loneliness that is so prevalent in our day. Correspondingly, the enormous blessing of valuing these relationships over time is they grow deeper and bless our lives in such powerful ways.

I mentioned the core of six couples of which Debbie and I are a part, that has met together for forty-seven years. I have also experienced tremendous blessing in a number of other small groups over the years. Each is unique, but all of them have contributed to a deeper understanding of *koinonia*, the amazing fellowship the Lord invited us to experience as we journey with Jesus and others. The Apostle John wrote about this, saying, "We want you to be with us in this—in this fellowship with the Father, and Jesus Christ his Son … If we are really living in the same light in which he eternally exists, then we have true fellowship with each other, and the blood which his son Jesus shed for us keeps us clean from all sin."[255]

As we think about our "investment portfolios," what should really stand out is the eternal investments we are making, rather than emphasizing all the things we won't be taking with us. Unfortunately, most of the world is running after all those things that truly fail to make us happy.

I recall during a question-and-answer session years ago, with a group of very relational people, Doug Coe was asked how many of these close "covenant relationships" one could make with friends around the world. His answer drew a collective gasp from that large crowd of people. Eyes flashing, he answered, "Thousands!" What I believe he was revealing was the truism that the deeper we go with a few in vulnerability, commitment, affirmation, confidentiality, sharing of time, assets, and friends—the deeper we can go with many. What a valuable "acquired taste" that is for any of us as we get older!

For those who are growing in this area, becoming an initiator is so important and so integral to these kinds of relationships. I love the response of a friend who, several minutes into a phone conversation, gets asked, "Well, what do you want?"

And his answer is, "I was just thinking of you."

---

255 1 John 1:3, 7, PHILLIPS

There is nothing wrong with purposeful calls, but isn't it a blessing on occasion to know the caller doesn't want anything except the presence of a valued friend?

One final observation on relationships is related to longevity and faithfulness. So many times when a friend goes through a painful setback in life or something dishonoring his reputation, it is so easy to discard the friendship. I find that is the very time when true friends need to emerge and stand close by.

A few years ago, I was wrongly implicated in the Russian collusion narrative. The press wrote many things that simply weren't true about what I had supposedly done with certain Russian leaders. I noticed some folks who distanced themselves; others drew closer. I always think about the 9/11 disaster, and all those who were running from the burning towers. There were a few who actually ran *toward* those buildings to find those who were in a bad situation.

I like to envision that picture as life's jolts take place for each of us—who are those who draw closer and want to help, as opposed to the ones who quickly disappear? I draw inspiration from the beautiful proverb, "A friend loves at all times, and a brother is born for adversity."[256]

Father Wounds Can Heal

I mentioned earlier the deep love I have for my dad, who passed away a number of years ago. My love and regard for his memory comes with a recognition that, due to a broken relationship with his own father, he was not able to affirm me in those important growing up years. I vividly recall the only one of my athletic events he ever came to—it was mid-way through a little league baseball game, and I came up to bat with the bases loaded. My dad was behind the backstop imploring me, "Come on, Doug, hit it a mile!" The count went to three balls and no strikes, and ball four was coming in high and away. I reached out and smacked it over the right fielder's head, and as I raced around the bases, I was choking back sobs. It was so important to get his approval!

My dad never realized that, but years later, through counseling, I was able to understand this wound and forgive my dad in my heart. I'm grateful that our relationship changed for the better before he passed away. Ironically, twenty years

256 Proverbs 17:17

after his passing, one of my sons shared with me a special encounter he had with my father months before he died, in which Dad shared at length how proud he was of me—he just wished he could tell me!

Because of Jesus' redemptive work in my own life, I have been able to understand and empathize with many who have struggled with a father wound. I think it is important to note this is not an attack on our fathers. I don't believe most dads intended to do this; they quite likely had similarly been wounded and lacked the understanding to impart the needed affirmation to their sons or daughters. Psychologists tell us that most importantly at puberty the father becomes a primary parent in terms of needed affirmation and acceptance. For girls, often the lack of it creates disastrous results as they desperately search for love and affirmation.

A significant part of my own growth occurred through a several-week experience called an "intensive," which I had the privilege to undergo in the early 80's. It helped me to see my dad through the eyes of Jesus and myself in that way as well. A father figure, the late C. Davis Weyerhaeuser, blessed me by offering this experience, and in turn did the same for many more young people in the Young Life family. This subject often comes up as I listen to young people.

I asked permission to share the story of my close friend, Carlos, a longtime colleague raised in El Salvador. His father left the home after severely abusing his wife early in Carlos' life. He then left a second family he created and started a third. Carlos grew up with anger and resentment toward his dad. He became a guerrilla fighter in the Civil War in El Salvador, but met Jesus after a close friend was killed and the realization of the fragility of life was made clear to him.

As Carlos began to grow as a young believer, the desire to reunite with his father became more important. He began to search, finding the second wife, and they were encouraged to board a bus on which his father occasionally was seen. The chances of reuniting in the large metropolitan area were dim, but amazingly, as Carlos surveyed the crowded bus, he saw his father! He had rehearsed the speech over and over—it was a well-choreographed forgiveness of the father for all of his misdeeds and the immense hurt he had caused. As Carlos began to speak to the father he had not seen in a decade, the Holy Spirit took over. He heard himself asking his father TO FORGIVE HIM for all the years of bitterness that he had held toward him. Isn't that just like Jesus! He gives us just the right words to truly heal.

Carlos went to live with his dad for over a year just to cement that all-important relationship together again. Today, Carlos is a man who can empathize and encourage many other men and women as they seek healing from the devastation of a father-wound.

The beautiful picture all of us can cherish is the words of the Father at Jesus' baptism, "You are my dearly-loved Son, in whom I am well-pleased."[257] Ironically, the next verse notes, "Jesus himself was about thirty years old at the time *he began his work*."[258] This loving affirmation was before the three years of public ministry—it was heartfelt and unconditional love of the Father to his Son. What a blessed example to all of us!

Deeply Invest in the Next Generation

I have frequently mentioned that there has not been a time in my life when investing in young people was not at the top of the list. Some years ago, I flew from Moscow to JFK airport in New York City after a several-week trip. This was back in the days when you wrote on an immigration card the countries you had visited. As I stepped up to the immigration officer after a long wait in line, he read out loud the nations I had visited, "Kazakhstan, Ukraine, Armenia, Russia. What is it you do?"

A little surprised he was asking, given the length of the line behind me, I responded, "I work with young people and leaders of government."

He responded, "Well, that is an odd combination!"

Without thinking, I heard myself respond to him, "I would pick the young people every single time!"

As I walked away, I thought about that statement that had just escaped my lips. It really was not meant as a criticism of the wonderful people in authority I was privileged to meet with during those weeks in a part of the world I had frequently visited for many years. I treasured the opportunities to come alongside and befriend many of these folks who often had impossible jobs to do with much

---

257 Luke 3:22, PHILLIPS

258 Luke 3:23, PHILLIPS, emphasis mine

criticism and very little affirmation. It was a joy to initially meet with them in their offices, often to invite them to the National Prayer Breakfast in Washington, and to see a positive effect in their lives. Many of them became good friends, we have shared deeply over the years.

However, the incredible openness of young people and the frequency of seeing them make a transformational decision to follow Jesus, with their whole lives ahead of them, is a blessed experience that never gets routine. I now understand why Jesus chose to deeply invest in the twelve disciples, when it is thought that they were all young, unrefined men.

I am often asked why I continue to work with the young men at Ivanwald (the discipleship house at The Cedars in Virginia, where I live and work), especially at my age. I always respond with a wide grin that these young men help to keep me young. As James Stewart wrote, "When Jesus and youth come together, deep calls to deep."[259] Our Lord passionately understood that investing in young lives was incredibly important, and they had many years ahead to grow and give leadership to the next generation. I have long treasured this poem about the amazing gift of connecting with young people:

THE PRIORITY OF YOUTH

Will Allen Dromgoole

An old man, going a lone highway,
Came at the evening, cold and gray,
To a chasm, vast and steep and wide,
Through which was flowing a sullen tide.

The old man crossed in the twilight dim;
The sullen stream had no fears for him;
But he turned when safe on the other side
And built a bridge to span the tide.

259 Stewart, James S. *The Life and Teaching of Jesus Christ.* Edinburgh: Saint Andrew Press, 1995, p.56.

"Old man, said a fellow pilgrim near;
"You are wasting strength with building here;
Your journey will end with the ending day;
You will never again pass this way;
You have crossed the chasm, deep and wide—
Why build you the bridge at eventide?"

The builder lifted his old gray head;
"Good friend, in the path I have come," he said,
"There followeth after me today
A youth whose feet must pass this way.

This chasm that has been naught to me
To that fair-haired youth may a pitfall be.
He, too, must cross in the twilight dim;
Good friend, I am building the bridge for him.

The Earth Is the Lord's

"The earth is the Lord's, and everything in it, and the world, and all who live in it." (Psalm 24:1, NIV)

I remember the first time I traveled across the world as a twenty-year-old, waking up in Leningrad and going to the hotel window and watching with wonder as babushkas swept the streets with primitive brooms. It was the beginning of a lifelong adventure of traveling to countless nations fueled by a desire to share the love of Jesus. Somewhere along the way, I came to realize that God didn't call me to work for him, but he wanted me TO WORK WITH HIM. What a difference that made! Rather than trying to strategize how I could help God with his work around the world, I asked him if I could join him. It has taken me to some of the remotest parts of God's great world—Eastern Siberia, North Korea, the Cape of Good Hope, the mountains of Peru, the Ivory Coast of Africa, the Great Wall of China, the southern tip of Australia, even to Bethlehem, where Jesus chose to begin his earthly journey.

In each special place, the question is the same, "Lord, can I join you in what you are doing here?"

In one journey in the mid '80's to what was then Outer Mongolia, I recall an unforgettable encounter that helped to shape my understanding of God's world. A handful of friends were on a three-week journey to numerous countries. It was the first long trip I took with Doug Coe.

As we prepared to leave, he challenged us to consider our goal for the experience. His first suggested answer was a bit surprising to me: that we would love God more when we returned than when we left—hard to argue with that, but I was expecting a more task-oriented response. The second goal was that we would love one another more deeply—we read the Book of Acts together each day and even suggested God might still be writing new chapters! When it got to the third goal, I thought we finally would get down to brass tacks, but Doug's surprising words were, "And God might even let us love on some people along the way"—almost an afterthought!

About midtrip, we came by rail from Lake Baikal in Siberia to Ulaanbaatar, the capital of then Outer Mongolia. Several days into the time there, we took a drive several hours out into the countryside. At that time, Outer Mongolia had less than one hundred known believers, and was a godless, Soviet satellite nation. We had been studying a chapter in Acts, sitting on the mountainside.

Doug suggested we drive off the dirt road to meet a group of yak herders down in the valley. Our translator, who met Jesus before we left and is still a close brother, Basaan-hu, got out of the van and approached the yak herders. They lived in yak-skin tents, and I had the thought, *If this isn't the end of the world, you might be able to see it from here!* Not only did this group of herders not know what America was, I doubt that any had even heard of Mongolia.

After we each went for a short "joy ride" on the dusty beasts, we sat and talked. After a few minutes, Doug asked the elderly leader if he had ever thought about who created all of this spectacular beauty before our eyes. He nodded affirmatively. Then Doug asked if he could tell him the Creator's name … and he told him all about Jesus, a herder of yaks himself! It was one of the greatest moments of my life. As I listened, Psalms 19 echoed in my thoughts, "The heavens DECLARE the glory of God. The skies PROCLAIM the work of his hands. "[260] Two days later, as our train rolled out of Ulaanbataar, Basaan-hu stood by the window with tears streaming down his face, and Jesus newly settled in his heart!

Doug often challenged us, "Don't convert others. Convert yourself." That trip helped me understand this truth much better—we didn't convert anyone, but Jesus showed up and touched all of us.

One other experience was very formational for me in experiencing God's world. It was in the mid-'90's and I had been doing "Jesus Conferences" in all fifteen former Soviet republics. I got the idea to gather twenty to thirty key young leaders from each country and have them together for five to six days. The central point of this vast land comprising twelve time zones appeared to be Omsk, a city of over a million in Western Siberia that just happened to have a hotel we had previously used, with a theater seating over 300. We met in May of 1995, with some groups traveling up to four days by train to join us. I brought a number of close friends, including Doug, to be a part of this gathering.

We had been together about four days when Doug asked me to gather forty of the top young leaders. As was often the case, he didn't tell me his intentions. I listened as he regaled the group about the possibility of being like Peter, James, and John or Mary, Joanna, and Susanna (in Luke 8:3), and getting up in the morning, reading the Gospels, and then doing whatever the Holy Spirit told them (the young leaders) to do. It wouldn't be under the auspices of any organization or denomination, but they would work with all of them and speak well of them.

I remember thinking, *He is trying to go back to the Book of Acts!* Twenty-five years later, we are finding it works! Ten cores began in five different nations, and the three became the twelve, then the seventy, etc. Much of Young Life's work in the former Soviet Union was spawned by some of those folks, and thousands of disciples have been raised up in cities and towns across the former Soviet Union.

The takeaway for me is for us to go across the world and join Jesus in what he is doing. The Scriptures are our invaluable guide along with the faithful

---

260 Psalm 19:1, NIV, emphasis mine

leadership of the Holy Spirit. "The earth is the Lord's!" What a delight it is for us to be able to join him!

Keep Short Accounts

> *"As far as your responsibility goes, live at peace with everyone." (Romans 12:18, PHILLIPS)*

If there is one thing the devil loves, it is broken relationships—especially among the followers of Jesus. As we have noted earlier, one of the strongest nonverbal messages we as followers of Jesus can send is our love for one another. I am convinced the new normal for each of us needs to be that we cannot be aware of anyone who has something against us with whom we haven't taken initiative to make it right,[261] and we can't think of anyone who has sinned against us to whom we haven't gone.[262]

As we noted in chapter four, discussing the ministry of reconciliation, Jesus is very specific about our responsibility to reconcile with one another. Some of the greatest experiences of my life have been reconciliations with family and friends that appeared irretrievably broken. Only Jesus can fit all those broken pieces back together and heal our hearts in the process.

There appears to be a very close connection between my truly experiencing God's love personally and passing it on to all of those I meet. "Yes, we love because he first loved us. If a man says, 'I love God' and hates his brother, he is a liar. For if he does not love the brother before his eyes, how can he love the one beyond his sight? In any case, it is his explicit command that the one who loves God must love his brother too."[263]

As Paul writes to his young son in the faith, Timothy, he summarizes what the goal of their ministry is: "Whereas the object and purpose of our instruction and charge is love which springs from a pure heart, a clear conscience and sincere faith."[264] Nothing interferes with these three precious qualities more than

261 Matthew 5:23-24
262 Matthew 18:15-17
263 1 John 4:19-21, PHILLIPS
264 1 Timothy 1:5, AMP

broken, unresolved relationships. At the top of our list of priorities must be right relationships.

I would note that the most important place to practice this is within the family unit. I count my wife, Debbie, and our four offspring, John, James, Katie, and Peter, as five of the greatest gifts in my life. I am honored to do life with them and now spouses and sixteen grandkids. Right relationships are the blessed gift we can share together, because Jesus is showing us how in the everyday lives we each are living. Most certainly: JESUS + RIGHT RELATIONSHIPS = JOY!

How Big Is Our Jesus?

I want to conclude with this daunting question: "How big is our Jesus?" I don't mean the Jesus seated at the right hand of the Father. I mean the one you and I have living in our hearts. Wouldn't it be truly exciting to sense that this Jesus is growing bigger and bigger within us?

I have experienced one exciting way that my Jesus seems to grow bigger and more real in my own heart, and I want to share it with you, my reader. I call it the ninety-day challenge.

There are twenty-eight chapters in the Gospel of Matthew, sixteen in Mark, twenty-four in Luke, and twenty-one in John's Gospel. That is eighty-nine chapters altogether. What if each of us dedicated the next ninety days (with one day off) to taking one chapter each day to meditate on. That is, beginning with Matthew chapter one, we read it three to four times, each time slower and more methodically. As we are digesting each chapter in this careful way, we ask several key questions to write in our journals: *What did I learn about Jesus today that I didn't realize before? How he walks, talks, lives, thinks, loves? And secondly, how does that apply to my life?* It should take a minimum of thirty minutes to explore the chapter, mining for nuggets of gold from the life and ministry of Jesus. I have challenged thousands of friends to join me in this holy pursuit of knowing Jesus better. I have found that "my Jesus," the one who lives in my heart, seems to get bigger as I journey through these four incredible accounts of the life and ministry of the Son of God.

It is enjoyable to read books about him written by his followers. They inspire us and encourage us, but there is nothing like immersing ourselves in the "God-breathed"[265] accounts of the life of Jesus as set forth in Matthew, Mark, Luke, and John. If you decide to take this challenge, I would be greatly blessed to hear from you after the ninety days. [266] It is truly amazing what happens in our lives as Jesus grows bigger in our hearts!

J.B. Phillips, in his book, *New Testament Christianity*, tells the story of a senior angel taking a novice angel on a tour of God's great universe.[267]As they travel from galaxy to galaxy, seeing the millions of stars making up this colossal universe, the angel saves the best for last on this picturesque excursion. Heading to one of the smaller galaxies, the Milky Way, the senior angel hones in on one smaller star, known as the Sun to us.

As they get closer, he points out some orbs rotating around that star. The climax of the trip comes as he breathlessly points to a single orb or planet about three away from the star. In hushed tones, the senior angel joyfully exults, "That is the visited planet." The young angel could hardly conceive of the irony that the immense Creator God sent the fullness of himself in Jesus to that dirty, colored ball to show those inhabitants what he is like.

When they begin to discover what he is like, they realize for themselves that "Jesus changes everything."

---

265 2 Timothy 3:16

266 Email me at Jesus changes everything 2021

267 Phillips, J. B. *New Testament Christianity*. Eugene, OR: Wipf & Stock, 2012. (originally published in 1957)

About the Author

Doug Burleigh has been on the frontlines of ministry for Jesus for over fifty years, serving on Young Life staff for twenty-five years (the last five and a half years of which he served as national president), and the past twenty-five-plus years with The Fellowship in Washington, D.C.

Throughout the years, Doug has led over sixty-five "Jesus Conferences" for young people in all fifteen nations of the former Soviet Union and every region of Russia. He has been a relentless advocate for discipleship and Jesus-centered living around the U.S and the world, from business to political to ministry networks and beyond. He is a frequent speaker and sought-after advisor on the topics of discipleship, mentoring youth, and cultivating a dynamic and sustained personal relationship with Jesus Christ.

Doug holds a B.A. in Political Science and Russian from Willamette University, an M.A. in Political Science from the University of Washington, and an M. Div. from Fuller Theological Seminary. He has been married to the former Debbie Coe for forty-six years; they have four grown children and sixteen grandchildren and make their home in Annapolis, MD.

Doug can be reached by emailing jesuschangeseverything2021@gmail.com.

Additional Resources

Recommended Reading

I include this list here of all the works quoted in this book, as they have been an invaluable part of my journey with Jesus. I hope you will find them equally valuable to yours. -D.B.

Aldrich, Joseph C. *Lifestyle Evangelism: Crossing Traditional Boundaries to Reach the Unbelieving World*. Portland, OR: Multnomah, 1981.

Barton, Bruce. *The Man Nobody Knows: a Discovery of the Real Jesus*. Chicago, IL: I.R. Dee, 2000.

Batterson, Mark. *The Circle Maker: Praying Circles around Your Biggest Dreams and Greatest Fears*. Grand Rapids, MI: Zondervan, 2016.

Benner, David G. *The Gift of Being Yourself: The Sacred Call to Self-Discovery*. Downers Grove, IL: IVP Books, 2015.

Blanchard, Kenneth H., and Phil Hodges. *Lead like Jesus: Lessons for Everyone from the Greatest Leadership Role Model of All Time*. Nashville, TN: Thomas Nelson, 2008.

Chambers, Oswald, and James Reimann. *My Utmost for His Highest: Selections for Every Day*. Grand Rapids, MI, MI: Discovery House Publishers, 1995.

Coleman, Robert E., and Billy Graham. *The Master Plan of Evangelism*. Grand Rapids, MI, MI: Revell, 2006.

Francis, James Allan, Kenneth H. Blanchard, Mac Anderson, and Gandalf. *One Solitary Life*. Naperville, IL: Inspired Faith, 2007.

Guyon, Madame. *Experiencing God through Prayer*. Cedar Lake, MI: Read A Classic, 2009.

Lucado, Max. *God Came near: God's Perfect Gift*. Nashville, TN: Thomas Nelson, 2013.

McLaren, Brian D. *The Secret Message of Jesus: Uncovering the Truth That Could Change Everything*. Nashville, TN: Thomas Nelson, 2007.

Metaxas, Eric. *Bonhoeffer: Pastor, Martyr, Prophet, Spy*. Nashville, TN: Thomas Nelson, 2015.

Ortiz, Juan Carlos. *Disciple: A Handbook for New Believers*. Orlando, FL: Creation House, 1995.

Phillips, J. B. *New Testament Christianity*. Eugene, OR: Wipf & Stock, 2012.

Stewart, James S. *The Life and Teaching of Jesus Christ*. Edinburgh, UK: Saint Andrew Press, 1995.

Stott, John R. W. *The Incomparable Christ*. Downers Grove, IL: InterVarsity Press, 2004.

Trueblood, Elton. *The Incendiary Fellowship*. New York, NY: Harper & Row Publishers, 1967.

Wells, H. G., G. P. Wells, and Raymond Postgate. *The Outline of History: The Whole Story of Man*. Garden City, NY: Doubleday, 1961.

Wright, N. T. *Simply Jesus: a New Version of Who He Was, What He Did, Why It Matters*. New York, NY: HarperOne, an imprint of HarperCollins Publishers.

Suggested Memory Work for Each Principle and Attribute

1. The Purpose: Deuteronomy 6:4-9; Matthew 22:35-40
2. The Work of God: Mark 9:23-24; John 6:28-29; Hebrews 11:6
3. The Message: John 5:39-40, 14:6; Colossians 1:26-28
4. The Ministry: Matthew 5:23-24, 18:15-17; 2 Corinthians 5:16-21
5. The Church: Matthew 18:18-20; Ephesians 4:1-6
6. The Method of Leadership: Mark 10:42-45; John 13:1-4,17
7. The Kingdom of God: Matthew 6:33, 13:44-46; Luke 17:20-21; Romans 14:17
8. Jesus Before Others, Self, Possessions: Luke 9:23-25, 14:26-27,33
9. A Person Who Loves the Brothers and Sisters: John 13:34-35; 1 Corinthians 13:4-8
10. A Person Who Takes the Scriptures Seriously: John 8:31-32; 2 Timothy 3:16-17; Hebrews 4:12-13
11. A Person Who Makes Disciples: Matthew 28:16-20; 2 Timothy 2:1-2
12. A Person Led and Empowered by the Holy Spirit: Acts 1:8; 1 Corinthians 2:9-13,16
13. A Person Who Bears Fruit: John 15:7-8; Galatians 5:19-23

14. A Person of Unity: John 17:20-23
15. A Person of Prayer: Luke 11:9-13
16. Spiritual Warfare: Ephesians 6:10-18
17. Authority: Romans 13:1-2; Ephesians 5:21, 6:2-3; Colossians 3:23-24; Hebrews 13:17
18. Message Sequence: Isaiah 53:6; John 1:1,14, 3:16; Acts 2:38; Romans 3:23, 5:6-8, 6:23; Colossians 1:15-20; 1 John 5:11-12; Revelation 3:20

CPSIA information can be obtained
at www.ICGtesting.com
Printed in the USA
BVHW030348110321
602152BV00002B/5

9 781631 954115